PRAISE FOR *THE FINAL RACE*

Many know the story of the Flying Scot, Eric Liddell, whose Christian conscience would not let him run in the 1924 Paris Olympics on a Sunday. Though he had trained for the 100-meter event, he had to switch to the 400-meter instead—and won the gold! It was all told in the book and movie *Chariots of Fire*.

What more is there to say? Plenty! Another Eric (named Eichinger) now tells the *rest* of the story in his fascinating book *The Final Race*. With gifted pen, he tells of Liddell's subsequent career as a missionary teacher in China and how his efforts there became a powerful witness to Christianity and culture in the Far East. As a celebrity, doors were open to him, and he faithfully used them to do the work of the Lord in remarkable fashion.

What happened *after* the Olympics was by far the most significant part of Liddell's life, and Eichinger nobly rescues it from oblivion, offering a true account, brimming with triumphs, tragedies, love, and violence—all set against the brutality of the Japanese invasion of China at the start of World War II. In these pages, Eric Eichinger has given us the genuine sequel in Liddell's life, providing a true tale that will grip readers and fire their spirits.

PAUL L. MAIER
Bestselling author of *A Skeleton in God's Closet*

The Final Race is a gripping read of the rest of the Eric Liddell story. This chariot of fire of God's grace didn't merely bask in Olympic glory but sacrificed it all to run the race of his life and to share the gospel of Jesus in China. Author Eric Eichinger does a wonderful job showing Liddell's humanity, his struggles, his tenacity, and above all his persevering faith. It's a riveting story of the love of Christ leading the way amidst the hurdles of culture and resources, as well as the overwhelming atrocities of war, concentration camps, poverty, and false ideologies. In the midst of it all, Liddell's life is a compelling story of the love of Christ, a race that he ran to win so that others would be blessed, to give God glory. Truth be told, his service was just a reflection of his Savior, the one he always wants you to meet through it all. Eichinger compellingly brings to life this story that will have you turning the pages in anticipation. It's a story that surely will bless all who read it.

GREGORY P. SELTZ, PHD
Executive director of the Lutheran Center for Religious Liberty, Washington, DC, and speaker emeritus of *The Lutheran Hour*

The story of Eric Liddell after his *Chariots of Fire* Olympic glory is both inspiring and challenging. Pastor Eichinger takes us on a thrilling yet heartbreaking journey of courage and self-sacrifice. He digs deeper into not only what made Liddell an all-time great on the track but also the difficulties of balancing God's calling with the demands of responsibility to family. Set in World War II China, *The Final Race* is a timely reminder that true faithfulness often leads to great sacrifice, but also great reward.

JIM STINTZI
Director of track and field and cross-country, Charleston Southern University; seven time All-American; and head coach of thirty years in the Big Ten

Pastor Eric Eichinger has done a masterful job of introducing us to Eric Liddell's life after *Chariots of Fire*. Since he both served as a missionary to China and ran track in college, Rev. Eichinger is able to capture Liddell's story in a unique and engaging way. Far from picturing the Christian life as one of pure glory and victory, *The Final Race* reminds us that following Christ means bearing a cross, having to sacrifice what we love at times and even living in uncertainty. Yet in all of this, Liddell's life points to the reality that God's grace always prevails and that the blood of Christ offers the only true hope there is. *The Final Race* is sure to inspire and encourage all of us who have to bear a cross.

REV. BOB HILLER
Senior pastor, Community Lutheran Church, Escondido, CA

The Final Race recounts the heroic story of Eric Liddell with passion and grit. Author Eric Eichinger shares how Liddell finished the ultimate race of life with commitment, determination, and self-sacrifice. Faith, family, war, romance, struggle, and victory combine to show that Eric Liddell was much more than an Olympic hero. He was a hero who changed lives for eternity.

MICHAEL NEWMAN
Author of *Hope When Your Heart Breaks* and *The Life You Crave*

Eric Liddell's life of loving service is a testimony to his Lord and Savior, Jesus Christ. His story is worthy of remembrance and celebration, and *The Final Race* is an enriching and rewarding testament. Like the Apostle Paul before him, Eric Liddell has "run the race," entering the joy of his Master. This book will help you enter into that race as well. I encourage you to read and be refreshed.

DR. JORDAN J. BALLOR
Research fellow, Acton Institute for the Study of Religion and Liberty

The Final Race offers a refreshing, compelling reminder of someone who lived by his principles regardless of circumstance. With this engaging account of Olympic hero Eric Liddell's life story, Eric Eichinger has given a solid example that should be considered by all endeavoring to live a life of virtue today.

DAVID AND JASON BENHAM
Entrepreneurs and bestselling authors of *Whatever the Cost*

Like Eichinger and Everson's remarkable work, I have been captivated by Eric Liddell's story for over thirty years. It was immensely gratifying to discover that *The Final Race* holds true to the man's incredible legacy while crafting a beautiful tale. Highly recommended.

DAVIS BUNN
International bestselling author

THE FINAL RACE

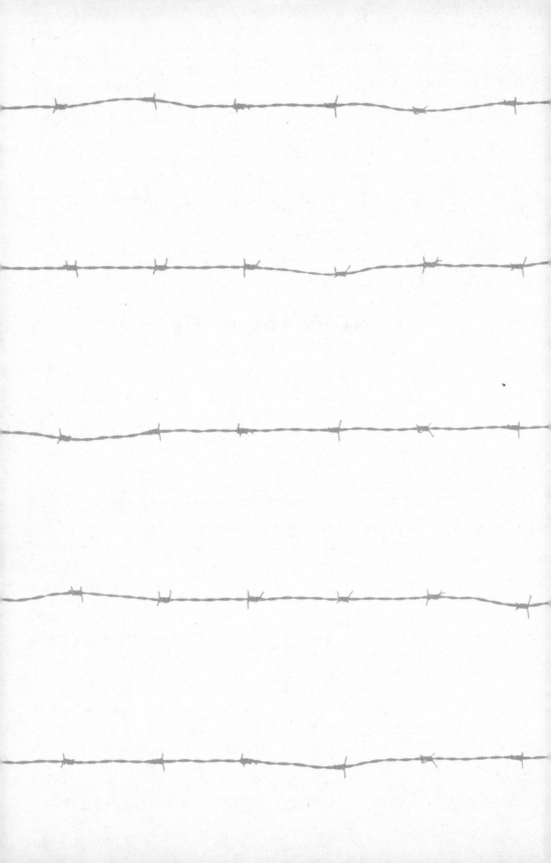

THE FINAL RACE

**The Incredible World War II Story
of the Olympian Who Inspired
CHARIOTS OF FIRE**

ERIC T. EICHINGER
with EVA MARIE EVERSON

TYNDALE
MOMENTUM®

*The nonfiction imprint of
Tyndale House Publishers, Inc.*

Visit Tyndale online at www.tyndale.com.

Visit Tyndale Momentum online at www.tyndalemomentum.com.

TYNDALE, *Tyndale Momentum*, and Tyndale's quill logo are registered trademarks of Tyndale House Publishers, Inc. The Tyndale Momentum logo is a trademark of Tyndale House Publishers, Inc. Tyndale Momentum is the nonfiction imprint of Tyndale House Publishers, Inc., Carol Stream, Illinois.

The Final Race: The Incredible World War II Story of the Olympian Who Inspired Chariots of Fire

Designed by Jennifer Phelps

Eric Eichinger is represented by SON: The Spirit Of Naples and Southwest Florida, Inc., 1100 Fifth Ave S, Ste. 201, Naples, FL 34102 www.SONStudios.org.

For information about special discounts for bulk purchases, please contact Tyndale House Publishers at csresponse@tyndale.com, or call 1-800-323-9400.

ISBN 978-1-4964-1994-1 (hc)
ISBN 978-1-4964-3245-2 (International Trade Paper Edition)

Printed in the United States of America

24   23   22   21   20   19   18
7   6   5   4   3   2   1

FOR KARA

You are my best "running partner." You ran this ultramarathon
with me every blistering step of the way.
Eric

AND FOR ERIC EICHINGER

Because you shared writing the story of Eric Liddell with me,
I have grown spiritually in ways I never imagined possible.
Thx, EE.
ee
Eva Marie

CONTENTS

AUTHORS' NOTE

THE WRITING OF THIS BOOK draws from a wide variety of research over a number of years, each experience more humbling than the last. Having been a competitive runner at a high level and a teacher in China, I already felt I had caught a glimpse of what it was like to stand in the shoes of Eric Liddell. While living in China, I decided to stride down that path a bit further to Weihsien, where Eric Liddell is buried and a memorial is dedicated to him. I sneaked into the condemned hospital structure where he died and surveyed the landscape as the familiar score from *Chariots of Fire* played in my mind. Somewhere on my return home from that pilgrimage, I knew I had to tell this story in a way that had not yet been done.

I am thankful for the numerous and dedicated biographers who came before me, including the primary source of D. P. Thomson's writing, as well as the Day of Discovery video documentary with David McCasland. The Eric Liddell Centre in Edinburgh, Scotland, is a trove of delight, and I warmly appreciate their hospitality. Having tea and dashing through the streets of Edinburgh to visit Eric's old haunts with his nieces, Joan and Sue, is a moment in time I will never forget. I am especially thankful for the audience granted to me by Eric's daughters Patricia and Heather; their open and continued communication; and for the voluminous correspondence with Eric's youngest daughter, Maureen. It has also been an extreme pleasure working with Eva Marie Everson, a servant-leader in her craft, who made the manuscript flow with narrative quintessence.

Rev. Eric Eichinger

The first time I heard the name Eric Liddell, I sat in a movie theater, shortly after the birth of my daughter, Jessica, in 1981. My husband and I had been given free tickets in exchange for our opinion about a soon-to-be-released movie, *Chariots of Fire*. I clearly remember being stunned as the final words appeared across the screen, informing moviegoers that Eric had died in China during World War II. Years later, as I entered the world of publishing, one of the first books I came across at a booksellers' convention was a short biography about Eric. *Oh*, I remember thinking, *he was the runner who refused to run on Sunday and who died in China.*

In 2015, I received a call from Rebeca Seitz of SON Studios in Naples, Florida, asking if I would look over a few chapters by a pastor from Clearwater. "He's not a novelist," she said, "and this is a novelization. With your experience, I think you can give him some pointers." As soon as I opened the manuscript and saw that the story was about Eric Liddell, something inside me said, *See this through.* Over the next six months, the good reverend and I worked on his project, and a year later, my agent called one fine afternoon and said that "EE" (as I call him) had been offered a contract to write a biography on "EL," but that Tyndale wanted a fiction writer's influence. Enter "ee."

The opportunity to work again with EE, to sit across the desk from him and pore over books and video notes and other research, to read the numerous accounts of EL's life, to speak on the phone with Eric Liddell's daughter, Patricia, on several occasions (oh, her patience in talking with me!), and to take the moments in Eric Liddell's life and weave my artistic thread through their fabric (and to do so from only his point of view) has been more than a project for me. *This* manuscript has changed my life. It has changed my walk with God.

This is a biography. We wanted to maintain the factual integrity of a traditional biography while also making the book readable and understandable. We wanted to make Eric Liddell's presence more immediate and relatable to readers. So each chapter begins with a fictionalized snapshot from Eric's life based on true history but told using the conventions of fiction. Obviously, when fictionalizing someone's life, writers don't know *exactly* what happened (Was it really raining? Did he really eat roast beef that night for dinner?), but I have tried to stay as close as possible to what we *do* know for certain and to enhance that part of the story to help draw readers into the life of a truly remarkable human being. My prayer is that, like EE and myself, you will come to feel that you actually *know* Eric Liddell . . . and that running this part of the race alongside him will make your journey with Christ that much more precious.

Eva Marie Everson

OUR RACE

ALMOST A FULL CENTURY HAS passed since Eric Liddell's running career began and his renown caught fire. Once he made his decision to withdraw from the 1924 Olympics 100-meter event due to religious observance, his iconic legacy was seared in time.

A prized favorite to win gold for Britain, his name was dragged through the homeland mud on the heels of his announcement. Yet Liddell navigated gold-medal glory via a different route, the 400 meters, a distance with which he had minimal experience.

Against all odds, he ran victoriously and in the process inspired millions. In so doing he preserved his routine commitment of honoring God by resting on the Sabbath and provided a rapturous reason for Britain to celebrate. The flame that had been lit beneath his celebrity exploded throughout the world.

Eric's incredible display of faith during the Olympics was just the beginning. He had another race in his life yet to run—a more important one, with a much greater prize. This final race of faith was not marked out using the familiar lines of a track. He did not know where it would end. He could not have imagined how his world would be torn apart before it was all over. And he certainly couldn't have fathomed the magnificent extent of how God would continue to use him in the generations that would follow. All Eric could do was prepare day by day and by faith run his race to the best of his abilities. He ran in his own unique theological lane as he persevered through hardships and ultimately achieved the everlasting crown of righteousness.

Many glowing embers of Eric Liddell's example remain today. They serve as luminaries for the race we have yet to run, and indeed are running—the race of faith in Christ Jesus. The baton of Christian faith has been passed to us. We don't know what our next century will bring or what tumult lurks around dark cultural turns. We can't know for certain what we will be asked to do. But we can prepare, as Eric did, in the days of comfort. Then when our days of hardship come, we'll be ready to meet them—so that we, too, might not run aimlessly but in order to win the prize.

Eric Liddell was prepared to run his final race of faith. Are we prepared for ours?

CHAPTER 1

ANOTHER RACE

*A man's pride will bring him low, but
a humble spirit will obtain honor.*

Proverbs 29:23, NASB

July 19, 1924

Journalists crowded London's King's Cross railway station platform like hunters in midstalk. They milled around, searching the faces of passengers urgently headed toward their respective train compartments. Their office-issued pads and nubby No. 2 pencils were poised to jot down the perfect quote, which by morning's print—and with the right framing—would become the next sports page headline. Cameramen, not to be outdone, vied from equal vantage points. They readied their flashbulbs in hope of seizing their unsuspecting victim and, in doing so, capturing their prize—an exclusive photograph of the nation's most recently crowned hero.

They had not been so lucky earlier that warm Saturday afternoon at the Stamford Bridge track, where a special relays meet between the British Empire and the United States of America had been held. Eric Liddell, the newly minted 400-meter gold-medal champion, was to run in the relay, only a week into his Olympic glory. Because his medal still had not arrived by mail, the sheen of his athleticism had yet to hang around his neck.

In the whirlwind seven days since breaking the world record in the 400 meters, Eric had received his bachelor of science from the University of Edinburgh, had been capped ceremoniously by Sir Alfred Ewing with a crown of oleaster sprigs, and had been carried out of McEwan Hall by his fellow classmates. He had given speeches, been honored at a dinner, and then made his way by train to London and Stamford Bridge. There, surrounded by a stadium built to hold more than forty thousand spectators, he and Horatio Fitch (Britain's and the United States' best sprinters, respectively) waited for their teammates to hand them the baton for the final 400-meter leg of the mile relay.

This race was the last event of the meet, and Britain was starved for some homeland firepower near the end of a disappointing race day. They were down to the last leg. Fitch got his baton first and took off.

Liddell—dubbed "the Flying Scot" on sports pages across his country—received his baton four yards behind in chase.

During the Olympic Games held in Paris the week previous, these same two men had dueled during the heats, quarterfinals, semifinals, and finals of the Olympic 400 meters. Fitch had run in the first semifinal, breaking an Olympic record to come in first place at 47.8 seconds. Eric had run in the second semifinal, coming in first at 48.2 seconds. The odds had been in Fitch's favor.

But Eric Liddell had something to prove—something beyond the Olympics. His was another race. His, a greater prize.

Much to Fitch's shock—and the world's—in 47.6 seconds, Eric Liddell had trounced all competitors and odds, crossing the finish line with a first-place win and in world-record time.

A week later, at Stamford Bridge, Fitch had retaliation in mind. The win should have come easily—Eric Liddell had spent the past week at graduation and banquets, leaving him no time for practice. The man's muscles would be practically atrophied, surely.

At two hundred yards, Liddell had made up two of the four yards between the men. Then, as they rounded the last turn, Liddell's head went back, a sure sign. Often it had been said that when the Flying Scotsman's "heid went back," he "culdna' lose."

Eric Liddell took over in the last straightaway, outrunning Fitch by a commanding four yards. His split time equaled his gold standard from the Olympics, and the hunger of the London crowd had been satisfied once again, but without compromise from Liddell.

With the race over, and in his typical fashion, Liddell shook hands with Fitch and the others, quietly gathered his belongings, waved to the crowd, and left the limelight as swiftly as he could.

No gloating. No interviews.

Since his boyhood, Eric's nature—to ward off pride and avoid attention when at all possible—had always been contrary to many self-promoting athletes and fame-seeking performers. Aware of his ascent in the public's eye, he had been careful to not allow success to go to his head. Over the course of the past week, he had realized that winning gold for his nation—in the way he had won—had catapulted him into a new stratosphere of unanticipated celebrity.

Now, as the late-afternoon sun beat down on King's Cross, Eric caught wind of the reporters awaiting him. The attention did not appear to be ending anytime in the near future. But what he wanted—what he needed—was to retreat into a solitary bed compartment and sleep in peace for his ride home. He hoped to find a way to circumvent the onslaught of questions, which would invariably add volume to his own vanity. And if he didn't answer correctly, his responses could easily be misconstrued. He looked around for a solution, but all entrances to his train were blocked.

Eric sighed, realizing he had little choice but to endure the questions and the blinding flashes of camera bulbs.

As he accepted his unusual defeat, Eric spied a baggage porter. Head bent under his trademarked hat, the older man nimbly pushed a luggage rack through the sea of travelers. Eric ducked his chin and, weaving through the crowd, made his way to the porter.

"Excuse me, sir," he said, keeping his voice low. "I wonder if you might do me a favor."

The porter listened as Eric explained the situation. "Would you be so kind as to loan me your cap and luggage rack?"

The porter's eyes scanned the crowd, whose voices had risen in the rush of the usual good-byes. He smiled at the conspiracy, then removed his hat and handed it to Eric. "My pleasure, Mr. Liddell," he said, smoothing back his disheveled hair. "Just add your bags to the rack here and make your way to that car over there."

Eric dipped into his pocket and slipped a sizable tip into the porter's hand. "Thank you, my good man," he said before shrewdly pushing the luggage rack. As the porter had done, Eric kept his head down, but he cast his eyes to the train cars and walked straight through the unsuspecting media.

After loading the luggage, he boarded the train undetected while the porter watched from the outskirts, a smile curling his lips.

THE PUBLIC AND LOCAL MEDIA could not recognize or appreciate the extraordinary pressures Eric Liddell was under. Questions of when to conclude his running career, when to leave for China, whether or not to enter seminary, how long to be apart from his family, the ever-closing window of opportunity to secure a wife—all were methodical drips increasing a dull pound in his thoughts. No matter which avenue he chose, all ultimately meant what seemed unthinkable to most—he would turn his back on fame.

For good.

And he was not about to open his heart to prying journalists as he mulled over his decisions. Had he indulged their inquiries, they could not have come to terms with the seriousness of the dilemma and the magnitude of the situation. The choice to leave his full life in Britain—to trade it for the obscurity of the Far East—seemed senseless to them.

To everyone. Nearly.

The public knew of Liddell's missionary lineage and had caught wind that he might possibly join in the efforts of his family eventually. But capitalizing solely on the potential of his success kept their interest. The Flying Scotsman had achieved so much, and so much more lay at his fingertips. Fanning the flame of stardom was a necessary act. They simply would not understand why he—or anyone, for that matter—would willingly walk away from the admiration and celebrity status they continued to lavish upon him.

To sacrifice everything earned and live a life of practical anonymity seemed more drastic than necessary. If he made the choice for China, he would walk into a place and time where no one knew him and where British citizens were despised.

Besides, couldn't he stay in England and do more for Christ there than in China? He already drew huge crowds of people—people who came to listen as he shared his Christian faith. A tremendous platform had already been set up for him.

How could he top that?

But journalists and fans alike could not know the depths of their newly crowned gold medalist. Where most people would give anything for the attention, Eric had learned to avoid it when possible. This was no feigned avoidance. At only twenty-two, he already recognized that these had been his "days of comfort," and that temptations befall a man when narcissism comes into play.

Not only was Eric the most famous Brit of his time, he was also an eligible bachelor. It wasn't easy getting to know a young lady who didn't recognize him or who already had high expectations of what he was like. Genuine seriousness was hard enough to identify for any young man seeking someone to marry, let alone for the most popular individual in the country. Still, he reasoned, the probability of finding the love of his life in China seemed astronomically low.

For Eric, the crossroads of life had never been dull. This one was no exception.

* * *

Once safe and unrecognized in his train compartment, Eric looked through the window dotted with a child's recent nose prints and chuckled at the reporters who realized, as the crowd thinned out, that they had missed their chance. Again. He situated his belongings, then stretched out, closed his eyes, and let out a long breath, releasing the tension his body had held unconsciously since stepping onto the platform.

Pride cometh before the fall.

The words danced about in his head. Oh, yes. He knew the line well, and he had no intention of dooming himself to its clarion prophecy. But uncertainties abounded, and how he would navigate the waters that lay directly ahead of him had to be determined soon.

But soon would come quickly enough. For now, what he really needed was to rest.

The whistle blew, and with a jerk, the train pulled away from the station, heading toward Edinburgh. With any luck, he'd make it home in time to get a little sleep in his own bed before morning. Before another set of responsibilities lay before him.

After all, the following day was a Sunday.

PART ONE

The First 100

Prepare for the Day

CHAPTER 2

FOUNDATIONS

*Train up a child in the way
he should go; even when he is
old he will not depart from it.*
Proverbs 22:6

September 14, 1909

Sweat beaded across the brow of seven-year-old Eric Liddell that warm September afternoon, and he wiped it toward the line of blond hair slicked with perspiration. "Come on, Rob!" he shouted. "Throw the ball!"

Rob, Eric's older brother, darted along the dry grass of Blackheath's meager playing field, his eyes searching for the best teammate to pass to. Finding a ready classmate, he tossed the oval rugger ball, then started toward his brother.

"Look!" he said, reaching Eric. "Mummy and Jenny are here!"

Eric turned in the direction Rob pointed. For a year now, since he and Rob had been enrolled in the London boarding school of Blackheath, their mother and younger sister, Jenny, had visited often, although not usually during class time.

"Should we go . . . ?" Eric began, stopping as Rob pulled him by the shirt sleeve toward their mother and sister.

Mary Liddell bent down to wrap each of them in a hug, then stood again. "I've—we've—" She looked down at Jenny. "We've come to say good-bye."

Eric cocked his head as his mother swallowed hard. Was this the day his mother had told them about, the day she and Jenny would leave England for China, where his father had returned a year earlier?

"Are you leaving, then?" Rob asked. "For the boat?"

Mary nodded as wisps of dark hair fell away from the pins that held her thick tresses in place at the nape of her neck. She squatted before them, taking their hands in hers. "I want you boys to promise me you'll be good for the headmaster. And study hard, and write to me as often as you can."

"Will you write to us, Mummy?" Eric asked, feeling the tremor in his mother's hand.

She squeezed in assurance. "Every week. Like clockwork." She looked each of them in the eye. "Now, do you promise?"

"We promise," they said together.

Their mother gathered them into her arms again, pressing her lips against their moist cheeks. Eric breathed in the fresh scent of her; she smelled like the heather that grew along the hills of Scotland. "I love you both so much . . . and I'll miss you most terribly. Never forget that."

"We won't."

Mary stood again and drew in a shaky breath. "Say good-bye to Jenny then."

Both boys gave their sister a hug as their mother continued her instructions. "All right. Off you go, my boys. Back to your play."

Eric lagged behind his brother in the return, then looked over his shoulder to see if their mother was still watching them. But she and Jenny had already begun to walk away, hand in hand. "Rob," he said loudly enough for his brother to hear over the voices of the other boys.

Rob cast him a backward glance.

"Do you think it will be many days before we see them again?"

Rob nodded. "Many, many days. Years, Eric."

Eric's brow furrowed. Years . . . years without his mother. Without his father. Without Jenny. He took a final look toward the fading figures of the two most important females in his life.

Ah . . . but years with Rob. At least he had his older brother.

BY 1920, SEPARATION WAS nothing new for Eric Liddell. He'd lived with it nearly his entire life.

Born the second son of missionaries to China in the frostbitten winter of 1902—only seventeen months after his older brother, Rob—Eric had left his birthplace at the tender age of five and crossed vast oceans to Great Britain, where he and Rob entered boarding school.

Shortly after Eric and Rob were enrolled, and in the tradition of the day, their parents, James and Mary, returned to China . . . leaving Eric with the first pangs of separation. Separation from his mother and father. Separation from his little sister, Jenny. Separation from all he had known up to that point. Separation from his nanny, Qi Nai Nai; the home within the London Missionary Society compound located in Siaochang; and summers spent at the beachside resort of Pei Tai Ho.

Separation from everything and everyone.

Except Rob.

Since birth, one of the few constants in Eric's life had been his older brother. But as the boys grew into young adulthood, even Rob had left him, after graduating from London's Eltham College—an elementary through high school educational institution for the sons of missionaries.

By this point, Rob and Eric had only seen their parents—along with Jenny and their younger brother, Ernest—a handful of times since arriving at school. And while their relationships with their immediate family had been maintained by letters passed between China and Great Britain, their relationship to each other had been set on a firm foundation of scholastics, faith, and sports, first in Blackheath in their elementary years and then at Eltham in 1912.

Back then, like their classmates, the Liddell brothers—known as Liddell i and Liddell ii—could not have been more delighted to move out of the drafty dormitories of Blackheath and into a larger, newer, and more advanced facility, a facility made up of more than brick and mortar. *This* facility sported a real game field—acreage of green grass that would change the course of young Eric's life.

Excelling at sports was one thing. Academically, Eric's bulb had never shone the brightest. But as he developed, his mind gravitated toward chemistry, thanks in part to one of his instructors, D. H. Burleigh. Through Master Burleigh's teaching, Eric learned that his young Christian mind did not have to be at odds with the scientific world and that God and his creation have a unique parent-child relationship.

Another teacher who had long-lasting impact on Eric was A. P. Cullen, better known by faculty and students as simply "Cullen."

Back in the early days, Cullen often said (with a chuckle) that he believed Eric wasn't as angelic as he appeared to be, because of Eric's bent toward mischief-making. But what he could never have known—or begun to figure out—was that he would be the only non-relative Eric Liddell interacted with through the three major phases of his life: childhood, young-adult athletics, and the missionary years in China during World War II.

It was Cullen who was with Eric in his childhood . . . and it was Cullen who would be with Eric in the days of war and imprisonment.

• • •

In Eric's mind, Rob had been the real sportsman all along; Eric had only played in his brother's shadow. But once Rob left Eltham for the

University of Edinburgh to study for a medical degree, Eric's talents in rugby and cricket rose to new levels.

Of the two sports, Eric tended to favor rugby. Schoolmates couldn't help but take notice. The life Eric had led—whether knowingly or unknowingly—in his brother's shadow was swiftly coming to a close as he began to outstrip Rob.

"Get the ball to Eric," teammates said, because they knew if Eric had the ball, the win belonged to them.

So while the high school student may not have shone in the classroom, on the grassy field his star made a slow ascent—so much so that during his final year at Eltham, Eric broke the 11-second barrier in the 100-yard sprint, and his running times began to flirt with some of the 100-yard sprinting records, not only in England but also in the world.

Popularity—something Eric had always enjoyed—gave way to *celebrity*.

Despite the sudden acclaim, however, Eric remained remarkably modest without change to his character. As his star climbed ever higher, he seemed to already display a keen sense that there were more important issues in life on which to focus.

Because when Eric wasn't busy with sports and studies, his focus zeroed in on the other constant in his life—church.

The Liddells were members of a Congregational church, a smaller and lesser-known church body compared to the much larger Scottish Presbyterian Church. Eric had picked up portions of his parents' Congregationalist doctrine in China, but in Scotland he found himself immersed in its rhythm, traditions, and instruction.

Compared to the state religion, Scottish Congregationalists, by profession, were much more ecumenical in nature and had no issue mixing with other varieties of Christianity. Independence and freedom in Christ were important virtues for Scottish Congregationalists, and in that Eric was no exception.

. . .

In March 1920, Eric moved out of Eltham and in with Rob. Once again, the Liddell brothers were under the same roof. But a larger blessing was that their mother, along with Jenny and Ernest, was set to arrive within the month, and James would follow soon thereafter.

Mary's role in arriving early was to secure and create a home for her family. Five years earlier, when Rob and Eric had said their last good-bye to their parents and siblings, they'd been two schoolboys. Now as grown men they would meet the woman who had brought them into the world. And this time, one of them—Rob—would have a young woman at his side.

Nerves plagued him. Ria Aitken had become more than a passing flirtation. Ria, he hoped, would one day become his bride. The family's acceptance of her, therefore, was critical.

The family moved in to their furnished flat at 21 Gillespie Crescent in Edinburgh and began reacquainting themselves. Eric managed to find a French tutor to aid him in passing the last of his classes. He also took a job as a farmhand just outside the city. Each morning, long before the rooster crowed, Eric hopped on his newly purchased bicycle and pedaled to the farm where he put in a hard day's work. In the evenings, he returned home to a family he loved dearly but from whom he had learned to live apart, despite that affection.

By autumn the Liddell family moved to Merchiston Place and began worshiping at nearby Morningside Congregational Church, one of four churches located at a pivotal crossroads within the city called the "Holy Corner." Rob had joined the church two years earlier. Now his family sat on the polished pews beside him.

At Morningside, Eric became active in the Young People's Union. While so many other young men and women his age sought new ways to carouse and carry on, Eric made faith the central focus of his life. Without a backward glance, he wholeheartedly poured himself into his role within the church and his walk with God.

What Eric could not have known then—and perhaps didn't realize until much later in his life—was that his walk would become a run, leading him to do more of God's work outside the church than he could have ever imagined.

.   .   .

On February 23, 1921, Eric Liddell officially signed his name in the books and became a student at the University of Edinburgh. A few months later, Rob and Eric stood on the train station platform to welcome James. The senior Liddell had a short time to be with his family before his work took him to the various Congregational churches in Britain. But James wanted more out of his trip home than work-related visits and time with family. He'd begun to hear rumors about Eric's sporting accomplishments. So in addition to wanting to spend time with Eric—a rarity for the Liddells—James's heart held a great desire to see his second son run.

But for Eric, sports had taken a sudden backseat to his zeal for examining creation in the shadows of Edinburgh's academic legends, such as Charles Darwin and David Hume, both of whom had walked the green courtyard and age-old halls of the university generations before. He became exposed to and familiar with Darwin's theory of evolution and Hume's major thesis born out of the Enlightenment: The laws of nature are inviolate; miracles violate the laws of nature; therefore, miracles do not exist.

Rather than allowing these thoughts to turn his heart from Christ, Eric enjoyed the challenges and appreciated the complexities of theology, philosophy, and science. He noted that these and numerous other theories omitted Christ's divine role in these matters. However, as a devout Christian and principled man of faith, he pressed forward, knowing that it was best to keep God factored into the equation of his scientific studies.

When educational responsibilities proved to be exhausting, Eric returned to the physical release and exhilaration of athletics. Playing alongside Rob, who had already established himself on the university rugby team and made a name for himself in his own right, rekindled Eric's joy for the game. Together the two became stars for the Edinburgh University rugby team's fifteen-man roster. When the Liddell brothers were on the paddock in winged tandem, it was a special time for them . . . and a special year for Edinburgh. Eric cherished every scrum, try, and goal because he knew *this* would be the last athletic season he and Rob would share at this caliber of play.

But the end came sooner than Eric anticipated. With Rob rigorously studying medicine and preparing to be a doctor, attempts to balance both medical academics and athletics at a high level became too much of a challenge. Rob decided to throw all his energies into becoming a doctor, which meant—in some ways—Eric found himself alone again.

May 1921 brought the university's annual sports day, which was primarily dedicated to track and field. The previous year an extremely talented and versatile athlete, W. L. Hunter, had graduated from the university. Hunter's completion of his studies left an athletic void no one expected to be filled anytime soon. And certainly no one had their eye on any of the freshmen.

But when Hunter left, Liddell entered.

A new dawn was about to break.

CHAPTER 3

THE STARTER'S PISTOL

Do you not know that in a race all the
runners run, but only one receives the prize?
So run that you may obtain it.
1 Corinthians 9:24

March 1921

Nineteen-year-old Eric Liddell squinted one eye against the afternoon sunlight as he returned his teacup to its saucer. Across the outdoor table sat a school chum from Eltham, one who had also matriculated to the University of Edinburgh. "Run in the sports day games?" Eric asked with a shake of his head. "I don't think you realize how busy I am."

His friend laughed easily, hunched over the table, and reached for his tea by the cup's rim. "And I don't think you realize how good you are."

A blush warmed Eric's cheeks, already toasty from May's heat. "I appreciate that—I do—but—"

"But what?" The young man leaned back and crossed one leg over the other. "Come on. You've been all about the books lately. Don't you miss sports? Even a little?"

Eric thought a moment. Oh, yes. He missed the games. But

shouldn't his focus be solely on schoolwork now? Schoolwork and church?

"All work," the friend said with a lilt in his voice, "and no play makes Eric a dull boy."

Eric laughed. "I'd have to train and—"

"I could help. Get you ready for the 100."

"You?"

"Sure. Why not?"

Eric folded his arms across his chest. "What do you know about training for the 100?"

The young man paused. Blinked. Then grinned. "Nothing. But I say we give it a go. We have a few weeks. If you don't win—or don't do well at all—why, I won't bring it up again."

Eric inhaled deeply. With spring in full bloom, the fresh air had made him feel alive again after hunkering over books during the long winter. "Nothing ventured, nothing gained?" he asked.

"Right."

"Okay, then. I'll have a go at it."

GAMES WERE JUST THAT—GAMES. And Eric had not put serious thought into them. His true focus had been elsewhere, in areas he felt it should be: his spiritual life and academics. This was not to say that Eric didn't genuinely love running, because he did. Running well—and running fast—came as naturally to him as breathing.

Eric agreed to train for the annual sports day—and so far it had gone well—but he didn't put a lot of stock in what winning might mean.

Not that *anyone* expected much from the university freshman. But that warm afternoon as the heather began to bloom beneath the sun's light on Great Britain's hillsides, Eric took his place at the starting line against Edinburgh's current fastest sprinter . . . and history took a slow turn.

Perhaps the older student looked at Eric sideways and chuckled inwardly, confident he'd leave the younger Liddell in his dust. Or perhaps he furrowed his brow, wondering, *Who is this new man on the track?* Either way, when the races were done, Eric had taken a shocking first in the 100 yards and barely got nipped for second in the 220-yard race.

A surprising accomplishment for a freshman—so much so that a Glasgow newspaper declared that Eric "is going to be a British Champion ere long, and he might even blossom into an Olympic hero."[1]

With such a success, Eric committed to running track for the University of Edinburgh and, with each event, steadily raised eyebrows with his blazing speed and the times he posted, despite what was becoming more of the focus: his unorthodox style.

As a runner, Eric had his own approach to racing, and it was one that would bring him great fame, even though—for Eric—it was simply the way he ran.

Duncan McLeod Wright, a talented Scottish marathon runner who went on to represent Britain in multiple Olympic Games, described Eric's unconventional style by saying, "In my half century's connection with Scottish sport, I have met many famous athletes, but I state in all honesty that I don't remember my first view of anyone as vividly as my first sight of Eric Liddell. It was at the Queen's Park Sports in 1921. I heard there was a real flyer in the Edinburgh University's colours. . . . Through a small window from the competitor's room underneath the Stand, I saw Eric for the first run in the 100 yards and was completely thrilled. Off to a slow start, he ran with blazing speed, chin up, head back on the shoulders, and his arms thrashing the air. 'Dreadful style' said the cynical critics. But his space-devouring legs raced on a straight path to the tape, and to me he typified the speed runner putting all his strength into his effort to gain victory."[2]

Practice and technique were given strong attention in Eric's training. Eric adopted what he could yet retained his peculiar style and stride. Years later, Eric recalled the first time he saw a cinder track:

Up to then I thought all professional runners would be first-class runners. They danced about on their toes as if they were stepping on hot bricks. Whenever they started to run, they dug big holes for their toes to go into, as if they were preparing for the time when their toes would dance no more. Surely they did not expect me to make such a fool of myself as all that? Yes, I found that they did. . . .

It was at this time that I got to know the trainer who trained me during my five seasons on the running track. He took me in hand, pounded me about like a piece of putty, pushed this muscle this way and that muscle the other way, in order, as he said, to get me into shape.

He told me that my muscles were all far too hard and that they needed to be softened by massage. He added that if they were not softened soon, some day when I tried to start, one of the muscles would snap. He took me out and told me to do a short run. After finishing the run I stopped much quicker than any of the others. When I asked him what he thought of it, he answered that if I wanted a breakdown I was going about it in the best possible manner, for it appears that one must never stop abruptly on reaching the tape.

Thus, being thoroughly humiliated, feeling that my reputation had been dragged through the mud, that my self-respect was still wallowing in the mire, and that if I didn't get into the clutches of a trainer soon, every muscle in my body would give way and I should remain a physical wreck till the end of my days—I was then in a fit mental condition to start an athletic career.[3]

Between his work within the church and his accomplishments on the track, Eric's popularity continued to grow. Remarkably, this had little to no effect on his character. Eric's humble profile remained unchanged.

Eric enjoyed spending time in the young adults group, teaching Bible classes at Morningside, and worshiping with his family. He sensed that within the walls of church and ministry he could still be the person he had always known himself to be, a circumstance that had become more and more rare. Morningside held true sanctuary for Eric in more than the obvious way. Eric had begun to recognize the increasing pressures of fame, and he not only recognized them, he *avoided* them.

· · ·

The three-legged stool of church life, studies, and athletics supported Eric, fortifying him through his remaining years at the University of Edinburgh. Each interest grew, strengthened, and enhanced him in every way imaginable. Eric became a fine science scholar, and his prowess on the rugby team ultimately gave way to an opportunity to play for Scotland's international team.

Eric played international rugby for Scotland over the course of 1922–1923. His blazing speed made him a natural wing three-quarter, and by the end of the season he had earned seven international caps and scored four tries. By pairing Eric up with another speeding winger, A. L. Gracie, Scotland enjoyed thrilling success.

"Is Eric Liddell better at rugby or running?" became a commonly heard question, since Eric's speed on the rugby field was as astonishing as his times on the track. This sparked an enjoyable debate among athletic fans. Many avid rugby fans chastised the faster wingers for leaning on their speed during matches. But "funking tackles" was no trait of Eric's. Though he never shied away from physical contact, he frequently used speed to do the work of multiple men.

In the seven international games in which Eric played, Scotland lost only one—and that by a mere two points. *The Student* made sure to pay tribute to Eric's prowess in the papers by declaring that he "has that rare combination, pace and the gift of rugby brains and hands; makes openings, snaps opportunities, gives the 'dummy' to perfection, does the work of three (if necessary) in defence, and carries unselfishness almost to a fault. Experience should make him as great a player as he is a sprinter."[4]

Ultimately, Eric's track times continued to descend, and running became his premier sport. Eric emphasized primarily the shorter sprints, eventually setting the school record for the University of Edinburgh in the 100 yards with a searing time of 10.2 seconds.

And his fame only increased with every rugby blue ribbon. Along the way, the "Flying Scotsman" moniker became associated with Eric in the press—and it stuck.

In the twilight of his university days, Eric Liddell became a household name and a bona fide star. He easily won the title of the most popular athlete in Scotland as an international rugby all-star and a favorite slated for Olympic glory. The 1924 Olympics were a year away, but the way Britain talked, Eric already had a gold medal clutched in his fist.

CHAPTER 4

MUSCULAR CHRISTIANITY

He said to them, "Follow me, and
I will make you fishers of men."
Matthew 4:19

Early April 1923

Eric glanced up from the book yawning open on his desk as some-one rapped at the front door at 56 George Square, the University of Edinburgh flat he shared with his brother.

"Rob?" he called out, hoping his brother had returned home and would answer the door.

Silence, followed by another round of insistent knocking.

Eric stood, the legs of his chair scraping against the floor-boards and echoing in the room. "Rob!" he called again as he made his way to the front of the town house, even though he felt fairly certain Rob wasn't home.

He opened the door, ready to apologize to whoever stood on the other side. "Sorry about that—"

A tall and lanky man stood between the Corinthian columns on the front stoop, looking from the scrap of paper he held in his hand to the number over the door. Then, blinking as though

23

he only just realized the door had opened, he extended a hand. "Eric Liddell?"

Eric accepted the handshake. "I am," he said.

The man smiled briefly, adjusting the round specs on the bridge of his nose. "But of course you are. Your brother gave me your address," he said, showing Eric the paper. "Said you should be here this time of day."

Eric stepped aside, aware of the gentleman's identity and his association with Rob. "Please," he said. "Come in."

The man ambled in, his shoes shuffling against the tile. "My name is D. P. Thomson," he said.

Eric smiled. "Yes, I recognize you from the posters I've seen, and Rob has said fine things about you." He gestured to the left. "Our sitting room is here. Please, have a seat, and I'll bring some tea."

Eric busied himself in the small kitchen, preparing refreshments and wondering why David Patrick Thomson, a young Church of Scotland pastor, had come to see him. From what Rob had told him, D. P. had—the year before and in response to the growing problem of spiritual disinterest among the young men of Great Britain—been part of forming the Glasgow Students Evangelical Union. The purpose of the GSEU, which drew its members from students in leadership, academia, and sports, was—pure and simple—Christian revival. But from what Rob had told him, the numbers of attendees had dwindled with each session.

Eric returned to the front room carrying a tray set with cups, saucers, and a pot filled with brewing tea. "I brought both milk and lemon," he said.

D. P. thanked him, then set about preparing his tea as Eric waited. "You can probably imagine why I'm here," the pastor said.

Eric remained quiet, something he'd learned to do along his short life's journey. *If you want to know anything, listen.*

D. P. peered at Eric over the rims of his glasses. "We've got a problem in our country, Eric," he said. "Our young men—from the students here at the university to the men sitting behind their prestigious desks to the boy working in the mines—they need the Lord. They need the message of the gospel."

Eric nodded as he prepared his own cup of tea.

"You know about our work, I'm sure—what with Rob—"

"I do."

"And you probably know that we're seeing fewer and fewer men show up for our meetings." The pastor took a sip from his cup.

"Rob has mentioned."

D. P. shifted in his chair and rested his elbows against his knees. "I'll get right to it, then. Here are my thoughts—we may not have much success getting the men to come initially to hear the gospel . . . but if we promise that they'll hear from Scotland's great athlete—"

A rush of heat filled Eric's face.

"I asked Rob if he thought you'd do it."

"Do what?"

"Come and speak. Share your love for the Lord."

"And what did Rob say?"

D. P. chuckled. "He said he didn't know . . . that you'd never done any speaking before, but that—that I should ask you."

Eric smiled. During their childhood, whenever Eric had been asked if he wanted to do something—he'd always said, "Ask Rob." Now Rob had said, "Ask Eric."

"When and where?" Eric asked.

"Friday night. In Armadale."

Eric nodded, his eyes searching the pattern of the floor's rug as his heart called out to his heavenly Father for direction. Within a moment, the answer came, and Eric looked from the floor to the man sitting only a few feet away, anxiousness etched into his face.

"All right," Eric said. "I'll come."

ONE DAY, when speaking of this meeting with D. P. Thomson, Eric would say,

> I was brought up in a Christian home where the stories of
> the Bible were often told and became familiar to me. In
> school, the stories of the Bible and the teachings of Christ
> were placed before me. The beauty of the Christian life
> began to appeal to me. The time came when the appeal of
> Christ became more personal and I began to realize that
> it was going to affect my life. In this experience of Christ
> there was a sense of sin but that was not nearly so great as
> the sense of being called to do a piece of work for which
> I was absolutely unqualified. My whole life had been one
> of keeping out of public duties but the leading of Christ
> seemed now to be in the opposite direction, and I shrank
> from going forward. At this time I finally decided to put
> it all on Christ—after all if He called me to do it, then He
> would have to supply the necessary power.[1]

D. P. decided that Rob should come and speak in Armadale as well. While Thomson was delighted and Rob willing, Eric felt the familiar inner butterflies that always showed up before a race. The morning after Eric's visit from Thomson, a letter arrived addressed to Eric from his sister Jenny. Her correspondence ended with a passage from Scripture, Isaiah 41:10: "Fear thou not; for I am with thee: be not dismayed; for I am thy God: I will strengthen thee; yea, I will help thee; yea, I will uphold thee with the right hand of my righteousness."

Eric, feeling ill-prepared for his new quest, was greatly comforted by this peculiarly timed oracle.

On Friday evening, April 6, 1923, Rob and Eric prepared to speak to the crowd of about eighty men. Rob spoke first and performed adequately but not as dynamically as Thomson had hoped.

Then Eric stepped up. Quiet and unassuming, he shared a few Bible passages and his faith in Jesus Christ and encouraged the young men with coal-dusted faces to trust Christ as well. To no one's surprise—save perhaps Eric's—his first speech was a smashing success.

The local newspapers picked up the story that the famous Scottish athlete Eric Liddell was speaking about his faith. The news rippled throughout the United Kingdom. After that, anytime it was announced that Eric would be speaking, large crowds responded. One week after the minor attendance in Armadale, Eric and D. P. spoke to a crowd of more than six hundred in Rutherglen. Everyone wanted to see the Flying Scotsman up close. Whether they just wanted to brush up against a rising celebrity or had a deep desire to hear his words, their motivations didn't matter at the outset. The most important thing was that people showed up.

Thomson was eager to train Eric in how best to articulate his faith. Dwight L. Moody, an American evangelist who encouraged a straightforward, winsome style of Bible teaching, had influenced D. P. Thomson greatly in his approach to ministry. Thomson found Moody's writings inspiring and enjoyed observing the results from implementing his methods. The unassuming tactics of decision theology—teaching people to decide to accept Jesus and to follow him—seemed to Eric easy enough to understand and communicate. Eric had little evangelism experience and only basic theological training, but he was sincere and committed to Christ.

Thomson, whose inspiring mentors also included Henry Sloane Coffin, possessed a slightly different, more pragmatic definition of living faith than Eric had grown up with. "Brought up in a Christian home," Thomson wrote in his journal describing his early observation of Eric, "inspired by the highest ideals from childhood, guided in all he did by Christian principles, Eric Liddell had, I believe, long before that day, a faith in Jesus Christ at once simple and strong. To his own great impoverishment, however, as well as to that of others, he had been until then a secret disciple. Of his influence for good there could be no question—it was acknowledged on every hand—but he had never disclosed its secret, and had never openly confessed his Lord."[2]

Eric might not have agreed with D. P. about the secrecy of his faith, having publicly professed it earlier in school and at chapel and church services. Eric's Congregationalist values were open to alternative philosophies. Congregationalists generally had no issue with exploring doctrinal nuances, the role of baptism, or the interplay between law and gospel from the broad spectrum of Christianity. But when Eric spoke before the growing crowds, he simply told his personal story, explained the strength behind his faith, and encouraged those listening to believe.

Eric's raw but genuine delivery would soon be honed under the watchful tutorial of Thomson.

Eric's rising popularity led to more opportunities and to larger and larger crowds at events now known as "Muscular Christianity Campaigns." Students and local athletes were invited to a "campaign," where they had fun participating in or watching staged matches or competitions. Eric took part in these, much to his delight . . . and the crowd's. Above all, those in attendance came to understand that Christianity bore no resemblance to weakness or boredom. Rather, being a Christian was exciting.

One afternoon the postman delivered a large stack of mail to Eric—something he had become uneasily accustomed to. But this particular stack held an envelope with an interesting bit of correspondence. A young girl, Miss Elsa McKechnie, informed Eric that she had formed the *official* "Eric Liddell Fan Club" and was eager to hear back from him. Eric always tried to correspond with everyone who took the time to write him. He took special consideration for the youth, artistically weaving his playfulness with his passion for God. Elsa was no exception, since it was "official" business after all.

Through it all, Eric did his best to remain humble as he polished his oratory skills with each new speaking opportunity. He engaged people with the prospect of faith in Christ and how that might factor into their lives and futures.

•　•　•

During the fall of 1923, Eric had to make preparations for the VIII Olympiad, which was swiftly approaching. Despite his valued contributions to Scotland's international rugby team, he decided to sacrifice his rugby play and focus exclusively on his running regimen. Knowing that he was the strong favorite to win the Olympic gold medal in the 100 meters, he decided that training for the sport and the race deserved his complete focus. With so much on the line, he didn't want to risk potential injury, especially with the hopeful eyes of the nation on him.

During this time, everything in Eric's life ran smoothly and efficiently. He enjoyed all the things prized by the superficial—athletic superiority, fame and adoring fans, youthfulness and health, respect and admiration from his peers, and a bright future. Yet as a man of faith, contentment reached its height with a sense of purpose and security in the belief that he was accomplishing what God had assigned him.

And then—just as everything seemed to be going well for the young Scottish athlete—news turned Eric's world on its head.

The opening heats for the 100 meters in the Olympics fell on a Sunday.

By this time, Eric had literally told tens of thousands of people about the role of Christ in his life and the importance of observing the Sabbath. How could he possibly compete on the Lord's Day, going against his own word—not to mention the Word of God—and throw sand in the eyes of everyone who had listened to him in the process? The very fabric of his integrity was at stake.

And he knew it.

What he didn't know, however, was that a single decision would send an otherwise humble man to the heights of fame, not only in his lifetime but for nearly a century afterward.

CHAPTER 5

OLYMPIC
MIND GAMES

Remember the Sabbath day,
to keep it holy.
Exodus 20:8

Late Autumn/Early Winter 1923

Eric stood at the sitting room window, staring out. The land he
loved lay beyond the street of the town house he called home.
He had not been born into this land; rather, it was the land of
his forefathers, the one that had adopted him early in his life
and that embraced him as a mother nurtures a child.

She had been good to him, providing him friends and an education, places to strengthen his faith and tracks to fortify his abilities in races and games. She had trained him, nourished him,
adored him.

And now . . . was it any wonder she had turned on him?

"Your decision not to run on the Sabbath has farther-reaching
consequences than national pride, Eric," D. P. said from a chair
behind him in the sitting room, the same chair where, only
months earlier, he had come to Eric asking him to join him in
Armadale.

Eric crossed his arms and felt every muscle in his back tense. "How's that?"

"The people are nearly out for blood—you were their shining hope in the aftermath of the war."

Eric flinched. "I didn't ask to be. I never—"

"No," D. P. agreed. "No, you didn't. But I daresay more than you imagine is at stake."

Eric turned and kicked at the fraying carpet with the toe of his shoe. "I know." He didn't look at his friend. He didn't have to. He knew instinctively the overwhelming concern that had worked its way across D. P.'s face.

"The more tarnished your image becomes, my boy, the more negative the impact it could have on the campaigns."

Eric sighed deeply as he walked to the same chair he had sat in the previous spring. "What do you suggest then?"

Thomson chuckled as he shook his head. "I would never dream of trying to persuade you, Eric—though I've surely been propositioned to do so." He stretched out his legs, crossing them at the ankles. "I wouldn't even be so presumptuous as to believe I could persuade you to change your mind. I only want you to understand the situation for those who have put their faith in you—"

"But I have put my faith in God," Eric said, the resolution rising in his voice.

"Some are saying this is a type of publicity stunt."

Eric's hand twitched. "You know me better than that."

D. P. chuckled again. "Ah, yes. Yes, I do, Eric. Your decision is based on principles from which you have never deviated. Not even by a hairsbreadth."

Eric closed his eyes against the words, remembering the agitation of those who had demanded something more of him than he could give. To go along with them meant to turn his back on God—the God of the Sabbath and the God of his life. And he couldn't. He simply couldn't.

Eric's eyes opened to find D. P. staring at him expectantly. But Eric shook his head. "I will not run," he said. "I will not."

PERHAPS THE BIGGEST MYTH surrounding Eric Liddell's life involves one highly scrutinized episode: that he deliberated over withdrawing from the 100 meters up until the week of the Olympic Games and that by serendipitous fortune, an eleventh-hour opportunity presented itself for Eric to run in the 400 meters, thereby paving the way to glory. What sounds like a Hollywood story indeed is presented beautifully, but inaccurately, in the critically acclaimed film *Chariots of Fire* (1981).

In actuality, upon hearing the news in the early fall of 1923—months before the Summer Olympics—that the opening 100-meter heats were set for a Sunday, Eric knew without question what his response would be. He would *not* run on the Sabbath—even for the Olympics. End of discussion.

Eric's deep-seated reverence for the Sabbath was rooted in the seriousness of his missionary upbringing, cultivated in the rigidity of his boarding school, and nourished by D. P. Thomson's strong legalistic theology. In Eric's thinking, it stood to reason that mankind should adhere to one of God's earliest commandments. But even to Christians of his day, Liddell's practice was in the minority and seemed like foolish extremism to non-Christians and those of weak belief.

After his conversation with Eric, D. P. helpfully framed Eric's Sabbath understanding to those who inquired by saying, "Eric [believes], as I myself have always done, that, one day in seven, different in every way from the others, gives new significance and value to the remaining six."[1]

While Eric considered his decision to be quite commonplace,

the majority of onlookers perceived it as a much bolder statement, especially considering everything at stake. Not only would Eric withdraw from the 100 meters, but his participation in two relays—the 4 x 100 meters and the 4 x 400 meters—would be withdrawn as well, since those events also fell on Sundays. Having Eric step out of three races would be a genuine deathblow to Great Britain's chances not only to lay claim to the fastest man on earth but also to mark a triumphant return to global sports dominance. In the wake of World War I, this was of immeasurable value for national pride and morale.

While Eric was more than equipped to make the sacrifice, he was not prepared for the ensuing aftermath. He had always been likable, with hardly a disparaging word spoken against him, and in recent years only good press followed wherever he went. All that was about to change.

Everyone, it seemed, had an opinion about his decision.

After Eric refused to run on Sunday, Britain ran through the stages of grief. They said Liddell would ultimately change his mind. When that hope went unrealized, they grew angry, calling him a coward and asking how he could turn his back on his country. They bargained, suggesting that he dedicate the race to the Lord or that the Sabbath ended at a particular time of day.

"My Sabbath lasts *all* day," Eric replied.

There was even speculation that the British Olympic authorities should appeal to the International Olympic Committee to reschedule some events, owing to religious observance. Any such controversial conversations that may have taken place were behind closed doors, unpublicized, and without success. Ultimately Great Britain dissolved into depression as the winter months set in, accepting that Eric—their greatest hope for national pride and glory—could not be swayed from his beliefs.

•   •   •

Eric genuinely lived according to the doctrines of his faith—which he believed and clung to—and he would not waver or consider it shrewd to compromise. He did not see the wisdom in competing on the Sabbath, nor did he worry about what his choice cost him. Seeking the glory and praise of other people was not his purpose. He would have accepted never competing in the Olympics at all, without losing any sleep in the process, had no reasonable solution come forward.

Lost in all the nearly political hullabaloo was the fact that Eric still planned on competing in the 200 meters, held on a Tuesday and Wednesday. But a wounded nation preparing for battle saw this only as a pale olive branch.

And then there was the 400 meters, which was not scheduled on a Sunday, and there was still time to qualify. However, there was one glaring problem. Eric had never—*ever*—seriously competed at that distance before.

This jump might not sound like much to a novice, but to the seasoned competitor, it bordered on preposterous. Those who had spent years training and competing in the 400 would surely leave Eric in their dust. But in some attempt to continue to do right by his country without turning his back on God's order, Eric sought out his coach, Tom McKerchar, to explore the prospect.

The year before, during the 1922 track season, Eric had run the 400 meters after his featured events in the 100- and 200-meter races, but only twice. They served, more or less, as extra events to sneak in a full workout on a race day, thereby strengthening him for later in the season. His times were decent for a world-class sprinter, but nothing to write home about. They were surely nothing to assure a gold at the Olympics.

Except for one event . . .

Eric's performance at this Stoke-on-Trent event during the summer of 1923 convinced McKerchar that Eric should at the very least try.

Eric ran the event without the benefit of lanes. Legally, the runners could cross in front of each other but were prohibited from boxing in other runners. From the firing of the gun, Eric fell behind. Then, fifteen yards down the track, another runner, J. J. Gillis, fouled Eric, who rolled onto the grass infield. When Eric heard the judge cry "foul," he assumed the ruling was toward him. But just then another judge screamed at Eric to get up.

Eric stood and stared down the track. The other runners were now twenty yards ahead.

Once he had his bearings, Eric took off at lightning speed. By the 300-yard point, he had caught up to the others. Then spectators watched in awe as his "heid went back." Legs pumping and heart pounding, Eric passed Gillis, who was in the lead, and won by two yards.

The Scotsman, in its article on the race, wrote, "The circumstances in which [Liddell] won made it a performance bordering on the miraculous."[2]

Eric fell to the infield grass, his heart pounding as though it might erupt from his chest. A teammate helped him onto his feet, then over to the pavilion. He suggested Eric have a drop of brandy to revive him. But Eric, in semiconsciousness, replied, "No thanks, Jimmy. Just a drop of strong tea."

His time was 51.2 seconds, almost three full seconds off the world record—and every tenth of a second in a race that short was a major barrier.

Yet the question remained: What could Eric have run had he not fallen?

• • •

Both McKerchar and Eric believed there was a possibility—albeit slim—that they could transform Eric—a 100-meter champion—into a world-caliber 400-meter man in time for the Olympics. But they only had six months to do it.

Eric and Tom knew one area to address: Eric's starting technique. Precious time had been lost there, and there was room for improvement. Years later, Eric remembered the difficulty:

> One of the hardest lessons to learn is how to start. Time after time you go to your holes, rise to the "get set" position, and wait for the pistol to go. Someone tries to go off before the pistol, and so we all have to get up and start from the beginning again. Even after I had been at it for four years, the papers now and then reminded me that my weak point was the slowness with which I started.[3]

When the announcement came that Eric Liddell would, in addition to the 200 meters, compete in the 400 meters, more than a few eyes rolled. As if such a goal—one Brits were sure he would fail at—would make up for losing the 100.

And by losing, they meant *not running*.

By now, all eyes had turned toward Harold Abrahams, an English star sprinter at Cambridge, who had become the de facto favorite after Liddell's refusal to run in the 100. Eric had sorely beaten Abrahams in the 100-meter head-to-head in July of 1923. Even so, British sports enthusiasts believed Abrahams could give them the gold at the Olympics.

Odds stacked against him. Naysayers lined up. Patriotic pressure mounted.

Eric remained grounded in his faith. He had somehow managed not to get caught up in the pandemonium played out in the press, which had begun to oscillate back ever so gently. The December 1923 edition of *The Student* offered,

Ninety-nine men, gifted with Eric's prowess, would now be insufferably swollen-headed, but here we have the hundredth man. Here is a man who hates praise and shuns publicity, yet is deserving of both. Here is a man with a mind of his own, and not afraid to voice his most sacred feeling on a platform if, by so doing, he thinks it will help his fellows. Here is a man who has courage, and delights to accept a challenge, be it for the sake of his School, his 'Varsity, his Country, or his God. And lastly, here is a man who wins because he sets his teeth, quietly but firmly, and always plays the game. Everyone is fond of Eric.[4]

CHAPTER 6

INTO BATTLE

Count it all joy, my brothers, when you meet trials of various kinds, for you know that the testing of your faith produces steadfastness. And let steadfastness have its full effect, that you may be perfect and complete, lacking in nothing.

James 1:2-4

April 1924

Eric had only been back home from America for a few hours when he found himself sitting across the dining room table from his brother, enjoying his favorite dinner of sausage and cheese and, of course, haggis.

"So, how'd you find America?" Rob asked him.

"By boat," Eric teased as he reached for the cup of tea resting to the right of his plate.

"Funny."

Eric shook his head, setting all banter aside. "It began badly enough. I should have known the Penn Relays would follow suit."

Rob smiled and rested his fork and knife against the plate. "How's that?"

"First I left my luggage on the dock and had to run back for it. Then there were the storms. Nearly pitched the ship, they were so ominous."

"Hyperbole."

"You think I'm kidding."

"I do."

Eric waved his fork in the air as if to dismiss his previous words. "All right, you win. But they were pretty bad."

"You didn't get sick like before, did you?" Rob asked with a wink.

Eric studied his plate, trying to decide what to dive into next. "Not quite the same . . . but yes," he answered quietly, remembering the trip the family had made when he'd first come to England. He'd been sick with dysentery and had lost so much weight, he had barely been able to support himself to walk across the deck. "Remember that woman? She was one—"

"—one of the missionary wives. She said with you unable to walk, you'd never be able to run," Rob responded. "I guess you showed her."

Eric chuckled as he bit into a slice of sausage. "Maybe not. My times at the games were quite awful. I came in fourth in the 100 and second in the 200. A lousy performance . . . and against international competition at that. The papers are sure to bring this up."

"Don't fret about it," Rob said, his voice returning to a more serious tone. "Won't do you a bit of good. How'd the others do?"

"Not a one of us came home with a first."

"Better for you, I'd say."

True, but Eric frowned at the thought. What would all this mean to the Olympic team in July? "One bright note," he said then. "On the trip back I got along quite famously with Arthur Marshall. He's one of the seven from the Cambridge University Athletics Club." He grinned. "We went to a masquerade ball one night. Had a smashing time." Eric chuckled.

"What's so funny?"

Heat rushed to Eric's cheeks as he replied, "Oh . . . it's nothing. Just that . . . Arthur and I met two very nice young ladies."

A twinkle caught in Rob's eye. "Did you now?"

"They told us they'd be in Paris for the Games and that—well, you know—perhaps we'd meet up after the races are done." He waggled his brow at his brother. "Speaking of young ladies, your wedding day is practically on top of us."

Rob grinned brightly before his somber face returned. "And soon thereafter we'll leave for China. I won't be there for you. For the Games."

Eric pressed his lips together. "No," he said. "You won't."

Yes, soon after the Games, Rob and his new bride, Ria, would leave for his birthplace. Everyone—Eric's entire family—would reside in China. Everyone but him.

And, once again, Eric would be alone.

AFTER ROB'S WEDDING, Eric continued to train for the world's greatest games.

He ran two races the following month but did not put forth an effort in the 400 meters until the end of May and on his home field at Craiglockhart, the University of Edinburgh. His first report card read:

- 100 yards—10.2
- 220 yards—23.0
- 440 yards—51.5

Only six weeks stood between Eric and the Games in Paris. He and Tom McKerchar both knew they had a lot of work to do, especially concerning his time in the 400.

At the next competition, Eric's times showed some improvement:

- 100 yards—10.2
- 220 yards—22.4
- 440 yards—51.2

As June wore on, Eric continued to improve. Eric won the 100 yards with a record-breaking (for the meet) 10 seconds flat. He also won the 220 yards with a time of 22.6 and the 440 yards with a sustained time of 51.2.

By Friday, June 20, at Stamford Bridge, London, Eric had dropped his 440-yard time to 49.6, a mark that began to flirt with the best times in the world at that distance. The following day, Eric lost the 220-yard finals to a runner from South Africa, finishing in second place by two and a half yards—devastating for a runner in serious competition.

Yet also on that same day, Eric won the 440 yards in 49.6 seconds. Still, he was not favored to win the 400 at the Olympics. Still, his countrymen looked at him as though he'd betrayed them.

Still, Eric remained on the outside looking in.

· · ·

Two of the most famous scenes in the 1981 movie *Chariots of Fire* are those that bookend the film—the British Olympic team running down the beaches of Broadstairs, Kent, in preparation for their departure to Paris.

Would choosing God's way result in victory?

Would Eric cross the finish line as—or behind—the winner?

Or not at all?

British fans provided great fanfare as their Olympic team embarked from Victoria Station. The elaborate send-off propelled the team into the opening ceremonies, allowing them to establish momentum early. On Sunday, July 6, while Eric worshiped at Scots Kirk, Harold Abrahams qualified for the 100-meter semifinals, which were to be held the following day. On Monday, Abrahams went on to win the gold medal in the 100 meters with a time of 10.6.

Britain breathed a sigh of relief at Abrahams's triumph, staking claim to the fastest man in the world with a new Olympic record, while no one said a negative word about the fact that Liddell had been exactly where he'd said he'd be—at church—the day before. Abrahams's achievement relieved Eric of a small amount of pressure, but the reprieve would be short lived when both men dug themselves (and Britain) into a hole.

On Tuesday, July 8, Eric faced his first Olympic challenge: the 200 meters. He took first in his opening heat, posting a time of 22.2. Later that day he dropped his time to 21.9. Eric safely advanced to the Wednesday semifinal heats, as well as into the finals—and Abrahams along with him.

But in the finals, Eric finished a disappointing third, barely nipped by Jackson Scholz and Charley Paddock of the United States, with a time of 21.9. Eric was not the only one who recognized the defeat. The main post in Edinburgh, *The Scotsman*, seized the opportunity to add more pressure:

> Liddell failed to reproduce the strong finish by which so
> many of his races in this country had been won. He was
> well placed and had his spurt been forthcoming he would
> undoubtedly have won.[1]

The paper seemingly forgot to report that Eric *did* win the bronze. Nor did it state that Harold Abrahams finished dead last.

Eric felt the foreboding weight of reality the night before the opening heats for the 400 meters. The eyes of the world seemed to be on Eric, his faith, and his God, all of which would be unfairly evaluated based on his performance—particularly if he made a poor showing. In retrospect, winning the bronze medal for the 200 meters would be a proud achievement marking a worthy effort against formidable opponents, but Eric knew he had much more to prove. His family was a half a world away, and he recognized that—even with his teammates and coach cheering him on—he was surrounded by people but alone.

Save for God.

Thursday arrived.

Eric started well, winning the opening heat with a slow time of 50.2. With three anticipated races to go, runners typically save energy in hopes of the greatest performance possible in the finals—provided they can make it there. This strategy worked well. Eric ran the fastest time of his life later that day, 49.3.

But Eric knew that while his time ensured him a spot in the Friday semifinals, it only placed him *second* in the heat. Eric had become the dark horse favorite. He knew it. But more important, so did everyone else.

The next morning, after a muscle-loosening massage, Eric's masseur handed him a note. Eric looked at the folded piece of paper, then slipped it into his pocket. "I'll read it when I get to the stadium," Eric said.

Eric went through his usual warm-ups and stretches, and he gentlemanly shook the hands of all his opponents before the start. Before digging his starting stance in the cinder, he removed the note, and—before one of the biggest moments of his life—read,

In the old book it says, "He that honours me I will honour." Wishing you the best of success always.

Eric did not disappoint in the semifinals. He delivered an astonishing 48.2 in the second of two heats. Even Horatio Fitch, the American odds-on favorite to win the gold, who had won the first heat at 47.8, took notice.

Eventually, the last call for the 400-meter finals rang through the stadium, and Eric took his position. Before the Games, both he and McKerchar had been pleased to hear that the races would be run on marked lanes, thereby eliminating the chance for being boxed in. But Eric had drawn lane six, the outermost lane—the most difficult position and least-desired assignment. The staggered start around the track's curve thrust him far out in front, which prevented him from being able to see any competitors during the majority of the race.

Eric's visible advantages had been all but removed, but he had an undetectable edge few others could see, let alone understand. He ran not only for Britain, but first and foremost for God. No matter what transpired during the race—whether he won or lost—Eric knew he already possessed an eternal peace that surpassed understanding.

The spectators' eyes went to Eric. Here stood the Scottish sprinter who refused to run on Sunday. The magnitude of the unfolding story line had swelled with each heat. Electric anticipation galvanized the stadium when Eric and the other runners crouched into their starting stances. Eric held more of a raw sprinter's mind-set and more experience in the shorter distances than his opponents. If he had raced against these same runners in the open 100 meters or 200 meters, there would have been no question who would have won. He had superior turnover leg speed. But this was the 400 meters.

Could Eric maintain his speed during the second half of the race?

The gunshot reverberated through the stadium, releasing the tension of both the sprinters and the crowd. Eric Liddell's moment of reckoning had arrived. He burst out swiftly, building a gradual lead on the runners, and maintained command of the race down the back straightaway. The other runners chased after him, fully expecting to reel him in. The closing turn of the track would assure this. Or so everyone thought.

Everyone but Eric.

As the finish tape waved in the late afternoon heat, Eric tilted his head back in his unorthodox style and dug in hard for the finish. His gait was not as fluid as the other runners', and as his muscles tightened in the second half of the race, Eric's stride appeared more hindered. He propelled forward, pushing through the turn, and led into the final straightaway.

The last 100 meters of the open 400 is the most grueling end to a race of any distance. The sheer speed needed to run a sub-50-second quarter rivals the shorter sprints yet calls for inordinate strength for a closing kick, which the longer distances require. The most difficult aspects of both ends of the running spectrum marry in those last one hundred meters.

Eric presided over these two demands marvelously as he flew down the track toward vindication. The other runners crept closer as they passed through the curve, but Eric showed no sign of slowing. The crowd stood in uproarious appreciation as #451 drew closer to destiny—his head back, his face lifted toward God.

In the last few strides one challenger fell. The pace had proved to be too much. Eric crossed the line first, setting a new world record of 47.6, as spectators gasped. Eric had broken his own record from earlier in the day by six tenths of a second—an astonishing feat by any stretch of the imagination.

Colombes Stadium thundered in frenzy and adoration as Eric breathed at a rapid pace, all the while taking in the moment. He shook hands (notably with two of the runners who had fallen) and flashed a smile, which simultaneously exuded exoneration and joy. He rested his hands against his hips, willing his body back to normal, reveling in his unexpected triumph.

Within seconds, journalists flocked to Britain's freshly reinstated darling in astonishment, but as soon as the band played "God Save the King," Eric Liddell quietly slipped out of the stadium.

CHAPTER 7

A VICTORY LAP

*For everyone who has been born of God
overcomes the world. And this is the victory
that has overcome the world—our faith.*

1 John 5:4

July 1924

The reporter grinned at Eric with his pencil poised, ready to write on the palm-sized pad of paper cupped in his hand. "To what do you owe your victory?"

Eric swallowed back a smile. "I ran the first 200 meters as hard as I could." He paused long enough to raise his brow, to prove—once and for all—the conviction that burned within his heart. "Then, with God's help, I ran the second 200 harder."

The journalist and those around him chuckled good-naturedly.

"Eric," one of them called out. "Harold Abrahams said . . ." He looked down at his notes. "That people may shout their heads off about your appalling style. 'Well, let them. He gets there,' he said. Do you have anything to add to that?"

Now it was Eric's turn to laugh. "We each have our own way to perform the gifts God gave us."

Another reporter raised his hand. "One paper—*The Scotsman*—said you achieved immortality in Paris."

"No, sir," Eric remarked quickly. "My immortality comes from Christ—not a track and field stadium in France."

FORTY-FOUR NATIONS COMPETED at the 1924 Olympics in Paris, France. Germany and China were absent from participation. The British traded blows in the short sprints with Charley Paddock and Jackson Scholz of the United States. Ultimately the British prevailed, winning gold in the 100 meters, the 400 meters, and the 800 meters, by Harold Abrahams, Eric Liddell, and Douglas Lowe, respectively. Finland equally dominated the longer distances. Albin Stenroos took gold in the marathon; Paavo Nurmi in the 1,500 meters, the 5,000 meters, and the cross-country run; and Ville Ritola in the 10,000 meters and the steeplechase, as well as silver in the 5,000 meters and the cross-country race. The "Flying Finns" were a formidable force with which to reckon.

With 126 events tallied from seventeen different sports, the United States finished first with forty-five gold medals, then Finland with fourteen, and France with thirteen. Great Britain ranked fourth with nine medals—and an unforgettable performance, especially for the Flying Scotsman. Not only had Eric been the first from Scotland to win a medal in the 200 meters (the bronze), he was the first Scot to medal in *any* Olympic event since 1908, when Wyndham Halswelle won gold in a final that became controversial when, after an American runner became ineligible due to illegal maneuvers, the race was rerun with Halswelle as the only contender.

Despite the joys of victory, what Eric looked most forward to was returning to normal life. But he soon discovered there was nothing normal about being a gold-medal champion.

After Eric returned to the United Kingdom, he shifted from

training for the Olympics to preparing for graduation from the University of Edinburgh, which was only a few days away.

On Thursday, July 17, 1924, Eric walked into McEwan Hall of the University of Edinburgh with his classmates, each one dressed in graduation-day finery.

These were the days before microphones and PA systems, so graduation marshals were required to use the power of their lungs and voices from the center of the stage. As the graduating class of 1924 received their diplomas, family and friends sat quietly within the massive Italian Renaissance–inspired room when the students' names were called. As the graduates received their diplomas, the applause came as light patter, the people being respectful of the reverberations caused by the large dome ceiling. Then Principal and Vice Chancellor Sir Alfred Ewing called out, "Bachelor of Science degree, *Mr. Eric Henry Liddell.*"

Eric took the steps, and as his foot met the highly polished floorboards of the stage, the crowd—both observers and students—rose in deafening applause. Long minutes passed as Eric cast his smile from the teary-eyed faculty and distinguished guests who sat on red velvet seats, to his fellow classmates, then outward to the rest of the audience. The tide had turned in his favor—and Eric had been made a better man because of it, in spite of having been in fine standing to begin with. He'd endured the confusion of his countrymen—those who, even of the same beliefs, could not quite understand his steadfastness. He had returned from the Olympics as a gold medalist and as a national hero but—more importantly—as a man who'd stood his ground.

Finally, Sir Alfred raised his hands and requested silence. Slowly the people quieted and returned to their seats.

"Mr. Liddell," Sir Alfred began, "you have shown that none can pass you but the examiner!" A light chuckle met Eric's ears, and he smiled. Sir Alfred continued,

In the ancient Olympic tests the victor was crowned with wild olive by the High priest of Zeus, and a poem written in his honour was presented to him. A Vice-Chancellor is no High Priest, but he speaks and acts for the University; and in the name of the University, which is proud of you, and to which you have brought fresh honour, I present you with this epigram in Greek, composed by Professor Mair, and place upon your head this chaplet of wild olive.[1]

Sir Alfred then placed a wreath made of oleaster atop Eric's head. (He used oleaster because olive trees do not grow in Edinburgh, but oleaster, which does, is a garden derivative from the olive plant.) Again, the crowd cheered.

The epigram, translated into English, read as follows:

Happy the man who the wreathed games essaying
*   Returns the laurelled brow,*
Thrice happy victor thou, such speed displaying
*   As none hath showed till now;*
We joy, and Alma Mater, for thy merit
*   Proffers to thee this crown:*
Take it, Olympic Victor. While you wear it
*   May Heaven never frown.*[2]

After the other names had been called and the diplomas received, neither Eric's friends nor the crowd had any interest in modesty. They hoisted Eric up on a chair supported by poles at its base and paraded him like a pharaoh, navigating him through a cheering crowd of men, women, and children, all the way to the doors of St. Giles' Cathedral, the birthplace of the Presbyterian Church, for the traditional service of thanksgiving. Overtures quickly came for Eric to give a response to the accolades.

Eric recalled his trip to the Penn Relays in the United States and mustered an extemporaneous response. "Over the gates of Pennsylvania University," he said,

> are inscribed these words: "In the dust of defeat as well as the laurels of victory there is glory to be found if one has done his best." There are many men and women who have done their best, but who have not succeeded in gaining the laurels of victory. To them, as much honor is due as to those who have received these laurels.[3]

After the service at St. Giles', Eric moved onward to the graduation luncheon at University Union. Though it was not normal for a recent graduate with only a bachelor's degree to be so honored, Eric became the central focus. Professor Richard Lodge, a noted historian, gave a special tribute to Eric: "Even a bachelor of science graduate should have no difficulty in translating his fancy Greek epigram, since the recipient is both a Liddell and a Scot."[4]

Those in the room laughed at the jest toward the popular *Liddell and Scott Greek-English Lexicon.*

After Professor Lodge concluded his speech, the crowd again pressed Eric to say a few words.

Eric said,

> I ask you to remember today that I suffer from a certain defect of constitution. I am a short-distance runner, a sprinter. Because I suffer from short-windedness, therefore I will not detain you for long.
>
> The papers have told you that my form, my action, is extremely bad. But this condition can probably be traced to my forefathers. As we all know in Scotland, the Borderers used to visit England now and then, and escape back as

quickly as possible. It was no doubt the practice of my forefathers to do this. The speed with which my forefathers returned from England seems to have been handed down in my family from generation to generation. They had to get back as best they could, and one did not look for correct action. So this probably explains my own running action.

The crowd laughed.
Eric continued:

A man is composed of three parts—body, mind, and soul. And if the University system continues to teach toward what each is entitled to, it will get the best and truest graduates from the University. When it is realized that they not only store the mind with knowledge, but that they also have to educate the body for the strenuous life it has to go through, and remember that they were of the spirit as well, the University will pass down graduates who are really worthy of taking their place in any field of life.[5]

With the luncheon over, the festivities continued. If Eric had grown weary of the accolades, he would be forced to endure them for a while longer as both he and Sir Alfred Ewing entered a "carriage" pulled by muscled athletes rather than horses. Sir Alfred and Eric were taken to Sir Alfred's home for afternoon tea.

"Never," Sir Alfred later said, "have I ever basked in so much reflected glory."[6]

●　　●　　●

The next day a dinner was held in Eric's honor at Mackie's Dining Salon—an idea that had originated from a group of congratulatory men who had sent Eric a telegram while he was in Paris. Noted theologian and jurist Lord Sands, the provost Sir William Lowrie Sleigh, and Sir Alfred Ewing were all present in the company of more than one hundred distinguished guests.

This was a unique moment in the history of Edinburgh, Scotland. The corporation of the city had surely welcomed and celebrated many worthy guests in the past—soldiers, statesmen, and elite leaders—but this was their first chance to do so with an Olympian. Eric Liddell was, simply put, the finest athlete Scotland had ever produced.

During his keynote address, Lord Sands said,

[I] had always understood that the quarter-mile was one of the most sporting and interesting of races. It was also one of the most gruelling, and it was somewhat remarkable that it happened to be the only Olympic race which had been won by a Scotsman. In these days of moral flabbiness it was something to find a man who was not content to shield himself behind such easy phrases as "It was once in a way" or "When you go to Rome you must do as they do in Rome."[7]

Lord Sands also arranged for a cablegram to be sent to Eric's parents in China stating cordial congratulations on "Eric's wonderful feat, and still more on his noble witness for Christian principles."[8]

Sir William Sleigh presented Eric with a gold watch inscribed with the arms of the City of Edinburgh and the words "Presented by the Corporation of Edinburgh to Eric H. Liddell, B.Sc., in recognition of his brilliant achievement in winning in record time the 400 metres at the Olympic games—Paris, 1924—W. L. Sleigh, Lord Provost."[9]

Eric spoke to the assembly in his soft voice, but his character refused to allow him to revel in the limelight. Humility and humor were hallmarks in Eric's delivery. On arriving at the dinner, he noticed his initials on the program—E. H. L. He said, "My parents had first named me Henry Eric Liddell, but before it became officially registered, a friend suggested to my father that the initials H. E. L. might be rather awkward. This evening would certainly have been an occasion on which they would have been awkward."[10]

Understanding that those in the room would want him to say something—*anything*—about his Olympic experience, he shared the story of having received the note in Paris that reminded him of God's Word in 1 Samuel. "He that honoureth me, I shall honour," he quoted.

"It was perhaps the finest thing I experienced in Paris, a great surprise and a great pleasure to know there were others who shared my sentiments about the Lord's day."[11] Eric spoke a few additional words to remind them of his ultimate goal to return to China as a missionary. In spite of what many may have hoped, he would not make athletics his long-term career. God had made him fast, yes, but God had also made him for China. Decisions of when and specifications of how loomed. He would at some point within the next year depart as a missionary, and he was not sure what the future held exactly for his running during that time. But he was more than content to focus on serving Christ in the mission field.

In closing he asked for their help and prayers. "Thank you very much indeed for giving me such a great honor tonight," he said.

A perplexed peace infused the gathering. It was as if the time for celebrating had abruptly come to an end, and the page of the Olympics had been turned. It was an unprecedented mood—most men in Eric's position would have milked the honor he seemed to so easily shun—yet it was salvaged by the possibility that there might at least be one more season to enjoy his running.

The Student did its best to provide words for the utterly astounding deflection of fame:

Success in athletics, sufficient to turn the head of any ordinary man, has left Liddell absolutely unspoilt, and his modesty is entirely genuine and unaffected. He has taken his triumphs in his stride, as it were, and has never made any sort of fuss. What he has thought it right to do, that he has done, looking neither to the left nor to the right, and yielding not one jot or tittle of principle either to court applause or to placate criticism. Courteous and affable, he is utterly free from "gush." Devoted to his principles, he is without a touch of Pharisaism. The best that can be said of any student is that he has left the fame of his University fairer than he found it, and his grateful *Alma Mater* is proud to recognise that to no man does that praise more certainly belong than to Eric Henry Liddell.[12]

That night, Eric boarded a train for London to compete in a post-Olympics relay competition between the United States and the British Empire, which would be held the next day—which also happened to be the day of Rob's missionary installation. Just as Rob had missed Eric's big race in France, Eric would miss Rob's big day in Britain.

No open races were run, only four-man relay teams. The United States got the best of the Brits in the majority of the events, but Eric gave another memorable performance that saved the day . . . if not a bit of national dignity. During the anchor leg of the 4 x 400, Eric received the baton well behind the American star, Horatio Fitch. Eric drew in close at the finish and surpassed him soundly for an emphatic win by four yards, matching his Olympic medal time with a 400-meter relay split of 47.6.

After the race, journalists crowded London's King's Cross railway station platform, their eyes searching for the Flying Scotsman.

But Eric Liddell had spied a baggage porter . . .

Minutes later, he boarded the train undetected, ready to return to Edinburgh.

Ready to return to life . . . and to another looming question.

CHAPTER 8

DOCTRINAL DISCERNMENT

Pay close attention to yourself and to your teaching;
persevere in these things, for as you do this you will ensure
salvation both for yourself and for those who hear you.

1 Timothy 4:16, NASB

Late Autumn 1924

"I don't believe I've ever known anyone who couldn't say no quite like you, Eric," D. P. told Eric at the end of another campaign.

Eric stretched his legs from the seat he'd nearly collapsed into, one directly opposite the seat his friend slouched on. He glanced out the small window of the train, smudged with a child's fingerprints from an earlier passage, to the platform on the other side. With a start the train took off, and—plank by plank—the station slid from view. "It's impossible to estimate what a simple yes can measure out to be."

D. P. closed his eyes. "Still . . ."

"Would you have me say no?" Eric's smile broke easily as D. P.'s eyes opened at the mention of the two-letter word. "And, if so, to which request?"

"Still," D. P. repeated. He adjusted his long frame into a more comfortable position. Then, as his gaze found Eric, he continued,

"But one day, Eric, when they ask me about you—and they will—I'll have to say that as a leader—as a speaker—you've made more strides in the last six months than anyone I've ever encountered. You're hardly the same man as the shy thing I asked to come to Armadale back when."

Eric leaned his head against the cold leather of the seat, then pulled his overcoat more tightly around him. "It helps that we get along so well," he teased.

Again, D. P. closed his eyes. "It doesn't hurt, my friend. But I'll tell you this—I've never known a man with finer character than you."

Eric looked down at his hands, taking note of his thumbnails.

"And when they ask me," D. P. continued as the night's darkness fell around them, "I'll say, 'There was never a hitch or a shadow in our friendship.'"

"No," Eric whispered.

"Due to you entirely, Eric."

Eric studied what little he could see of the calmness of D. P.'s face, then shut his own eyes. He was tired . . . so tired . . . and sleep—with the rocking of the train—should come easily now. "Not entirely," he mumbled.

"Yes," D. P. said from what sounded like a world away. "Due to you entirely." He paused. "Pure gold is what you are, Eric. Pure gold, through and through."

AFTER HIS STUNNING OLYMPIC performance in the summer, of all the thrills and emotions Eric saw in people's faces, none had matched D. P. Thomson's. Thomson knew that with Eric's crowning athletic achievement, the crowds would not be able to resist coming to hear him speak. The time was ripe to harness the zenith of Eric's fame with the evangelism efforts in Britain.

D. P. felt that if Eric left for China soon—as Eric was considering doing—it would bring that opportunity to a premature end. "Stay in Edinburgh," D. P. suggested. "Begin seminary. That way you'll be better prepared for missionary work in China."

Eric listened with an open heart. He was determined to be a missionary, so it stood to reason that he should be equipped with some formal theological training.

"You can continue your love of running," D. P. continued, "as well as serve the Lord as an evangelistic missionary in Britain."

His friend and mentor made a compelling case, but Asia had a great need.

Eric returned to his flat—now in Gillespie Crescent—where he found another piece of correspondence from young Elsa McKechnie. The Eric Liddell Fan Club had grown—a great deal, she told Eric— and their legion was all ears for more inspirational words and advice from him. Eric received the message, in more ways than one.

God wanted him in China, but he could not argue with the window of opportunity he had to proclaim the gospel of Jesus Christ in Britain. A short while after his Olympic victory, Eric enrolled in the seminary at the Scottish Congregational College in Edinburgh and moved into a house in Merchiston Place, much to D. P. Thomson's delight.

•   •   •

During the month of September 1924, Eric and D. P. Thomson spoke in public meetings, first in Scotland and later in England. Their last event was held in Kilmarnock, a large burgh of forty thousand people located about twenty miles southwest of Glasgow. Each and every one of the Protestant churches there took part in the event.

Later, D. P. wrote to his mother, saying,

Kilmarnock has been a great experience. It finishes on
Sunday and promises to finish grandly. Never has there

been a finer spirit among the team, and never have we enjoyed such inspirational fellowship. We have gained five new members, splendid fellows all. 500 men turned out to hear Eric Liddell on the opening Sunday, and 1300 to the mass meeting at night. We had six meetings daily. On the second Sunday night we had 1700 at the Mass Meeting— One innovation proved very successful—a late meeting for young fellows attending evening classes.[1]

After Kilmarnock, Eric and D. P. traveled to Glasgow to hold meetings at the Dundas Street Congregational Church, where James Liddell had been ordained so many years before. Between 450 and 600 people showed up each night of the campaign. Eric "steadily gained in confidence, in clarity of thought, and in preaching power," D. P. penned in a letter home.[2]

Seminary began in October. In addition to Eric's new studies, he continued to serve as Sunday school teacher at Morningside, remained president of the Young People's Union, and honored his commitments to the weekend speaking events with D. P., which often included a pre-meeting race or rugby match.

The life of the seminary student, Eric had quickly learned, was one of discipline and devotion to God. To walk in the footsteps of the seminary professors was an important aspect of theological training. Mere head knowledge would not do.

Eric plunged headlong into the hermeneutical debate shaping the ecclesial landscape. He became familiar with Harry Emerson Fosdick's theological writings. Fosdick was an American Baptist pastor who resided in New York and served at a Presbyterian church in Manhattan's West Village. He'd become a leader in the rising controversial issue between fundamentalist and modernist theologians. The fundamentalist-modernist controversy had spilled over into multiple denominations and centered on how to interpret the Bible.

The modernists speculated that the Bible contained a certain amount of history, a kernel or husk of truth that had bloomed into myths, legends, and folklore. The fundamentalists argued that this way of thinking was a perilous road littered with potholes of presupposition. If the Bible were not infallible, that could mean that man had not been made in the image of God. Furthermore, miracles would be nonexistent; so much for Creation, the Virgin Birth, the deity of Christ, his resurrection, and his atonement for the world. To follow that path to its logical conclusion, the fundamentalists argued, would lead toward agnosticism and ultimately atheism.

Fundamentalists rejected the false impression that they employed an ignorant use of hermeneutics, the branch of knowledge dealing with interpretation. They defended only a *literal* interpretation of Scripture, where the context of each passage was king—poetry should be read as poetry, descriptive literature as descriptive, prescriptive as prescriptive. The limited range of possible interpretation meant that truth was apparent even in translation, so translations of the Bible could be confessed to be God's infallible Word, speaking to his people in the nuances of language that he created for them to use.

And this debate shaped and reshaped Eric Liddell.

Ultimately, Eric endorsed primarily a literal interpretation of the Bible, even though many in the Congregationalist Church were drifting toward modernist thinking. Years later, while writing his own discipleship book about studying the Bible, he quoted a sermon by John Wesley: "If any doctrines within the whole compass of Christianity may be termed 'fundamental,' they are doubtless these two: . . . justification . . . relating to that great work which God does *for us*, in forgiving our sins . . . [and] the new birth . . . relating to the great work which God does *in us*, in renewing our fallen nature."[3]

Eric took seriously the four disciplines of the seminarian—systematics, exegetics, history, and practical application. But every theologian gravitates to one, and Eric easily zeroed in on the practical discipline—simply conveying the gospel to people.

D. P. Thomson continued to arrange for speaking appointments for himself and Eric. In his campaign speeches with Thomson, Eric led with a subdued voice, offering a vivid picture of what a Christian life was like based on his own uniquely interesting experiences. Then Thomson followed up with a thunderous voice as the closer, calling those in the audience to commit their lives to Christ.

Although they were different in their approaches, Eric understood that much of the intense zealousness in Thomson's message had been born out of pain. He'd lost a brother and five cousins in the tragedies of the Great War and was occasionally prone to despair.

D. P.'s drive was in knowing that time was of the essence. Therefore, he didn't skirt around the issues in his messages or his emotional delivery.

D. P.'s one remaining brother, Robert, was equally passionate about evangelizing. Eric enjoyed Robert's company greatly on those occasions when he joined them for campaigns.

For D. P., Eric's continuing enthusiasm and his following brought great rejuvenation.

Although Eric understood D. P.'s fiery decision theology, he wrestled with reconciling the relationship between the law of God's Word and the gospel as he slowly tried to work out how to strive under the law and yet, at the same time, be content to live under the gospel. His approach when speaking was to compare faith to common ordinary experiences he could easily draw upon, such as from the science lab or the sports field. "We are here to place before you the call and challenge of Jesus Christ," he would say.

> Many of us are missing something in life because we are
> after the second best. We are placing before you during these
> few days the things we have found to be best. We are putting

before you one who is worthy of all our devotion—Christ. He is the Savior for the young as well as the old, and He is the one who can bring out the best that is in us.

Are you living up to the standards of Jesus Christ? We are looking for men and women who are willing to answer the challenge Christ is sending out. If this audience was out and out for Christ, the whole of Edinburgh would be changed. If the whole of this audience was out for Christ, it would go far past Edinburgh and through all Scotland. The last time Edinburgh was swept, all Scotland was flooded.

Then he would pause for effect. *"What are you going to do tonight?"*[4]

Eric and D. P.'s dynamic evangelism teamwork bore much fruit, but they were not without critics who questioned their tactics of playing on the emotions of the crowd. But thanks to his pre-Olympics experiences, critics were not new to Eric.

Leaving the critics to question him was fine . . . as long as he was okay in God's eyes.

•   •   •

As had been his habit for most of his life, Eric continued corresponding with his parents. When he shared both the positive and the negative press he and D. P. had received, his father wrote to the London Missionary Society secretary expressing his feelings and offering some perspective on the situation:

It is certainly very gratifying that Eric has so fully entered into this spiritual experience, and is desirous of passing on what is his possession, that others might also enjoy the same. My wife and I are perfectly sure he has the illumination that will be as an anchor for life if he keeps in touch with Jesus

Christ. We are very glad the team is not stressing theology as such, but getting the young life to face their personal relation to the Saviour. . . . From what we know of Eric we are sure he will not seek to harrow any one's feelings, or seek to publicly uncover what any one wishes to be kept sacred. But I guess he'll want very honest dealing as between individuals and their Lord. We could never dream of connecting Eric with sensational methods. Our hope is that the churches will be helped, and many young people make the great decision.[5]

Eric's speaking engagements with D. P. drew such crowds, and were so frequent, they hampered Eric's studies during that school year. Eric counterbalanced working through his own theological perspectives via reading, studies, lectures, chapels, sermons, and worship with subtly applying these perspectives in his own evangelism efforts.

But a new problem arose.

Eric had become involved with the Oxford Group—a term coined for Rev. Frank Buchman's theological and lunchtime gatherings of Christian men. Buchman was a mission-minded Lutheran minister from the United States. The Oxford Group subscribed to a number of Christian principles Eric already believed in, but they also afforded him the opportunity to consider new thoughts and principles that Eric then embraced, embodied, and would later reflect as bedrock disciplines of the Christian. Eric's old ideology contrasted with some of the principles he picked up from the Oxford Group.

Saying yes to every request felt easiest but only proved to be exhausting. Every man has his breaking point, even one described as being "pure gold through and through." Eric lamented his struggles to his parents, which prompted his concerned father to write again to the LMS: "We hear that Eric is having strenuous times between work and meetings. We hope he will not undertake too much while still doing study. He is one who finds it difficult to refuse work."[6]

Studying, speaking, training, racing, traveling, and keeping up with correspondence and endless requests pulled Eric in too many directions. Something had to give.

Soon.

The resident pastor at Morningside Congregational Church, Rev. Moffatt Scott, had always been supportive of Eric's ministry and active Sunday school leadership. He offered Eric the opportunity to preach to the youth a few evenings a week from the pulpit. Despite the nearly crushing schedule he lived under, this was a wonderful chance for Eric to partner with his closest support system and to serve the immediate community that had ministered so much to him.

Eric could not refuse.

But during his preparation for the task, terrible news from London blindsided him. Robert Thomson had died after a short illness. Both D. P. and Eric took the news of D. P.'s last brother's death exceedingly hard. The fleetingness of time and the fragility of life began to plague Eric as he worked through his own myriad emotions.

What if God had a different path in mind for him?

What if a seminary degree amounted to no more than words on parchment?

• • •

The season of Advent gave birth to wonderful news. Eric's coach, Tommy McKerchar, and his wife welcomed a new addition to their family: a son they named Eric Liddell McKerchar. Eric was dumbfounded by the honor, and when asked to be the child's godfather, he quickly agreed. Despite his demanding workload, when the time came for little Eric's baptism, the senior Eric had no issues clearing his schedule.

In January, Eric received a letter from his brother Rob. Rob and Ria had begun a six-month training in medicine and language skills. The letter also stated that Dr. Lavington Hart, the principal of Tientsin Anglo-Chinese College, had arranged for the money Eric would need for his passage to China.

TACC needed a science teacher, and Eric fit the bill. If Eric could arrive by spring, Hart would be the most ecstatic man on the planet.

But Eric wasn't ready to move to China quite yet. As spring arrived, D. P. and Eric continued with their meetings, now focusing on the United Kingdom's YMCAs. The most remarkable of these meetings, D. P. reported years later, was the one that took place at the London Central YMCA in Tottenham Court Road.

The men there gathered in the men's lounge. They sat on sofas and in armchairs, were allowed to smoke, and were encouraged to ask questions. But there was to be no singing of hymns, as D. P. and Eric had grown accustomed. There was to be no reading of Scripture and no call for a decision at the end of the meeting.

Within five minutes of Monday night's opening service, as Eric spoke, cigarettes and pipes were extinguished. While the men listened intently, none of them asked questions. By Wednesday evening, no one so much as lit a match.

"We will finish with an after-meeting in the chapel," D. P. told those in attendance. Eighty-plus men followed him and Eric out of the lounge that night.

The Glasgow Herald reported on Eric's work, saying, "Their leader, Eric Liddell, . . . stands for the Christian youth with a clean breeze about him, and his lungs well filled with the air that blows from the Judean hills. There is not a tincture of conventional piety about any of them; they are interesting and winning."[7]

As the weeks passed, Eric's unique path toward China became more imminent. Despite his rigorous schedule, he continued to find it difficult to refuse the appeals of those who wanted a small bit of him. One such request came with an interesting twist at a Wednesday evening church function. A young Sunday school teacher, Miss Effie Hardie, reached out to him with a request. Since Eric was headed to do missionary work, Effie thought it would be a lovely idea if he became a pen pal to her class so they could learn about life for the Christian missionary. Eric, always wanting to help everyone in every possible way, agreed to consider. His intentions were as noble as Effie's were optimistic.

Other than the short games before a few of the meetings he held with D. P., Eric had given up playing rugby. But he was relieved that spring brought one more go-round on the track and field circuit. The physical exertion through sport and competition was a welcome break from his daily pedagogical aerobics. Simply put, running gave his mind a rest.

He had stayed in strong enough shape for the intense six-week stint. And during his final season, he rarely lost. The public loved him all the more for it.

But running only intensified the public's interest in hearing him speak. He addressed a crowd with D. P. Thomson at Edinburgh's St. George's United Free Church. Between 1,100 and 1,200 people flocked to listen.

Eric had always been intrigued by gospel emphasis, but articulating salvation entirely by God's work was difficult. He consequently engaged his crowd with strong use of instructions and requirements, demonstrating how to live a good Christian life, which was what he was familiar with. It was easy enough to fall back on. Eric found it simpler to explain abstract truths by offering practical steps listeners should take. This method made complete sense to Eric, yet he would soon discover that relying on human effort would be an exhausting way to live a life of faith in Christ.

Eric's last meet of the year, and what would be his final race on British soil, took place on June 27, 1925, in the Scottish Amateur Athletic Association, held at Hampden Park in Glasgow with a crowd of over fifteen thousand. Eric walked away with four first-place finishes, in the 100 yards (10.0), 220 yards (22.2), 440 yards (48.9), and one-mile relay—only the fourth person in the history of the meet to do so. It put an emphatic exclamation point on his athletic career and forever marked him in the annals of the sporting world. With that, he headed back to Edinburgh for his last full day in his beloved city.

Eric could now finally set his face toward China, with his athletic career officially behind him. He believed with all his heart that he'd find his real calling in the mission work in China, in spite of escalating tensions there. For most of those who knew him—and even for those who only thought of themselves as knowing him—the idea of walking away without hesitation after achieving the pinnacle of success was unthinkable. Most could not appreciate the full magnitude of what he was doing. The opportunities at his disposal seemed infinite.

Yet Eric Liddell wanted only to follow God, his parents, and his other family members back to the mission field. He traded fame and the potential for lucrative opportunities for a life of comparable anonymity.

The most selfless route is typically the path offering the most peace of mind. Eric knew this truth beyond the shadow of any doubt.

And as the world was about to see, Eric Liddell lived it.

But before a final good-bye, Eric gave valedictory meetings in both Glasgow and Edinburgh. More than a thousand people were turned away from seeing Scotland's greatest athlete one last time.

June 29, a bleak morning, arrived with much more fanfare than Eric anticipated. First, the Glasgow newspapers ran a poem for his day of departure:

> *For China now another race he runs,*
> *As sure and straight as those Olympic ones,*
> *And if the ending's not so simply known—*
> *We'll judge he'll make it, since his speed's his own.*[8]

A second surprise came when a carriage pulled by friends arrived at his door at 29 Hope Terrace. After loading him in, the team of young students paraded him through his favorite city, through crowds and cheers to Waverley Station. There, he was astounded to see his principal, T. Hywell Hughes, among the throng. Hughes offered a handshake of gratitude as the well-wishers sang "For He's a Jolly Good Fellow" and "Will Ye No Come Back Again?"

Eric stood on the train station platform, surrounded by his fans. When they cheered for him to leave them with some parting words of wisdom, Eric blurted out, "Christ for the world, for the world needs Christ!"[9]

The words had always been Eric's credo, and he was proud to be given the chance to rattle off the powerful line one more time. Through singing, tears, and cheers, Eric slowly separated from one home and headed for his other.

And he prayed. He prayed that the Lord of the nations would unite them all together—one day. He prayed that, in Christ, he would do his part and that others would do theirs.

The last puff of train engine smoke vanished up and around the bend, as if a divine starter's pistol had signaled the beginning of a new race. After taking a seat and settling in, Eric recalled a line he had picked up in school: "We must prepare in the days of comfort, for when the days of hardship come, we will be prepared to meet them."

Eric Liddell was prepared to meet whatever challenges came.

Or so he thought.

PART TWO

The Second 100

Run the Distance

CHAPTER 9

A SORT OF HOMECOMING

*Go home to your friends and tell them
how much the Lord has done for you,
and how he has had mercy on you.*
Mark 5:19

July 18, 1925

Fourteen days after leaving London's Victoria Station, Eric stepped onto the station platform at Pei Tai Ho, the Chinese beach resort he'd not seen or played at for eighteen years. He scanned the small crowd waiting there until he found his father and mother, his sister, Jenny, and his younger brother, Ernest.

They spotted him as well and, within seconds, had him wrapped in hugs, his mother waiting until the last for her turn at him. He breathed in the oddly familiar scent of her. "Mother," he whispered as she pressed another kiss against his cheek. "Mother," he said again.

"Let's get your luggage," his father said, "and be on our way."

They looked good, all of them. His parents had aged, of course, but so had he—receding hairline and all. Ernest had grown to a strapping lad of twelve, and Jenny looked as lovely as he had remembered. "Where are Rob and Ria?" Eric asked.

"They'll join us next week," James Liddell said. "That'll give you five weeks total with the whole family before you get to work." He beamed at his wife. "Won't that be something, Mary? Five weeks with all our children?"

Mary didn't answer; she only nodded.

They loaded everything—including themselves—into a donkey-drawn carriage and settled in for the short trip to their summer cottage. They'd hardly pulled away from the station when Ernest begged, "Tell us everything about your trip."

Eric threw back his head and laughed. "Which part?"

"All of it!" Jenny exclaimed.

"How about the weather?"

Ernest wrinkled his nose. "Not that."

"Partly cloudy. Pouring rain in parts. Sunny in others," he teased, his eyes taking in the unfamiliar terrain. He'd hoped he could have remembered even a fraction of it. Of being there with Rob. The smells, the sounds . . . anything.

Jenny punched her brother's upper arm, bringing him back to the moment. "Anything but that. Did you meet anyone interesting?"

Eric nodded. Indeed, he had—a Lithuanian who spoke only of the poverty of his country, something Eric had not fully appreciated until their train passed through the country. Then he'd been able to take note of the people—a large number without shoes or decent clothing—and of the houses, most not decent enough for any human and yet inhabited by many.

He'd also met a Chinese man who sat next to him for a portion of the trip and carried a bundle wrapped in a skin.

"—and every so often the car would rock hard," Eric said, "and when it did, a large swarm of flies would rise up and . . ." Eric felt the pain of such poverty in the deepest part of himself and he frowned, aware that his younger sister and brother were looking at him now, waiting. "And then back down again."

"It sounds positively awful," Mary said. "That poor, poor man."

"And for you, Eric," Ernest said, "for having to sit so close."

An hour later, Eric stood next to his father on the beach. They'd cuffed their pants to their calves as the water lapped over their bare feet. "I read your report to the LMS while on the train," Eric said, resting his hands on his hips as he took in the beauty around him. Something familiar caught hold of his memory now, and he breathed it in. "Is it really so grim here now?"

James's chin rose a notch, something Eric had almost come to expect from his father, even though he'd so rarely seen him in his life. "Worse," he said finally. "This country has been brought to a sad condition, Eric. The work of the church has been more difficult than ever."

Eric blinked, furrowing his brow. Had he made a mistake by coming now? In Britain, he had the world at his fingertips when it came to his work. But here? No one knew him beyond his being the son of Rev. James Liddell.

But once Eric made up his mind to do—or not to do—something, little could change it.

IT HAD BEEN DECIDED that upon return to Tientsin at the end of the holiday, Eric would live in the upper room of James and Mary Liddell's home. At twenty-three, Eric had essentially been on his own for nearly two decades. He was an independent man, a scholar, and for all practical purposes, a world conqueror. And now? Now he lived in his parents' attic.

James and Mary, along with Jenny and Ernest, had called No. 6 London Mission in Tientsin home for several years. The comfortable and large brick residence was located within the London Missionary Society compound in the foreign-designated section of the city. The house boasted a tennis court in the front and, from Eric's vantage point in the attic, a commanding view of the grounds all around.

The Liddells, like most of the missionaries and Westerners, had various Chinese servants who helped in the house quarters, three of whom lived in the back portion of the house. They were paid a fair wage, but the situation created a noticeable dichotomy within the city.

Almost 80 percent of the million-strong city were native Chinese, and they lived a rugged lifestyle, working across a wide spectrum of agriculture and domestic labor, particularly in relation to the wealthy foreign class. The Chinese section of the city was much larger but not nearly as upscale as the way the resident aliens—the British, Germans, and French—insisted on living.

During his first days back home, Eric purchased two large albums and organized the newspaper clippings, photographs, and programs he'd collected over the past few years. He then employed a carpenter to build a small cabinet that would house his medals, nearly two hundred in all. In this way, whenever visitors came to call and inevitably asked to see the medals, Eric could easily display them rather than having to take them out of their individual cases.

He also spent time familiarizing himself with a new way of life and the political sentiments of the country.

Tientsin, being a port city, was valuable for international trading partners, similar to Shanghai and Hong Kong. The British influence over the years had thrived in this context. The British ran the taxes, policed the city, and exercised government. They had their own restaurants, a country club, and a racetrack, all with the goal of getting China open to business, work, and trade. The LMS, among various other Christian missionary entities, flourished in the midst of the growing Western influence.

Consequently, the Chinese resisted the westernization of their country. The wake of the previous generation's Boxer Rebellion uprising had left an unsettled sensation in the culture. The national pride of the Chinese was at stake, and many felt they were beginning to lose their culture.

These waves of sentiment crashed over Eric in a direct way. Enrollment in the Tientsin Anglo-Chinese College had dropped significantly, and a storm cloud of concern swelled over the turbulent missionary community, meaning that even though Eric had traveled from Europe to China, leaving behind everything he knew best, he had no guarantees of a position by the end of the year. He very well may have made the long trip to work as a teacher but not have any students to teach.

Dr. Samuel Lavington Hart, the president of Tientsin Anglo-Chinese College, was eager to connect with Eric. Dr. Hart, a seasoned man, wore a stately goatee, which seemed to punctuate the intensity of his work. He made it clear that he and his wife, Elsie, had tremendous hearts for sharing Christ in an academic setting.

Eric and Dr. Hart resonated with each other on more than this one level. Dr. Hart believed that *Christian* education was foundational for *all* education. Eric appreciated that sentiment. Like Eric, Dr. Hart had abandoned notoriety in Britain when he felt a call to China. A prominent physicist, he had left his influential post in 1892. He and his wife, along with his brother and his brother's wife, had undertaken the long journey, just as Eric had, each with hope and the belief that they were doing God's will. But Dr. Hart's brother and his brother's new bride both died of dysentery after their first year in China.

Afterward Dr. Hart and Elsie moved from Wuchang to Tientsin, where he founded TACC with the heartfelt desire to share the gospel with the sons of Chinese businessmen and government officials.

When Eric questioned whether, come fall, he'd stand before a classroom of empty desks, Dr. Hart assured him "the Authorities of the College have decided to open the college as usual in September. They will admit all, whether former students or new students, whose distinct purpose it is to devote themselves quietly to study."[1]

Eric and all the missionary community breathed a sigh of relief that their opportunity continued intact, fragile though it was. Immediately, Eric set up shop, buying lab supplies as best he could find in the local markets. When the school doors opened for his first year as a teacher, Eric joined a faculty of five other British missionary educators, including his old teacher A. P. Cullen.

And what a reunion! Cullen had enjoyed following Eric's athletic career and thoroughly endorsed his addition to the college. Cullen's voice stating, "We are fortunate to have Eric on campus" offered powerful validation.

But one thing had changed. Eric had always heard his old professor referred to as "Cullen." Within the extended LMS family, however, children referred to their elders as "Uncle" and "Auntie." Now, when Eric heard children call out for Cullen, they called him "Uncle Rooper" (based on an old nickname from childhood).

Eric easily became "Uncle Eric."

Eric thrust himself into his work like a champion rejoicing to run his course. He taught science in the morning and also participated in leading the college's morning services. His afternoons at the school became a laboratory of a different kind when Dr. Hart asked Eric to develop the athletic program. Afternoons were for playing catch-up, for tea, for Chinese classes with his private tutor . . . but Eric's old habit of saying yes came too easily, even in another country.

That year Eric organized races, games, and full-fledged track and field meets with his students. And for the students, Uncle Eric's participation became coveted. After all, how often does one have a chance at competing against a star Olympic gold medalist?

On the field, Eric could see another side to his students, and they him. He had always appreciated being able to offer Christ in, with, and under scholastic studies. This was no secret. But he preferred a kinetic way to inspire faith in others, and sports set the table perfectly for his appetite as well as that of the students.

The college flourished, even during extreme adversity.

• • •

By February, Eric had a firm footing in his work and took the time to respond to Miss Hardie and her Sunday school class back in Edinburgh. After referencing all the students by name, Eric delighted them with a unique tale of the circumstances around his work during the holidays:

> Just at Christmas time Tientsin was being attacked and for two weeks we could hear the guns going just about five or ten miles away. Slowly the attackers were winning their way until on the 23rd of December the fighting was going on in a part of the Tientsin city. Then on the 24th Tientsin was taken. It was all quite exciting with the fighting so near. Of course we were all safe as we live in a part that is ruled by the French. . . . I wonder how you would like a battle like that to go on just outside Edinburgh? . . .
>
> This has just been a very short glimpse of some things here. All the while it changes quickly, later on I may be able to give some idea of Tientsin.
>
> With all the best of wishes to each one in your class,
>
> Yours sincerely,
>
> Eric H. Liddell [2]

The ensuing year flew by with fierceness. Success had never taken long to blossom for Eric in Britain; China appeared no different. He established himself among the faculty at the college, in the classroom with the students, on the sports field with the greater community, and at Union Church with its members. Eric acted as the superintendent of the Sunday school, taught a class for the boys there, and facilitated Bible studies in some of the area's Chinese congregations.

And as though he had more hours in the day than everyone else, he volunteered as chaplain to British troops rotating through their station in Tientsin port.

With every focus, Eric aimed for excellence and measured results. This way of life and faith had always worked for him, which was, of course, a hard point for anyone to criticize. Eric steered a ship of legalistic theology, which his family and surrounding institutions bolstered for him. His thinking and his convictions were strict, but not unyielding. He kept this nuanced tension in mind, as he would occasionally catch wind of straying theological tendencies from his Congregational denomination in Scotland. Consequently, Eric felt conflict over the direction the Congregationalists had begun to steer regarding the interpretation of Scripture.

Eric was a missionary, but not a theologically skilled, church-planting missionary. Church politics had never been a strong interest for Eric, nor had the arguments and divisiveness they created. As he grew deeper spiritually, Eric's own opinions developed, but he kept them tamed. His primary interest lay in sharing Christ with those who had never heard of him. If there was anything he could do to assist or aid someone in the assurance of their eternal salvation, he helped, and happily so.

* * *

Another LMS teacher joined Eric in early 1926.

Eric Scarlett and his wife, Dorothy, were initially sent to Tientsin to fill in for a few months at the college. But Scarlett's vibrant personality made him impossible to release when the time came. Together, the two Erics worked in the science department and developed an exciting course in practical physics.

That summer, Jenny Liddell announced her engagement to a businessman named Frank Turner, but a few months later she called the engagement off. Again unattached, Jenny often accompanied her equally unattached brother to various social events, sometimes to help ward off Tientsin's single women who were interested in Eric.

By late summer 1926, another missionary couple—the MacKenzies, of Canada—returned from furlough along with their children: Florence, Margaret, Norman, Esther, Finlay, Kenneth, and Agnes Louise.

Like Eric, Florence MacKenzie, who attended the Sunday school class Eric taught, tended to be more athletic than academic, and she was known for her wit and love of life. Without knowing it—and perhaps without Eric meaning for it to happen—the young Florence caught Eric's eye in a way he had not experienced before, which left Eric with a profound problem.

Eric was twenty-four years old.

Florence was only fifteen.

CHAPTER 10

A SLOW BLOOM

Love is patient and kind; love does not
envy or boast; it is not arrogant or rude.
It does not insist on its own way; it is not
irritable or resentful; it does not rejoice at
wrongdoing, but rejoices with the truth.

1 Corinthians 13:4-6

Autumn 1928

Eric sat hunched over his classroom desk holding two pages of unfolded stationery—one in his right hand that he'd already read, the nearly read second page in his left.

The door to his classroom rattled open, and he looked up to see Cullen stroll in. "Thought you'd be gone by now," he said by way of greeting.

Eric waved the paper in his right hand. "A letter from Annie," he said. "I brought it to read during lunch but had other issues to deal with instead."

Cullen smiled, his cheeks rising to the round spectacles resting on the bridge of his nose. "Ah, Annie." He slid into one of the front row desks and crossed his legs. "What does our favorite nurse have to say for herself?"

Like Eric and Cullen, Annie Buchan—Nurse Annie to most—had come to China from Scotland to serve on the mission field. She'd arrived in Pei Tai Ho for a brief vacation shortly after Eric arrived back in China, and then as summer gave way to autumn, she'd left again, having been given a difficult assignment in the Hopei plain. That Christmas she'd endured the holidays among the war-torn mission at Tsangchow, then went on to Nan Yuan. From there, she'd gone wherever God—and country, by way of the mission agency—called her. Through correspondence she'd managed to keep her fellow missionaries up to date on her comings and goings.

Eric returned to a portion of the first page and read it aloud to Cullen. "'This past May we were again forced to evacuate from the restored Siaochang station to Tsangchow because the warlord armies there behaved more like ghastly thieves than soldiers. We—my staff and I—climbed into mule carts and prepared prayerfully for the grim and harrowing journey. We found a Methodist mission along the way and took temporary refuge there. For reasons perhaps only God can know, the soldiers robbed the Chinese who passed along the way but left us alone.'"

Already knowing what came next, Eric blew out a long breath. "Shall I continue?" he asked Cullen.

"Please."

"She writes, 'We had been told of how soldiers plundered the poor village people, and now we were seeing them at work. They kicked open doors, pushed their swords through them. We heard the cries of the terrified people inside. There was, of course, nothing to plunder from us, but once again we felt ashamed to go free.

"'Soon another band of soldiers caught up with us. They blamed us for having a bodyguard and for breaking treaty rights. They made us walk while they took turns riding the carts. Things looked ugly for us. We had no supplies and yet here we were, caring for the war's victims. One general came along and, feeling sorry for us, sent over some food.'" Eric looked up at Cullen, reading the rest from memory. "'We heard he was murdered a short while later.'"

Cullen reached into his pocket for his pipe and a small pouch of tobacco. After preparing it, he struck a match, then touched it to the sweet leaves within the bowl. "There but by the grace of God, Eric," he said between puffs. "There but by the grace of God."

ALTHOUGH ERIC NEVER regretted leaving his great love of track and field for missionary work, he couldn't help but note that the winner of the 1928 Summer Olympics 400-meter race, American Ray Barbuti, won with a time slower than Eric's in 1924.

That fall, Rob and Ria, along with their new daughter, Peggy, arrived in Siaochang to help with the rebuilding of Siaochang Mission Hospital. Rob—now Dr. Robert Liddell—also became its medical superintendent and worked alongside Nurse Annie.

In October, Eric took part in the Far Eastern Games at Port Arthur, located at the southern tip of China's Liaodong Peninsula. There he ran the 200 meters in 21.8 seconds and the 400 meters in 47.8, finishing first in both races.

But his most challenging race came later along the streets of the seaport city and the long dock to the boat aimed for Tientsin.

Eric had run the 400 meters at 2:45 p.m. with two goals in sight—first, the finish line; second, the 3:00 boat leaving for home. With only fifteen minutes between the two—literally only a little more than fourteen after the run—Eric had hired a taxi to wait for him. His plan was a simple one: run the race well, stand for the playing of "God Save the King," dash to the taxi. The taxi would then hurry for the dock, and—on a wing and a prayer—Eric would board the boat with a few minutes to spare.

But after his win, in addition to "God Save the King," the band played "La Marseillaise" for the French runner who took second. As soon as the last note echoed between the stands, Eric grabbed his overcoat and his bag and dived into the waiting taxi, which then sped to the dock.

When the taxi slid to a stop and Eric jumped out, he discovered that the boat he needed to be on in order to make it back to Tientsin in time for church the following day had already left the dock.

Eric ran to the edge of the dock, his eyes wide, his mouth gaping. Just then, a tidal wave rolled the steamer back toward the dock. Eric threw his bag onto the deck, backed up a dozen or more steps, ran, and leaped across fifteen feet of dark waves, landing safely alongside his bag.

Comic books for young readers and sports pages in Scotland later appeared recounting the tale with the Flying Scot sailing over new horizons—Olympic records, Asian political adventures, and the rails of moving ships.[1]

* * *

As Eric grew in his role as teacher, local hero, and leader, Florence MacKenzie continued to develop into a fetching young woman, even as the world she lived in stood on the brink of civil war. Now nearing seventeen, Florence, like Eric, taught her own Sunday school class. Eric, who seemed to look for *any* excuse to be near the beauty with the long auburn curls, often dropped by her classroom if only to ask if she needed anything.

"Anything at all?" he would inquire.

Florence would assure him all was well.

He also managed to show up, quite naturally, at home during the hours Jenny instructed Florence in her music lessons. "I made it just in time for tea," he would say. In spite of their age difference, he noticed her more often at church socials, picnics, and the dramatic plays performed by the Sunday school classes. And he couldn't help but note that while the ten years between their ages had not changed—and would not—the older Florence became, the less peculiar his growing interest in her felt.

•   •   •

In late 1928, Eric sent a circular letter to several friends informing them of how life had been treating him that year and confirming that he was well aware of the things going on, both in Scotland and in China.

> The year has been one of ups and downs and like many others I have sometimes felt are we getting anywhere at all. At the beginning of last year (1927) we thought that as a college we would be able to finish our academic year (June) in peace, despite the fact that a great number of colleges round about had had to close down. Our wish was not granted for there was a sudden scare in Tientsin that the Southern Army would be advancing towards it before long. . . .
>
> We still hoped that the examinations would be able to be taken, but before long it was clearly seen that it would not be wise to go on so we closed down. The examinations were put off till September! It was rather a damper to have the work suddenly closed like that, but on thinking it over there were some things that could be said for the students. . . .
>
> The trouble fortunately passed over. The advancing southern force was stopped and ever since has seemed to lose rather than gain power.[2]

What neither Eric nor the recipients of his letter could have known at the time was that "power" would soon take on a new meaning and "trouble" would fall upon his world in ways that would test even the strongest of believers.

•   •   •

Christmas 1928 came, and Eric sent out a number of Christmas cards to family and friends in Scotland, including one to the little

Sunday school class of Effie Hardie. As 1929 dawned, Eric found himself faced with a new decision—his four-year commitment to TACC would meet its completion in June. His mother and father planned a furlough in June, and he thought to go with them to receive additional training and then return to the students—and Miss MacKenzie—in China. By then, she would be over eighteen. The timing seemed perfect.

But an announcement by Dr. Hart in late January 1929 changed all that.

In a February 1929 letter to Miss Hardie's Sunday school class, Eric wrote,

> Dear Miss Hardie,
>
> Thank you for the beautiful calendar which came for Christmas, it was good just to see a bit of Old Edinburgh once again. . . .
>
> This year I should have been returning home but I have decided to wait on another year. This decision has been aimed at owing to the ill health of our Principal. Dr. Hart has been at this college for 25 odd years and was hoping to stay another year, but this winter he has been seriously ill & the doctors advise him to return in May. I am staying on for the next year so as to save any trouble as regards two of us from the Science department being away together.
>
> The rest of my family all go home at the same time in a month so that I will be left on my own here. The pleasure of looking after a house will be mine?!! [3]

Within days of writing the letter, an unexpected change came to the Liddell home. James left for Tsangchow to attend the annual LMS District Committee meetings only to return a couple of days later, aided by Dr. Arnold Bryson. Mary gasped as she saw the condition of her husband and listened intently as Dr. Bryson explained to her that James had suffered a mild stroke not long after his departure.

James assured Mary that he now felt fine, but after a visit from their doctor, he was told to return to Scotland sooner rather than later for extended rest and relaxation. The following month, Rob arrived back at Tientsin. He and Eric escorted their parents, Jenny, and Ernest to Taku so the family could say their good-byes. This time their parents and siblings left China for Scotland, rather than the other way around, yet still leaving Rob and Eric behind as they had done so many times before.

"We'll see you back home soon," James assured Eric, gripping his hand. "Come when you feel the time is right."

"And we'll be back *here* as soon as your father gets better," Mary said to Rob as she hugged him for a final good-bye.

Eric and Rob watched the family board, then remained on the dock as the ship set sail, wanting to watch and stay as close to their loved ones as possible, for as long as possible.

CHAPTER 11

ORDINARY TIME, EXTRAORDINARY DAYS

Love bears all things, believes all things,
hopes all things, endures all things.

1 Corinthians 13:7

Early Summer 1929

"How about a game of billiards?"

Eric glanced up from the evening meal he'd been enjoying with his three flatmates, surgeon Dr. George Dorling, grass widower Gerald Luxon, and newcomer David McGavin, a handsome bloke by anyone's estimation.

Eric glanced from George to Gerald, then to David. "Are you speaking to me?" he asked.

"To all of you!" David exclaimed. "The evening is still young. What do you say?"

"Well . . ." Eric hemmed and hawed. "I've often enjoyed the order and geometrical precision of the game . . ."

David cocked his head. "The what?"

Eric threw his napkin next to his plate, as though dismissing his own words. "Sure, why not?" He pushed himself up from the chair. "Gentlemen? Shall we have a go at it?"

He raised his brow casually toward George and Gerald, who bit their lips to keep from laughing.

A short while later, after standing by idly while Eric won three out of three games, David turned to Gerald. "I may as well have asked if I could watch him sink ball after ball into the pockets."

The laughter Gerald and George had managed to withhold for too long now erupted from their chests. "We learned a long time ago," one of them quipped, "that playing billiards with Eric is not playing billiards with Eric."

David looked from them to the observant Eric, who now leaned his hip against the billiard table. One hand rested near the top of his upright pool stick.

An easy smile broke across his face, one he hoped wouldn't anger his new flatmate.

David slid his stick across the surface of the table with a grimace. "I see now, Liddell, where you misspent your youth."

LIKE MANY CHRISTIANS, Eric pursued the irresistible lure of God's law and its precision. One day, during their time as flatmates, Eric entered the room of the young Dr. George Dorling. He carried a copy of the New Testament in one hand, and his blue eyes held a deeper twinkle than usual. "Look at this, George," he said, opening the book and pointing to Matthew 5:48. "'Be ye therefore perfect, even as your Father which is in heaven is perfect.'" Eric straightened. "He said it, and he means it. You and I can and should be no less than that—perfect, even as our heavenly Father is perfect."

When he left the room, George pondered the way Eric lived, how he sought God earnestly, and how he weighed out his own actions when he fell short of that perfection he felt so called to achieve. Eric, George surmised, never spoke unkindly of anyone, always seeking to find the good in them, even if only the tiniest ember. "We three,"

Dr. Dorling said years later, "were miles below the standard Eric set for himself."[1]

*   *   *

Life continued at its usual nonstop pace.

Eric and his flatmates rose each morning to breakfast, served at 7:30 by Kwei Lin, their cook. After finishing the first meal of the day, each man returned to his own private quarters for quiet time, then left for work.

Eric taught from nine to four o'clock, followed by afternoon tea. Later the men enjoyed their dinner meal, typically an English one. And each day, Eric managed to sneak a peek at the young Miss MacKenzie and to note that she grew more and more beautiful. Because Jenny had gone to Scotland, Florence no longer took piano lessons in his old home, which meant Eric could no longer "happen by" for tea, or just "happen" to need a book from the room adjacent to the piano room.

Eric needed a plan B.

Keissling and Boder, a Tientsin German restaurant, was famous for its cakes and chocolates and ice creams. Of course Eric, a teacher, could not ask Florence, a student, to go for dessert alone, so instead of asking her only, he asked if her siblings might like to come along as well. "My treat," he said.

Before long, not only did Florence and "four or five of the younger MacKs" enjoy the fruit of Eric's pocket change, but their invited friends did as well.

At the opening of summer 1929, with another year behind him, Eric went to Pei Tai Ho for his annual vacation to spend time relaxing in the summer sunshine, to bathe in the warm beach water, to catch up on his reading and his napping . . . and to continue his pursuit of getting to know better the object of his growing affection.

The MacKenzie family was also vacationing in Pei Tai Ho. Seeing Florence on the beach or during group activities was easy enough, but he now knew for certain that if he was going to keep the younger men from attempting to court her, he'd have to monopolize her time a bit more creatively.

As he'd done in Tientsin, he managed to arrive on the front porch of the MacKenzies' cottage for afternoon tea. Then, as the sun sank toward the horizon, he'd ask Florence if she'd like to take a stroll along the beach. She'd accept, and while the world grew pink and brilliantly orange around them, they'd talk leisurely about anything and everything.

Florence's physical loveliness aside, Eric found in her a young woman of great Christian character, energy, and wit. And as with everyone who knew Eric, Florence found his gentleness and kindness, his mischievousness, his way with children, and his love of God to be exceptionally charming and drawing.

●　　●　　●

During this time, Eric continued his strong friendship with "the other Eric," teacher Eric Scarlett.

In a letter to friends, Eric wrote,

> Mr. Scarlett, one of the other foreign teachers, and I have been having our mid-day meal with the students lately, instead of going home. This is something that foreigners have not done in recent years and it certainly was a bit of an eye opener. . . .
>
> There is a good deal of talk about there being no need for foreigners out here etc. that I cannot agree with. We certainly have something to give to China just as China has something to give to us. The standards always seem to

decrease unless there is a foreigner at the head. (Ch'a bu dou) is a great expression with them, it means, good enough or near enough and it is an indication of the character of a great number of the people. Exactness they do not worry about.[2]

In August, before school started and while Eric was still on "vacation," the two Erics, known as Liddell and Scarlett, led a camp in Pei Tai Ho for over thirty poor boys (all but two of them Russian) from Tientsin. For two weeks, the two Erics engaged the boys in activities designed for both body and soul.

When their time together came to a close, Scarlett said, "They're not only more fit, they weigh more leaving than coming in." He suggested that they do it again in the future.

In the fall of 1929, with classes at TACC well under way again, Eric caught the news that Dr. Otto Peltzer, the reigning world record holder in the 500 meters, the 800 meters, and the 1,500 meters, planned to visit China. While he was there, someone suggested organizing a race between the two champions.

Eric had hardly been in training—and said as much—but acquiesced because of the fun the event would bring. He won the 400 with a time of 49.1 seconds; Otto—a lanky twenty-nine-year-old German with a dimpled chin—took the win in the 800.

When the races were done and hands had been clasped in congratulations, Otto turned to Eric and said, "You know, with training, you could be the world's greatest at the 800."

"Oh, no," Eric said. "I don't think so."

"You should do it. Train and then enter the 800 meters in the next Olympic Games. They're being held in Los Angeles in America."

"America? Won't that cost the Olympics in competitors?" Remembering how financially skinned he'd been during the 1924 Games, he added, "Most European athletes won't be able to afford the trip."

"Could be, but the Games are worldwide, you know, not just European."

Eric nodded in agreement.

"So, you'll do it?" Otto teased.

"No," Eric answered, his head dipping shyly. "I'm much too old now."

Otto laughed. "Oh, but I'm older than you," he said, "and I'm entering!"

•   •   •

On November 25, 1929, Florence celebrated her eighteenth birthday.

Shortly after, she and Eric took another of the long walks they'd both come to look forward to, this one because Eric sensed a burgeoning anxiety growing in her.

"Talk to me," he said.

"I'm not sure of what's ahead," she told him. "I have always wanted to go into nursing—that much I know—but the entrance to the school I want to attend in Canada is extremely competitive." She sighed. "In only a few weeks I'll have to take my exams, and I'm worried I won't do so well."

He took a deep breath and held it. He would pray for her, of course, but what if his prayer for her meant losing her? What if she went to Canada and never came back? With a sudden exhale, he said, "What I've really been hoping for quite some time is that you'll come back here and marry me."

Florence stopped and turned to him, her eyes wide. "What?" She blinked. "What did you say?"

Eric chuckled deep in his throat. "I've hoped—for quite some time—that you would marry me."

Florence's lips broke into a generous smile. "Are you *sure*?"

"I'm sure," he said. "What about you?"

"I—I—gracious, Eric. I've nearly worshiped the ground you've walked upon but you are ten years older and I didn't want anyone to think badly of you . . . because you shouldn't have to endure that and—oh, Eric. I *do* love you . . . and if *you're* sure . . ."

"Is that a yes?"

Florence nodded. "That's a yes!"

For the first time, Eric gave his new bride-to-be a chaste kiss, then said, "We'll have to keep this to ourselves. I must speak to your father first."

"Of course," she agreed. "Yes, of course."

•   •   •

Eric contacted Jenny in Scotland, asking her to send an engagement ring via a missionary friend headed to Tientsin. As he waited for its arrival, he spoke with Mr. MacKenzie, who gave his blessing but insisted that Florence complete her training to be a nurse first.

Eric agreed.

When it arrived, Eric placed the five-diamond token of his love on Florence's ring finger. Their engagement became official. They had a long, arduous wait before them, but at least they could openly declare their love for each other.

Florence, along with her sister Margaret, made arrangements to leave for Canada the following summer.

In March 1930, Eric asked the LMS for a two-year furlough to Scotland that would begin the same month Florence departed for school in Canada. His plan was to spend his time furthering his studies at the Scottish Congregational College. He would then return to China to teach at TACC and wait for Florence's return.

In early April, A. P. Cullen and Eric Scarlett left Tientsin for Pei Tai Ho to make certain the LMS cottages were ready for the summer's vacationing missionaries and their families. After arriving by train, they climbed on top of donkeys to ride the five miles from the station to the cottages. Cullen and Scarlett had barely gotten on their way when three men stepped out from behind bushes and demanded that the missionaries hand over their money.

Cullen, slightly ahead of Scarlett on the road and speaking in Chinese, demanded that they be allowed to pass.

The men pulled pistols from their waistbands and commanded that Cullen and Scarlett give them what they wanted.

"Now wait a minute," Cullen said, hoping to reason with them.

One of the bandits fired his gun. A sudden thud behind Cullen caused him to turn. Scarlett lay on the ground, face up.

The three men panicked. One grabbed Cullen, pulled him from the donkey, and stripped him of his wallet and gold watch while the other two opened the suitcases Cullen and Scarlett had brought with them, riffling through them in search of valuables.

"Hurry, hurry!" one of the Chinese men called out. They turned to go, but not before firing another shot, this one barely missing Cullen.

As soon as he was able, Cullen hurried over to Scarlett. "Stay with me," he urged as he ripped the shirt of his friend open to find blood pouring from a bullet wound just above the heart. Cullen felt for a pulse and attempted to apply pressure to the hole in Scarlett's chest. The pulse was weak, but at least it was still there. "Stay with me, Scarlett."

Cullen jerked his head up at the sound of footsteps. Townspeople, curious at the echoing of gunshots, now gathered around him. "Go get help!" Cullen called to some of the boys.

Again he felt for a pulse in search of a sign that Scarlett held on to life.

But there was none.

Two days later, Eric and his future father-in-law met the train carrying Scarlett's body at the Tientsin station. On Saturday, Eric helped carry the casket from the funeral service held at Taku Road Church to the Canton Road Cemetery. There A. P. Cullen led the graveside service.

Five days later, Eric Liddell sat at his desk and wrote another letter to the LMS foreign secretary:

> Since I last wrote you a good deal has happened so that my plans have had to be altered. The death of Mr. Scarlett means that it would place the College in a very difficult place were I to go home this year. . . . Would you please cancel any arrangement for deputation that you have made for me. I am sorry to do this, especially as Dad is none too well, but I am sure I am right.[3]

On April 12, the annual Easter baptismal service included nine students from Scarlett's class. In a letter to friends, Eric wrote, "This Easter Service, and the seeing of all these students taking their allegiance to our Saviour, was like a ray of light penetrating the darkness of the days we had passed through."[4]

In May, Mr. and Mrs. Hugh MacKenzie officially announced the engagement of their daughter to Mr. Eric Liddell. Shortly after, Florence and Eric said a painful good-bye as she and Margaret left China with another missionary family, heading first to Great Britain, where they would visit with Eric's family in Scotland, and then on to Canada.

Eric could and would write to her, of course, and she to him. But it would be a good, long time before they saw each other again or held each other in their arms.

Another separation, which Eric had become all too familiar with . . . but this time—even more than all the times before—drove a deeper sense of distance into his heart.

CHAPTER 12

ONWARD AND UPWARD

Many waters cannot quench love;
rivers cannot sweep it away.

Song of Solomon 8:7, NIV

Autumn 1930

Eric and Rob, shirt sleeves cuffed to just under their elbows, stood in the Tientsin home of their parents, carefully wrapping and boxing the items their parents had written to them about.

Eric held a crystal figurine up to the sunshine bursting through a nearby window to watch the light play within the prisms. "Mother always fancied this," he said, then looked at Rob, who raised his brow in agreement.

"I still can't believe we're doing this," Rob noted. "When they left for Scotland, I felt sure they'd return soon enough."

Eric nodded as he wrapped the figurine in a sheet of paper before nestling it in the packing box at his feet. Recent news that the LMS medical council had determined their father no longer physically able to return to China had come to them in an ink-stained letter. Along with the shock of it all had been the request that their oft-left sons sell their furnishings and send the rest to Scotland.

"Look at this," Rob now said, holding up a tiny framed photo of baby Eric swathed in a white christening gown.

Eric crossed the room and took the photo from his brother, who punched him lightly. "Sweet thing that you were," Rob teased.

Eric chuckled, then studied the colorized photo a final time—the blond of his hair, the blue of his eyes, the rose in his cheeks—before handing it back to Rob.

He couldn't remember the day, of course, but he'd heard his mother and father tell the story so many times he often felt as though he could.

"Eric Henry Liddell," his father had said as he poured water over his head, "I baptize you in the name of the Father, and of the Son, and of the Holy Spirit." James had spoken the blessing over his newest son, splashing his forehead the appropriate three times and, in doing so, uniting Eric in the eternal grace of Christ. James had told Eric that as a missionary, he delighted in sharing the joys of baptism with anyone. "But baptizing my own children . . . I savored those opportunities."

GLOBAL DEPRESSION CAME in more ways than one. Voices of opposition arose in Britain stating that the Chinese should teach themselves or that the college was too expensive and the missionaries should simply engage individuals on a one-on-one basis.

The opposition came from China as well. Earlier in the year Eric had taken a piece of London Missionary Society stationery from his father's desk. After crossing out his father's initials and replacing them with his own carefully penned E. H., Eric began a letter to Effie Hardie:

We have just had our half yearly exams and broken up
for the Chinese New Year holidays. We are not meant to
have a holiday this year as it is against the government

regulations. Still they cannot stop an old custom like that so easily. An order went out saying that all the little shops were to stop selling the usual little new year gifts & of course that meant absolute ruin to them. Some of the little shop owners committed suicide so that a petition went from Tientsin asking the government to withdraw the regulation. Fortunately they did. . . . Since then it has been increasingly hard not because the students are definitely making trouble but just because of the absolute slackness & indifference. I see that a College at Chi Nan has had to close altogether because the Provincial leader is against Christianity. I suppose we are getting some of the feeling from there.[1]

If Effie Hardie could not sense the foreboding in Eric's words then, she surely understood it later. He ended the letter with a note that he would be in Scotland by August.

Instead, by August, Eric had buried his friend Eric Scarlett, had notified the board that he would not return to Great Britain as planned, had seen Florence off at the train depot, and he and Rob—who lived and worked two hundred miles away in Siaochang—had packed up their parents' home.

As for Florence, she and Margaret had traveled from China to Scotland, where they'd been welcomed by the family that would soon be her own. Scotland had been an enchanting experience for the MacKenzie girls and of epic proportion for Florence. When the Liddells left China, young Flo—a little girl whose auburn curls bounced as she walked—had simply been the daughter of their friends. She had been Jenny's piano student and Eric's Sunday school class pianist. But when she arrived in Scotland with Margaret, she wore the ring Eric had sent to Scotland for.

The British public had also heard of their plans to marry, and as news spread westward, most received the eyebrow-raising news with joy. Certainly, Eric's family was among them. And after a brief vacation with them, Florence and Margaret continued on to Toronto where, oceans away from her love, Flo began the rigors of nursing school.

•   •   •

While Florence spent special days with Eric's family, Eric received the extended benefit of that treatment from her family in Tientsin. While he was not one to openly gush about his feelings in front of friends, no one in the MacKenzie household minded him bubbling over while talking about Florence. And Eric didn't mind the extra stories about his fiancée that only her young brothers could glee-fully tell. While such delightful anecdotes never seemed to receive distribution in wide release, Eric playfully reminded Florence in their private letters.

Eric knew their fledgling flame of love needed fuel to burn and glow, but he also knew that too much yearning too soon would not be helpful for either of them. They would be separated not weeks or months but *years* before they joined together as man and wife. This time of long farewells had been the formula of his childhood and young adulthood. Time and again he had said good-bye to fam-ily members. In some ways, he'd grown accustomed to this type of lifestyle. But Florence had not experienced such, and Eric had never been separated from someone he planned an intimate life of mar-riage with.

As Mary Liddell had modeled for her sons all those years previ-ously, Eric put his heart down on paper to Florence—under the letterhead of the Tientsin Anglo-Chinese College stationery, which bore the insignia "Onward and Upward"—as often as he could. In turn, Florence shared with Eric her excruciating schedule as a student nurse. Each week she spent nearly sixty hours between her clinical work and time in the classroom. Her day began each morning by five forty-five and went nearly nonstop until ten o'clock at night. More than anything, she kept her eyes on the calendar. With each day that passed, she and Eric drew closer to the day when they would see each other again, and closer still to the day when they would marry.

•　•　•

Life in China marched—as the letterhead stated—onward and upward.

Eric developed an appreciation of Dr. Lavington Hart's vision for the TACC, and his concept of Christian education fit Eric's ideals perfectly. Variant methods of missionary activity had been scrutinized to produce results. As Eric expressed in his letter to Effie Hardie, some argued against too much proselytizing and felt that Christians should simply live passively in their context, allowing God to do the work of bringing people to faith. This thinking fit well with the anti-Western sentiment of the Chinese. But Eric was an active missionary, which came out in how he thought, spoke, wrote, and lived. He constantly concerned himself with the salvation of others, especially his students. He designed daily readings for them, hoping to introduce them to walking in the Word and in prayer every single day.

Eric loved sharing his faith with the students in all facets of life, not simply in short bursts of contrived opportunity or random conversations. Devotions, classroom teaching, out-of-class study sessions, fellowship groups, sports activities, and private outings and gatherings fostered the growth of relationships. Eric especially appreciated the tutor model that Dr. Hart had established before his retirement. The current British missionaries—A. P. Cullen, Carl Longman, Gerald Luxon, and Eric Liddell—each served as a tutor-mentor for a particular class through that class's duration at the college. Over the course of four years, Eric had gotten to know a good majority of his students quite well.

During the years Eric served as a teacher, one of his greatest delights was the occasional invitation to Dr. Hart's office, where he would witness a handful of students who, toward the end of their time at the college, confessed their faith in Christ.

Eric expressed this passion to Miss Effie Hardie in a letter dated February 19, 1929:

> This is the last day with my class, as they leave in June.
> I am hoping some of them will definitely come out for
> Christ before that time and would be glad for your prayers
> definitely for them. What a work lies before them if only
> they get to know a living personal every day Saviour.
> Their work can be far greater than ours out here in their
> own land.[2]

Often on Sunday afternoons Eric invited students over to his study for tea. He aimed at learning more about each of them—their families, their homes, their interests—as well as conveying to them that he was interested in being not only their teacher but also their friend. This created a doorway of opportunity to share what Jesus had done for him, was doing for him, and promised to do for him— and for everyone.

Eric did his best to encourage his students to examine the Bible daily and suggested that they meditate on it. He found, like a farmer tending his crops, that not all the sown seeds would sprout or grow at the same pace. Tending to each student on an individual basis proved to be an intricate challenge.

•　•　•

The passing days didn't ease Eric's missing his friend and colleague Eric Scarlett. They had enjoyed batting around evangelical thought and experience as it played out in the daily lives of their students. Eric recalled how, only the year before, they had dined with the Chinese students at lunchtime. Now, Eric continued the tradition alone, painful as it was, especially when the students would want to debate about the necessity of the British presence in China.

Eric also kept up his athletic regimen of football (soccer), rounders (a European form of baseball), basketball, tennis, and running. He even had a minor taste of mortality, as he admitted to losing a 100-meter race to some of his younger Chinese students. The students would not always point out that Eric had given them a 10-meter head start. Still, Eric could tell his body felt different in his late twenties than it did in his early twenties.

A not-too-surprising request came early in the fall for Eric to serve as coach for the football team. Eric wrote to Florence, telling her of the assignment. "We have a long way to go yet," he shared, "before we get that spirit into our games that I should like."[3]

Coaching brought joy to Eric, giving him the opportunity to pass on his love of healthy competition even while teaching with the highest degree of integrity. Trial, error, painful lessons, and controversial decisions all helped his team learn respect, trust, discipline, and how to work together—touchstones of Eric's daily lifestyle.

Eric's sportsmanship values had permeated through the roster by season's end. His tendency to win, however, did not transmit so effortlessly. Still, his follow-up assessment of the season carried with it an air of moral victory when he realized that the students put more effort into a losing game and that they took the referee's decision in a better spirit than they had done previously.

Eric knew that winning was not always possible and didn't truly matter in the end. Fostering others to know victory in Christ was the real match.

Eric's 1930 end-of-year report states,

The Spirit of our Master slowly works his way into our games, work and services. We do not see, like a builder does, great changes in a week or two, but here and there comes a word of cheer and a sight that makes you sure that the work is slow but sure. Here a boy begins to face life and definitely decides that he will face it, building his life with Christ as its foundation, and there another in the quiet makes his surrender too. . . .

The past year has in some ways been disappointing—for one thing, the difficult problem of getting a suitable Christian Principal has not yet been solved—but nevertheless we face this coming year with confidence and cheer, for we hear our Master saying, "Be of good cheer, I have overcome the world."[4]

•   •   •

January 1931 ushered in a new urgency in Eric's pressing decision of how best to spend his academic focus in Britain. The previous year Eric had requested a two-year furlough from his local missionary board at the college. This allotted plenty of time to finish his seminary training and would closely coincide with Florence's completion of her nursing studies. Additionally, he reasoned, he could continue with advanced teaching education, which would make him even more effective in and out of the classroom. Eric figured that with his imminent return to the mission field and forthcoming wedding plans, never again would he have the singular freedom or time to invest in his studies.

The London Missionary Society's governing board surprised Eric with the news of their recommendation. They would grant him only a *one*-year furlough. His time in Britain would be of the essence. Eric mulled over and prayed a great deal about his decision. He truly loved teaching and, in particular, Christian education. He revered the environment Dr. Hart had created at the college.

The lingering financial depression seemed to be spreading around the world, with no sign of slowing. Accordingly, school officials held serious recurring conversations about the vitality of the college, especially after the closing of the school in Chi Nan. The survival of Tientsin Anglo-Chinese College continued to be held in question as the Chinese government pushed stricter standards on the Christian college.

Would there even be a school for him to teach at when he returned?

Eric read the proverbial leaves in his teacup and went with what positioned him best for his future as well as the future of his potential family. He enrolled in the Scottish Congregational College for two terms, which he needed to complete for ordination. Having his teaching degree, six years of experience, and a formal seminary divinity degree and ordination into the pastoral ministry would set him up for a wide variety of professional opportunities.

Eric loved his work but had no reservations admitting the fun that came from looking forward to the year ahead. His final term came and went, and Eric was satisfied with all he had accomplished. He had done all anyone could have or would have expected of him—he had extended his stay an extra year, two times over, which providentially brought him to the end of a sixth academic year. He would be entering his seventh year in the mission field—divinely appropriate for a Sabbath's rest.

For Eric Liddell, however, "rest" would be a relative term.

CHAPTER 13

A GAZE INTO THE LOOKING GLASS

*If we say we have no sin, we deceive ourselves,
and the truth is not in us. If we confess our sins,
he is faithful and just to forgive us our sins and
to cleanse us from all unrighteousness.*

1 John 1:8-9

Late August 1931

For the first time in six years, Eric stepped out of the train at Waverley Station in Edinburgh, Scotland, his heart and mind flurried by emotion. Two weeks earlier, he'd left Canada's shores after having spent blissful time with Florence—a time he wished would slow to a crawl, a time both he and Florence had enjoyed, in spite of knowing it would end.

They'd talked of everything, just as they'd always done. School and work. China and its political unrest. Family and friends.

Their upcoming nuptials.

"Are you counting the days?" Eric had asked Florence, and she'd assured him with the number.

"Easier to think in terms of weeks or even months," she had said. "*Days* makes it almost unbearable."

"Eric!" Jenny's voice penetrated his thoughts.

He turned, saw his family standing to the left of the crowd, and waved.

The familiarity of it all sent a shock wave through him, met by the unfamiliar parting the last time he'd stood on this very platform. Then, he'd been given a hero's farewell. Now, only blood relatives stood to welcome him.

After their customary hugs and kisses and Mary dabbing at her tears with a dainty handkerchief, eighteen-year-old Ernest hurried toward baggage to retrieve Eric's luggage. Jenny looped her arm with her brother's as they walked behind their parents and said, "I've got news."

Eric smiled down at her. "What's that?"

"I'm getting married."

Eric halted, Jenny with him. "No! And who is this chap?"

"His name is Dr. Charles Somerville," she rattled on. "He's a tad older than me . . ."

"Define 'a tad.'"

Jenny wrinkled her nose as she lowered her voice to admit, "Twenty-six years."

"Good heavens!" The words burst from Eric as they began to walk again. "I suppose Flo and I are in the clear, then. You've seen my romantic wager and have raised the bid significantly."

Jenny squeezed her brother's arm. "I'm crazy mad about him, Eric."

"When is the wedding?"

"April. Rob and Ria are coming. And, of course, you'll be there."

THE LONDON MISSIONARY SOCIETY had salivated at the opportunity of penning Eric in on their deputation schedule. Traveling on behalf of the LMS and raising funds for the further advancement of the mission was understood. But Eric was not the conventional speaker in rotation. As an Olympic gold medalist and national hero, the LMS saw him more as their poster boy, the kind which appears only once in a generation. He discovered almost immediately that his speaking schedule was monstrous, matching the ravenous financial need during the Great Depression.

And this was merely the timetable the LMS had planned. An outpouring of other requests rained upon Eric to the awkward point that a separate committee of the Congregational Church had to be put together to discern and deal with all the lecture requests. And, of course, D. P. Thomson's plans had to be considered.

On Saturday, September 4, 1931, Thomson recorded in his journal that he had spent time with Eric that day and found him fit and happy—the same old Eric, "obviously glad to see me."[1]

A few days later, Eric stayed at Thomson's home where they discussed plans for meetings for the short period they had together. Eric expressed to Thomson that he felt the pressure of the schedule that had been set for him.

"It must be realized," Thomson wrote in his book *Scotland's Greatest Athlete*, "that, apart from the pressure of public engagements and the obvious need for time with his own family, and for the necessary rest and recreation after those strenuous years overseas, Eric had undertaken quite a demanding course of study."[2]

By the last day of September there was no hiding the fact that Scotland's favorite son had returned—older, wiser, and darkened by China's sun, his receding hairline more pronounced by age. And on that day, St. George's West Church in Edinburgh found itself packed with interested representatives from the sporting and religious communities gathered for a public welcome.

Eric rose to speak. He deflected the praise to the best of his efforts. "I accept your welcome," he said, not in my own name, but in the name of a great many others. I accept your welcome in the names of those countless men, whose names are almost unknown, who went into places of danger and difficulty and hazarded their lives for the sake of Jesus Christ, and who came back after they had done those things and were never welcomed. In the name of these men and others I accept it. I think we should always remember the men who have made the task we go to far easier than otherwise it would have been.

In China, the evangelists are going out among the people. They are going into their homes. They are sleeping in places just the same as the Chinese themselves. They are trying to understand the problems those people have to face, and the greatest challenge there is to every Christian person asks for no great courage, but asks for patience and sympathy that we will be able to sit beside those whose opinions are different from our own, and try to enter into their problems and face them from their point of view.

Tonight I want to leave a message with you all. We are all missionaries. We carry our religion with us, or we allow our religion to carry us. Wherever we go, we either bring people nearer to Christ, or we repel them from Christ.[3]

Eric knew through observing others and by firsthand knowledge that some people reacted adversely to the presentation of the gospel while others readily embraced it. He had evaluated this in his own public speaking, private conversations, and the mission field. He had carefully observed numerous others proclaim and share the gospel, netting various responses. He was eager to determine through Scripture why this was and to discover the best approach to cultivate and invest his energies.

Eric loved Jesus because Jesus loved Eric—and the world. Eric found it inconceivable that anyone could reject that beautiful truth if they truly understood just how much Christ loved them and to what lengths he went to save them. The interplay of law and gospel, and more specifically how Eric might convey that distinction to his audiences, was again at stake. The handling of it seemed to carry heavier consequences than he had first perceived.

•   •   •

After an exhausting September, October brought autumn leaves and the final lap for Eric's formal academic studies. He reenrolled with the Scottish Congregational College and was greeted by the familiar and proud faces of D. Russell Scott, a professor and the chair of biblical languages and criticism, and Thomas Hywell Hughes, the principal and sitting professor of systematic theology.

Eric enjoyed what these father confessors brought to the table, as well as their enthusiasm and personalities, but languages were never quite in Eric's bag of tricks. He struggled with Chinese even while being immersed in it. Learning biblical Greek and Hebrew proved to be a formidable assignment. Though Eric valued the languages determining what a scriptural text *says* in its original form, he gravitated toward Hughes's systematic approach, preferring to dissect what the texts *mean*.

The interconnected network of doctrine making up the theological field of systematics is often likened to catechism on steroids. Eric appreciated always being able to reference certain Scriptures in conjunction with Christian thinking and began to develop early ideas for a book he hoped to one day write. His new theories challenged his experience in the mission field.

The Congregationalists had historically been known as staunchly nonconformist to Calvinistic thinking, which had dominated the Scottish landscape for centuries. Hughes rejected the concept of limited atonement, the concept that only a limited number of souls would be allowed to pass through heaven's gates. He instead taught and advocated an unlimited atonement. This different starting point for evangelism resonated with Eric for the mission field.

Eric also found it more liberating to proclaim to everyone that Christ had died, risen, and delivered them from their sin, as opposed to only the elect. He wanted to confidently articulate the gospel to, imaginably, the worst person in the world, saying that "Christ has forgiven you all your sins via the Cross." Eric knew that for salvation to take root, hearing the truth of the gospel was only the half of it. He also had to help people in any way he could to recognize and confess faith in Christ. All this served Eric and reconfirmed his zeal for mission work.

E. Stanley Jones became another theological influencer for Eric during his seminary days. Jones was an American Methodist missionary who had dedicated a great deal of his life to serving in India. He had contextualized himself into India's way of life as fully as he could and had become a friend of Mahatma Gandhi. Jones's writings had received much critical acclaim and sold in high volumes. His book *The Christ of the Indian Road* quickly became required reading for many Western-thinking seminaries.

Eric appreciated the full-immersion missionary experience on which Jones expounded, especially contextualization involving an attempt to present the gospel in a socially relevant way, considering indigenous cultures, customs, and traditions. Not only did Eric soak up Jones's ideas as good theory and practice, but he also was eager to test and apply them in the Chinese context when he returned.

Eric felt validated, stretched, and convicted, and he voraciously consumed all that Jones taught. He understood better why the Chinese resented the imperial presence of the West. Yet Eric believed God had *called* him to China, and therein lay the satisfying task of going about his work for the Lord within a challenge he could more clearly identify.

But as much as Eric studied theory and evaluated various methods of sharing the gospel, he knew not every part of native cultures should be embraced. Some issues were a matter of right and wrong, and he was never afraid to address them—even for his British brethren.

Amid his myriad speaking engagements, Eric declared that gambling and intemperance were "two of the greatest problems the church was facing; both vices were sapping the energy of their young people."[4]

He tied this point to an anecdote of addiction concerning a former great Scottish athlete who ended his days begging outside the same stadiums where he used to be cheered. Eric's popularity took a slight hit, but the glancing blow was well worth it. He never felt he judged anyone, but he was not afraid of being self-defined, particularly when looked up to by so many of Britain's youth.

By February, Eric's speaking schedule, academic demands, pressures of moral example, navigation of reporters, and disarming of the occasional dissenting debater in his audience had left him exhausted. And it didn't help matters that he had to wait another six months until his monthlong visit with Florence, with a looming eighteen months beyond that until their marriage. Their letters traversed back and forth across the ocean, and their emotions ebbed and flowed with them.

Maybe it was forging through the fog of academics one last time. Maybe it was suspended romance, which caused emotional heartache. Maybe it was feeling as though he was past his athletic prime, or maybe it was the miserable winter weather. Or perhaps it was the constant scrutiny of the public eye provoking him to project his best image. Eric had always tried his best to be perfect in every way and occasionally reinforced his striving by quoting from Matthew 5:48: "Be ye therefore perfect, even as your Father which is in heaven is perfect." Whatever combination of reasons, frustrations invariably set in, and Eric wondered why life had to be so compounding and difficult.

Eric had fallen short. He could not deny that the perfect law of God mirrored back to him his own imperfections. Slight as they may have appeared to the human eye, he knew the reality.

He retreated to his parents' home in Drymen during one of these spells of gloom. His family's presence was typically a source of solace, even as he had not always had the convenience of their physical support through much of his life. His trip proved fruitful in a surprising way. James and Mary Liddell happened to be hosting an Oxford Group speaker at their home during his stay, whose talk Eric attended.

The burden of the law, which was weighing him down as he failed to achieve perfection, dropped from Eric's shoulders as he listened to the speaker's message. The gospel is not something people *do*, he realized, but something they *receive*. Hearing more about the grace of Christ relieving the burden of the law stirred a new kind of peace in his heart and a sense of renewal. Christians serve God indirectly as they serve their neighbors directly. Understanding that Christ was disguised in his service to others, Eric was relieved of the pressure of striving for and failing at perfection; personal holiness was not the only way to serve Christ.

Much to Eric's delight, the Oxford Group, which Eric had become interested in seven years previous via fellow athlete Loudon Hamilton, had grown. The small gospel group had expanded internationally all the way to South Africa and had resonated with numerous key leaders in the United Kingdom. Two of those leaders were Stuart and Bina Sanderson, who ran a business in Galashiels.

Eric recalled how his "heart had burned within him" years before during his initial talks with Hamilton. Hamilton had been greatly influenced by the Oxford Group, and he had told Eric something that would be instrumental in his own life in the years to come. Living in such a way that God can say hello to us at any time of the day or night, Hamilton told Eric, begins by spending quiet time with God each morning. This early-morning quiet time with God is something that Eric practiced and treasured and passed on to his own students at TACC.

Eager to fan the flame from his earlier meeting with Hamilton, Eric decided to seek out the Sandersons in Galashiels, but with Jenny's impending wedding and Eric's rigorous schedule, he had to suspend his inquisitiveness . . . if only for another two months.

Jenny Liddell and Dr. Charles Somerville married on April 20, 1932. Somerville, a widower, came with three children in tow, which was a lot for Jenny to take on. But her new husband was no stranger to the missionary community, and their love for each other was undeniable. Eric could look on only in admiration as he dared think ahead to his own special day to come. Only a few more months and he would see Florence again. Focusing on a strong finish to his academic year, graduation, and ordination remained.

May provided a brief open window for Eric to trek to Galashiels and meet the Sandersons. Stuart and Bina were a unique couple. Married in 1914, they had become acquainted with Rev. Frank Buchman a decade later. Buchman's message had a major influence on them in how they practiced their faith, made decisions, and lived their life together.

Loudon Hamilton described them as "true pioneers" of the Oxford Group, and Stuart's own minister said, "If only every minister in Galashiels had an Elder like Stuart Sanderson, it would make a mighty difference to the churches in this town."[5]

Stuart and Bina were fiercely capitalistic business-minded Christians who ran a tweed mill. They were comfortable swimming upstream against popular culture and conventional wisdom. During difficult financial times, and even though it meant great personal financial loss, they chose to sell their large house and car. They simply valued their talented staff more. They moved into a cottage and humbly kept about their business.

Stuart's motto had always been "Whatever you undertake, put your very best into it." Their tweed mill became a continued success in the face of adversity, when many other businesses were closing around them. In the process, their home became a welcoming base for the Christian lay movement.[6]

For Eric, the Sandersons seemed also to possess a deeper, oracular knowledge that interested him. During Eric's stay at the mill house cottage, life and theology were discussed with a passion. Somewhere midconversation, Stuart addressed something he felt Eric had hidden in his life. Eric quickly denied it, but inside he was bothered.

Bothered because he had lied.

He concluded his pleasant visit with the couple and went on his way.

Eric returned to Edinburgh a different man. He was both relieved and agitated by his conversation with the Sandersons. Sunday arrived, and Eric could not bear it anymore. He *knew* he had lied. And he knew he had sinned not just once, but twice. Worse, God knew it.

The first lie had been the issue Sanderson had stumbled upon, and the second was his own covering of it. Even though they were simple enough crimes to have hidden away in his heart, and which he had already gotten away with, Eric could not forget.

For he knew *God* could not forget.

Bothered beyond reason, Eric did something he had seldom done before—he disturbed someone else's Sabbath. He picked up the phone and called the Sandersons. Stuart did not receive the interruption with the same hospitality he might have offered any other day or hour of the week. Still, he told Eric to drive out to him later that afternoon.

Private confession and absolution was a familiar practice for Eric.

However, naming the sin out loud, upon other human ears, was an ominous sensation no one looks forward to. Eric told Stuart, "I lied to you before." Eric apologized during the awkward chat and was comforted to hear forgiveness spoken to him.

Only God, Eric, and Stuart knew the specifics of Eric's sin—as should be the case. A guessing man might suspect the issue Stuart kicked up had something to do with the inner workings of Eric's private life, a fear only the pressures of fame can produce, which if discovered, would potentially tarnish his reputation. Regardless, with his slate clean, Eric felt like a new man. To hear audible grace spoken back after a confession of wrongdoing is a sensation unable to be simulated.

Now Eric had a stronger desire than ever to be associated with the Oxford Group. At a house party gathering in St. Andrews, he shared, "The Group has challenged me to a keener life for Christianity, I know I am going back to China leading a fuller Christian life than when I first went out. It has brought to me personally a greater power in my own life, discipline without the thoughts of discipline, and a greater willingness to share the deepest things in my life. In my time in this country I have met no body of people who are so vitally active and through whom the Spirit of God works so closely as the Oxford Group."[7]

These changes for Eric would serve him well in the hard days to come.

CHAPTER 14

PATIENCE AND TACT

We rejoice in our sufferings, knowing that suffering produces endurance, and endurance produces character, and character produces hope, and hope does not put us to shame, because God's love has been poured into our hearts through the Holy Spirit who has been given to us.

Romans 5:3-5

June 22, 1932

The morning arrived with private pomp and cloistered circumstance. Ordination day vacillated between endings and beginnings as Eric sat in an isolated chair at the front of the sanctuary in the Scottish Congregational College chapel—the chair designated for the ordination candidate.

Eric pressed his lips together, staring out at those who sat before him. His parents—both beaming—his younger brother, his sister and her new family, and a few other family members. He smiled toward them. His mother smiled back; his father nodded.

Principal Hughes walked forward, bid Eric to rise, and began the litany of questions Eric had been prepared to expect.

"Do you believe in one God, Father, Son, and Holy Spirit, and do you boldly declare Jesus Christ as Savior and Lord, and acknowledge him Lord of all and Head of the church?"

"Yes," Eric answered.

"Do you believe the Scriptures of the Old and New Testament to be the Word of God, and, inspired by the Holy Spirit, the unique witness to Jesus Christ and the authority for Christian faith and life?"

Again, Eric replied, "Yes." Because he did.

"Will you be a faithful minister of the gospel of Jesus Christ by proclaiming the Good News, teaching the faith, showing the people God's mission, and caring for the people?"

"I will, with the help of God," Eric confirmed.

Once the examination questions were answered, D. P. Thomson invited Eric to kneel. A warmth ran through him as D. P. placed his hand upon Eric's head and offered up a prayer of blessing. Tears welled in his eyes. Oh, how God had blessed him with D. P.'s friendship. With his encouragement. With his example and love.

The prayer over, D. P. changed guard with Professor Russell Scott, who proclaimed the gospel charge, his eyes never leaving Eric's. "Go, therefore, and be a shepherd of the Good Shepherd's flock; administer the holy sacraments; offer prayer for all God's people; instruct, watch over, and guide the flock over which the Holy Spirit has placed you. Do it not for earthly gain but with great joy, for you have been called not to lordship but to serve his flock. And when the Chief Shepherd appears, you will receive the crown of glory."

Scott bowed his head, and Eric did likewise. A slow breath eased from him as the professor prayed, "Merciful God and Father, you have graciously promised that through the preaching of the crucified Christ those who believe in him will be saved. Guide and bless your servant, Eric Henry Liddell, sent forth to witness in China. Graciously look with favor upon him for the sake of your Son, our Savior, Jesus Christ. Grant him confidence and great boldness; uphold and sustain him in hardship, and grant him faithfulness in all his labors that through the speaking of your Word, the nations may come to worship before your throne in spirit and in truth; through Jesus Christ our Lord, who lives and reigns with you and the Holy Spirit, one God, now and forever. Amen."

Eric stood, and Russell extended his hand. "Rev. Liddell," he said, a slight smile tugging at the corners of his mouth.

Eric's heart swelled. He was no longer Mr. Liddell. He was now Rev. Liddell, like his father before him. And as his father had been, Eric felt more confident than ever in the call to continue in service to the people in Tientsin, China.

Soon enough, he stood at Waverley Station, preparing to say good-bye—yet again—to his family. His mother waited, wanting to be the last one to hug her son before he boarded.

"Out in China," she spoke against his temple, "we dreaded the long good-byes." She leaned back, placing the palms of her hands on both sides of his face. "So as not to cry, we made them joyful."

Eric's heart was heavy. He would not see this face again for another seven years. She would miss his wedding to Flo . . . the birth of their children . . . and he would miss her. "How's that, Mother?" he asked past the knot forming in his throat.

"We always said, 'Those who love God never meet for the last time.' That made it a meeting, not a parting."

Eric slipped from her embrace. "I love you."

"And I love you, Rev. Liddell."

"REVEREND" DENOTES AN ACADEMIC DEGREE. "Pastor" designates a calling to a specific group of people in the body of Christ. Eric knew the subtle distinction—while the seminary forms the theologian, the people whom the theologian serves form the pastor.

Rev. Eric Liddell looked forward with vested enthusiasm.

Eric's time in Scotland had been the most special of seasons. But the time had come to leave . . . again. He boarded the SS *Duchess of York* and steamed toward Canada.

And Florence.

By now, Florence had moved in with her friend Betty Thomson and her family. When Eric arrived in Canada two weeks after sailing from Liverpool, he went directly to the Thomsons' home. His excitement at seeing his fiancée again fell flat when he discovered that Flo was at the hospital finishing her shift. While waiting, Eric sat on the outer porch banister and kept polite chatter going with Mrs. Thomson and Betty. But his keen eye was focused down the road, looking for the young woman he hoped would round the corner at any moment.

When she did, midsentence and without apology, Eric hopped over the porch railing and sprinted down the road. Seeing him, Florence ran as well. They embraced, their faces buried in the curve of the other's neck, and remained that way for a long time.

Betty watched with amusement, then said to her mother, "I don't believe I've ever seen two people more in love."

As before, the month Eric and Florence spent together went by too quickly. Soon enough—too soon—Eric boarded a train leading him away from Toronto, heading toward Vancouver. From Vancouver he would head back to China: to Tientsin and his students, to his friends . . . and to Flo's family, who had become much like his own.

He could now count the days until Florence became his wife with renewed energy, feeling certain that the pure joy pulsing through his veins would get him through another year and a half until they could marry in China.

●　　●　　●

As wonderful as it was to be back—and as quickly as Eric managed to fill up his time—he had to reconcile the fact that none of his closest loved ones were nearby. The joys of spending time with Florence in Canada and his family and friends in Scotland were a memory met by a fresh loneliness. His colleague and friend A. P. Cullen, as well as the entire MacKenzie clan, soon left China for their furloughs, which meant that those who would have helped push away the hollowness until Florence's return were now also absent.

The normally five-man-staffed college of British missionaries had dropped to three. Even after such a long stretch of time, a replacement for Professor Scarlett had yet to be found. Combined with Cullen's absence, extra pressure fell on the remaining members Eric Liddell, Carl Longman, and Gerald Luxon.

In addition to Eric's regular teaching duties, he took on Cullen's previous role as secretary of the college, and, as the man who had developed the Min Yuan Sports Field, he was promptly named chairman of the games committee. Additionally, the newly ordained Rev. Liddell added regular preaching assignments at Union Church to his schedule. There he was consulted with anything regarding religious supervision and found himself still functioning as acting superintendent of the Sunday school.

As if all this were not enough to occupy his time, he began a column for the *London Missionary Society Magazine*. He wrote articles describing life in China, the Chinese people, and the relationship between those who served and those being served.

Eric loved teaching Sunday school and particularly lessons from Christ's Sermon on the Mount. He had studied it so much that he put together a small booklet on the subject to aid the other teachers and students. Each Sunday in his class, Eric routinely dropped theological morsels to feast on, and many of these spiritually savory bits were extracted from the Gospel of Matthew—his favorite book.

Years later, Rev. T. T. Faichney, who pastored Union Church, recalled that Eric once defined the Kingdom of God in an extremely simple and satisfying way. "The Kingdom is where the king reigns," Eric had said. "If he is reigning in my heart, then the Kingdom of Heaven has come to me."[1]

Eric taught that it would be incorrect to think of the Kingdom as a fine pearl that a person should sell all he has to obtain. Instead, he instructed, we should see the merchant (Christ/the King) selling all he has (his life via crucifixion) to obtain the fine pearl (the hearer of the message). In this way, Eric stressed how the King reigns graciously over humanity.

Eric also designed an extracurricular daily Scripture reading card for his Chinese students, produced with the same overarching goal he set for himself—to designate daily quiet prayer time each morning and to seek the message the Bible had for them in their own lives.

Eric noted that the times and the culture continued to drift no matter where he was in the world or in which capacity he served. The trend had become evident in the culture of Eric's British homeland and in his own Congregational Church theology. It had also frustratingly revealed itself in the behavior of his Chinese students—a particularly unruly class, which Eric wrote about in a ministry report:

> The class has not been an easy one and it has driven me to
> a deeper life of prayer myself. There was one boy who was
> especially irritating so I put him down for special prayer. . . .
> This year he has been much better and for a time joined
> the Bible class, but there's a long way to go with him yet.[2]

In the time that waxed and waned between hard work and waiting patiently for "Flossie" (as Eric now called Florence) to complete her nursing studies and return to China, Eric strived to go deeper into his relationship with Christ. He did his best to be mindful of others' salvation as well and could not help but share the gospel with them when opportune. If those chances did not arrive, he frequently prayed for those in his immediate context. A unique chance presented itself in another way that stretched Eric even further, both physically and spiritually. Ku Lou Hsi Church, a Chinese congregation near Drum

Tower in the old city section of Tientsin, had been without a pastor for a while. They created an opening for Eric that required him to come in weekly and meet with a group of their men. Eric's issues with the Chinese language made themselves known again, but he had grown accustomed to allowing Christ to lead him down new avenues—especially when he felt ill equipped.

Eric continued in his report, saying,

> Ku Lou Hsi has been and still is a difficult problem. There
> is no ordained Chinese Pastor in charge and I think the
> evangelist feels his hands tied by one or two of the deacons
> who have been there for many years. In the class, we have
> the Evangelist, a man who has started a Christian bookshop,
> one or two of the Sunday School teachers, and some others.
> We have banded ourselves together to pray for one another
> daily for power, for we feel that we must start with ourselves.
> We want depth in ourselves first. I have tried to incorporate
> some of the Oxford Group principles which made such a
> difference to my own life.[3]

The final days of January 1933 brought news of a major health concern for Florence. Exhausted from an intensive three months of clinicals in a psychiatric hospital, she struggled with a bout of anemia and had been forced to spend two weeks in bed. This was an alarmingly long scare as she drew nearer to her nursing school graduation finish line in May. In the dark hours of the night Florence wondered if she would see Eric again. Eric figured a nursing school was as good a place as any to fall ill but tossed and turned as he waited for news that Florence had pulled through with renewed health and vigor.

That summer Hugh MacKenzie and Florence's brother Finlay returned to China. Florence had graduated with her class in May, they told him, but still had six months of work left to complete before she could come home to Eric and their wedding plans. After being apart for so long, Eric deemed the short span of time doable.

The good cheer and stories were welcomed, but other news shook him, such as when he heard of the sudden death of a missionary's young wife.

Eric penned a letter to the LMS Foreign Secretary Francis Hawkins:

> To think that she was at the May meetings being farewelled
> and then that within a few months God wanted her. . . .
> During my time at home last year I too was passing through
> a greater struggle than I had ever had before. It has brought
> me back here with a clearer message than before and a more
> personal Christ.[4]

By early autumn, Rob and Ria returned to China. Rob had been anxious to get back to medical service as hospital superintendent in Siaochang, where he and Eric had been small boys together. There, Rob and Annie Buchan went to work together.

As James and Mary had once left their children in England, Rob and Ria, on this trip back to their work, had done the same, leaving seven-year-old Peggy sobbing as their train pulled away from Waverley Station. She would now enter the School for the Daughters of Missionaries; they would not see her again for six years and, in their absence, she would go from little girl to teenager. As difficult a decision as it had been, Rob and Ria knew this was the way of missionary parents.

But Eric couldn't help but think that he had always had Rob to lean on as they grew up without the physical presence of their parents. When he heard of Peggy's tears, he found himself dreading similar experiences that might await him as a father. Knowing how it felt to be on the receiving end, he considered the other side of the perspective even less comforting.

* * *

On Sunday, November 12, 1933, Eric preached at Union Church. As he spoke from the pulpit, he felt the comforting presence of his father near him. The following morning Eric received a cable as he finished up breakfast. At only sixty-three years of age, James Liddell had passed away on Saturday at Eric's Aunt Maggie's home in Drymen, where he had gone to observe Remembrance Day. After taking a walk and visiting with friends, James had returned to Maggie's, sat in a chair, suffered a massive stroke, and died.

Eric sat stunned by the loss but comforted in the remembrance of all the love his father had bestowed on those he encountered in his too-short years.

CHAPTER 15

STEADFAST WEDLOCK

Therefore a man shall leave his father and his mother and hold fast to his wife, and they shall become one flesh.

Genesis 2:24

March 27, 1934

Nearly a decade had passed since Eric sprinted across the finish line in Paris, a leap that catapulted him to greater fame than he had known previously. Scotland's greatest athlete became an Olympic gold medalist.

Now, as he waited at the altar of Union Church in Tientsin beside his friend George Dorling, he stood ready to cross another line (single to married) and to add another title (husband).

Eric crossed his hands and held them low and in front. He breathed in the scent of the altar flowers. Then, as the church pianist played the final stanza of a song carefully chosen by Florence, he looked at George and smiled so broadly his cheeks hurt.

"Easy, boy," George teased in a whisper.

Eric allowed the smile to falter, but only a little. "Thank you, George," he said.

"Whatever for?"

"For being here."

The music changed, and the bridal march began. All eyes turned to the back of the church as Flo's sister, Agnes Louise, and George's fiancée, Gwyneth Rees, began their slow stride down the aisle. Eric glanced at George, saw the smile break across his face, and then spoke from the corner of his mouth. "Easy, boy."

George chuckled, and when the pastor behind them discreetly cleared his throat, Eric turned his attention to the young ladies coming down the aisle. He glanced at his top hat resting on the front pew and wondered if he made as dapper a picture as he hoped in the dark morning suit he wore. He knew without doubt that his bride would be beautiful and wanted only that she be pleased as well.

The music changed again, and the congregation—made up of Flo's family and their friends—stood. Eric's hands flexed as he saw her, her arm linked with her father's, her hair caught up beneath his sister's lace veil, her mother's wedding gown flowing about her. She carried a bouquet of pink carnations that trailed from her waist to nearly the hem of the dress.

And she beamed, her expression full of love—love for him. For him alone.

Oh, how he wished his parents could see her. Or even one of his siblings.

But as it had been so often in his life, even with dozens around him, Eric stood alone. Though after today, he mused, he would never be alone again.

AFTER A TEN-DAY HONEYMOON IN the Western Hills outside Peking, Rev. and Mrs. Eric Liddell returned to Tientsin. Toward the end of their trip, Eric noticed a pesky sensation in the back of his throat, and Florence confirmed it to be tonsillitis. Florence tended to Eric for two weeks after they arrived home in Tientsin. Eric did not mind in the least, but it was the first time in his decade of service to the college that he missed work.

The two young marrieds enjoyed their time together through the next year. The wait was well worth it by all estimations. There was relative peace in China—at least for the short time being—though the Chinese government had recently ordered one of the TACC classes to take military drills, and another class was required to attend two weeks of military camp.

Eric wrote to his old friend D. P. Thomson, saying that although he hated war and felt the attitude of Christian people to it would be one of the future's greatest challenges, he couldn't help but notice that the drills had smartened up some of his students.

Eric eased back into his teaching life as the couple joyfully discovered the roles of husband and wife. They hosted many people in their home for game nights, Bible studies, and meals. Hospitality became a new art form in the Liddell home, and most everyone coveted an opportunity to spend an afternoon or evening with the Liddells.

Florence's mother also enjoyed popping in for weekly visits, which evolved into semiweekly visits over meals, and then into daily tea. Eric certainly loved time with guests, and especially family, but he valued time with his new bride more. He wisecracked to a friend that his preferred hymn of choice might soon be "Peace, Perfect Peace, with Loved Ones Far Away."

Peace came in its own time. Before long, Florence shared with Eric the joyous news that, come the summer of 1935, he would be a father.

In the spring of 1935, the political climate brought changes to the world as well as to Tientsin Anglo-Chinese College. As Eric and Florence awaited the birth of their first child, the Japanese penetrated the Great Wall of China near Peking. In Germany, Hitler made plans to use the 1936 Olympics as a host to his Nazi propaganda, and the Chinese Communist Party continued to strengthen its army.

Closer to home, a new order came demanding that one of the TACC classes suspend their studies for three months of intense training at a military camp. Even though Eric was upset that their time away from the classroom represented a half year's work, he also saw these changes in the tide as an opportunity to hunker down spiritually. He organized a prayer breakfast for the staff of TACC and joyfully observed the changes brought by such time spent with God.

That year, a total of eleven students were baptized during the college's annual baptism service.

But an unintended headache arrived during this tender time in the form of a request. The LMS District Council, in the interest of finances, looked for ways to alleviate some of the burden on the college. The sentiment that too many missionaries were assigned to the college had been growing. Eric, being uniquely qualified as a pastor, received a request asking that he and Florence leave Tientsin and venture to Siaochang to serve the rural countryside mission in that capacity.

It was a rare occurrence and an unusual sensation for Eric to have to consider choosing between two callings. He had always tended to be a focused, linear, black-and-white thinker, but here there seemed to be no right answer. He recognized great need in both ministry contexts, and he did not dismiss the new opportunity lightly. He traveled to Pei Tai Ho where Florence had gone for the summer. There, Eric talked with Florence about the choice that lay ahead for him, revealing that many of the missionaries had strong opinions of not wanting to see Eric leave the college.

Eric wrote D. P. Thomson about having wrestled and sorted through his thoughts:

I was a tutor of the graduating class of 1935. I never
seemed to get a real grip of the class. In teaching, one of the
difficulties was the large difference in standard between those

at the top of the class and those at the bottom, but over and above this I never felt that I gained their loyalty or obtained any deep friendship. I know there is always the influence of which we are unconscious, and the way in which it molds the characters of the students, but I do feel that I should be able to see more direct results from my work.[1]

But even though Eric had doubts about his influence, he had been no slouch. In the years from 1922 through 1935, nearly 160 boys had come to profess faith in Christ. He could not help but be aware that he'd often had an indirect—but more often than not, a direct— hand in their confessions of faith. Despite the challenges of 1935, he could not argue with his overall impact. He continued his reasoning to Thomson:

I have discussed the possibility of my going to the country field for a year and a half to help, but we have come to the unanimous opinion that it would be a big waste to do such a thing. My Chinese does not put me in a position to start straight in at all well, and although I see the big personal advantage of doing so, in that it would give me the best grip of the language that I could ever get, I think it is really a waste. The choice would really have to be—give up educational work altogether now, and I don't feel a definite enough call to do that.[2]

Eric and Florence contemplated the move to Siaochang deeply but ultimately decided to decline the opportunity. The timing simply wasn't right, and, as Eric would later explain to the LMS officials, he would go if he felt the calling, but he believed his work at the college was of better service. Even still, their final decision left Eric feeling out of sorts. He had always struggled with saying no when requests came to him. He had also been accustomed to much more free time as a single man. A married man's life is different, he reasoned, as well as that of a family man. On top of everything else, their family would soon expand to three, and both he and Florence anticipated needing the precious time together.

Patricia Margaret Liddell came into the world in July 1935. The blonde, curly-haired child became a joy to everyone around her and gave a sense of life carrying on, even in troubling times. Eric proudly delighted in the added role of fatherhood and welcomed the few headaches from late-night cries and lost sleep.

* * *

The following year, a much-loved Patricia toddled at the beaches of Pei Tai Ho, playing on the very shoreline where her father had proposed to her mother. The Liddells were blissfully happy—they'd settled in well as young marrieds, their daughter was nothing short of a treasure, and to add to their joy, another baby was on the way, due in January of the following year.

But the world did not seem to share their bliss. Minor eruptions led by cultural upstart Mao Zedong continued. His communist revolution had gained a large following in opposition to the Chinese national government. Leaders ruled the main streets and capitals of China, but tension and uncertainty commandeered the side streets and alleyways. By late summer, the head of the Nationalist government Chiang Kai-shek was nearly overthrown by a group within his own government who urged him to unite the Chinese forces to evict the Japanese.

Talk of the inevitability of declared war increased over dinnertime's rice bowls and mah-jongg tables.

Tientsin's people grew worried. Stress mounted. Eric ministered and preached accordingly to his community. Not only did he have his own children to raise, but he also had his spiritual children in the faith to teach. He passionately continued to share Christ, develop relationships, and serve as a peacemaker, helping to settle disputes.

Eric continued emphasizing and reemphasizing freedom in the gospel that was disguised in the joy of adhering to God's Word. His was a voice of soothing comfort as the community braced for an uncertain future. But no pastor escapes the ministry without having to pivot on a few ideas. Eric's homiletic approach at this period in China contained more of a gospel-oriented delivery, which veered from the earlier law-oriented decision points he shared in D. P. Thomson's meetings. In one surviving sermon outline, Eric describes focusing on one's own work as irritating; however, when the eyes are placed on the work of God, the face is lit up. Eric's sermon text, Romans 10:17, answers the great question, "Where does faith come from?" It is not manufactured in an individual's heart by a decision, but "faith comes from hearing, and hearing through the word of Christ."

On one level, Eric preached this basic message to all hearers: that there is an emptiness in trusting in one's own works of righteousness but a relieving richness in recognition of God's righteousness working in and through humanity. A deeper consideration of Eric's sermon may reveal that Eric had been alluding to his own experience, as any good preacher tends to do.

The rippling effect of the Oxford Group continued to turn heads and raise eyebrows in China. Will and Margaret Rowlands, LMS missionaries stationed in Siaochang with Rob, hosted a weeklong fall spiritual retreat there with a number of the London Missionary Society workers and Chinese pastors. Gardner Tewkesbury, a China-born missionary like Eric, led the retreat. The teaching points of the Oxford Group were implemented throughout the week, and the retreat was a powerful spiritual awakening for all in attendance.

Missionary men and women, foreigners, and Chinese pastors

united under the Scriptures. Through quiet devotion times and Bible study, penetrating questions, soul-searching confessions, forgiveness, resolution of differences, and letting go of grudges revealed themselves at every turn. Many of the reports from the missionaries afterward alluded to the transformative effect the week had on them.

One missionary, Edith Owers, who had struggled with sharing space with other women in the group, said, "All this time, I had the privilege of living with the Bible-women in their new quarters, and none of us will ever forget that week. Life and work ever since has been on an entirely different footing."[3]

Alec Baxter, a short-term missionary, had mental reservations and personal dislikes but expressed, "I can never be sufficiently thankful for the steps which led to a complete resurrendering of my life to God, and for the new life and vitality engendered by this in my own spiritual progress."[4]

Will Rowlands summarized the experience in a report, saying, "There are many in Siaochang today who owe their release from besetting sin and new power in service to these heart-searching talks."[5]

The success of the retreat pleased Eric greatly. Feedback from Oxford Group sessions typically produced similar reactions to his knowledge. Walking as a Christian, especially in the face of adversity, had always been difficult. And the chatter of looming war made living the faith even more challenging. Any theological perspective that could help was a benefit, and the Oxford Group's perspective *did* help, even though some considered it politically and theologically controversial. The Oxford Group was unconventional in the way its meetings were organized—without singing, praying, or a fixed order of service, they didn't resemble church services of the time—and its members were far from united in their political opinions, which made some people suspicious of their teachings.

Eric's favorite mantra had become living a "God-controlled life," a life that adhered to the Oxford Group's principles. This way of thinking and living had spread through Eric's circles of influence. The ensuing peace that came with living this way contained a hidden reward. The controversy directed toward the Oxford Group's teachings was out of fear that one might be weighed down by submitting to the perceived oppressive will of God. Challengers of the Oxford Group's practices thought they might find more freedom adhering to their own will in addition to God's. Yet, ironically, it is only by being completely at peace with God's will—in his control—that freedom in God's grace is ultimately found. Great joy is found in the ability to live under discipline without the burdensome thought of discipline.

This distinct understanding and belief was vital to Eric and influenced how he grappled with his next big life decision—helping the rural Chinese discover faith in Jesus Christ. Eric could only chuckle during his quiet times with the Lord, wondering what possible way God would shake up his life with such a different call than he had previously imagined.

. . .

Humor had always been Eric's lubricant for life. He kept his sense of wit churning through the tense times as well as the times of ease.

A classic example of Eric's amusement happened shortly before Florence gave birth to their second child. Florence and Eric had debated the name of the new child. Florence had been vying for Heather, while Eric had been holding out for Carol, as the birth would be quite near to Christmas. One evening Eric told Florence he had written down the names on two individual slips of paper, then placed them in a hat. "I'll be fair and allow you to be the one to draw the name out of the hat," he told her.

Florence carefully considered the proposition as an air of seriousness took over her. This method seemed fair enough. She slowly reached a hand in, drew a slip, and unfolded it.

"Carol," she read as her balloon of hope burst.

But what Eric had not revealed to Florence was that he had written "Carol" on both slips of paper in the hat. His straight face did not last long. Florence sleuthed the truth out between Eric's giggles and smirks. After he gave his confession, she threw a cushion at him. Their laughter resounded through the new year.

On January 6, 1937, a second daughter arrived. Eric and Florence named her Heather.

A few weeks later, Rob and Ria rushed to Tientsin with their young son, seven-year-old James Ralph, who appeared quite ill. Doctors at MacKenzie Hospital confirmed their worst fears—James Ralph had tuberculosis of the spine and needed to return to Britain as soon as possible.

Rob booked passage for his wife and son, now secured in a body cast. Between the time it took for young James Ralph to recover and the political climate in China, Rob knew that when he said good-bye to them, they would not see one another's faces again until his next furlough, scheduled for two years out.

*   *   *

Eric took pride in his flourishing family, and he pedaled Patricia around Tientsin on the front of his bicycle. But his mind wasn't completely free for work and fun. He had been mulling over a now-familiar request—Siaochang.

In the summer of 1937, the LMS's district council decided to transfer Eric to Siaochang, where he would serve God for four months in a rural community, with an eye on a more long-term transfer.

The district council of the London Missionary Society had their hopes set high to ease the volatile situation TACC faced. The college needed to reduce funding by one staff member. Eric had always been the logical choice. Cullen had been ordained as well but was in

Early Days

A family visit during a furlough from China (TOP, L TO R: Eric, sister Jenny, brother Robert; MIDDLE: parents Mary and James; BOTTOM: brother Ernest)
1922

Eric winning a race
1923

I press on toward the goal for the prize of the upward call of God in Christ Jesus.

PHILIPPIANS 3:14

**I run the first 200m
as hard as I can.
Then, for the second
200m, with God's
help, I run harder.**

ERIC LIDDELL

Eric being paraded through
the streets of Edinburgh after
his gold medal victory
JULY 17, 1924

Crossing the finish line
at the British Empire versus
United States of America
relay in London
JULY 19, 1924

A Family Man

Eric and Florence with
their wedding party
MARCH 27, 1934

Eric's sense of humor
on full display at
a friend's wedding
1934

Eric holding
Patricia outside
their home in China
WINTER 1935

Eric, dressed for
work in Tientsin
1938

**In the dust of defeat as
well as the laurels of victory
there is a glory to be found
if one has done his best.**

ERIC LIDDELL, quoting an inscription
at the University of Pennsylvania

Siaochang mission
outpost where Eric lived
and worked with his
brother Robert while
his family stayed in the
safer town of Tientsin
LATE 1930s

Christ for the world, for the world needs Christ!
ERIC LIDDELL

Family picnic
on furlough in
Carcant, Scotland
1940

Florence Liddell in
Toronto with her three
daughters: Patricia,
Heather, and Maureen
NOVEMBER 1941

Patricia and Heather
admiring their new
baby sister, Maureen
1941

To The COMITE INTERNATIONAL DE LA CROIX-ROUGE,
GENEVE (Suisse).
Service Internés Civils
Service Civilian Internees
Civil-Gefangenen Dienst
Please transmit the following message:

DEMANDEUR—ANFRAGESTELLER—ENQUIRER

Nom-Name ERIC H. LIDDELL Nationality BRITISH
Prénom-Christian Name-Vorname ERIC HENRY
Camp-Gefangenlager CIVIL ASSEMBLY CENTRE
Matriculation No. 3/88 BLOCK 23/8
Localité-Locality-Ortschaft WEIHSIEN
Province-County-Provinz SHANTUNG
Pays-Country-Land CHINA

Message à transmettre—Mitteilung—Message
(25 mots au maximum, nouvelles de caractère strictement personnel et familial)—
(nicht über 25 Worte, nur persönliche Familiennachrichten)—(not over 25 words,
family news of strictly personal character).

LARGE AIRY ROOM WITH ELEVEN OTHERS. HEALTHY,
ENJOYING SOME READING. CONSTANTLY REMEMBER AND
PICTURE YOU ALL. DEAREST LOVE TO ALL,
EVERYTHING SUFFICIENT. LONGING FOR YOU, LOVE
ERIC.

Date-Datum AUGUST 24th 1944

DESTINATAIRE—EMPFÄNGER—ADDRESSE

Nom-Name LIDDELL ( ) Nationality BRITISH
Prénom-Christian Name-Vorname
Rue-Street-Strasse UNITED CH
Localité-Locality-Ortschaft To
Department-County-Provinz O
Pays-Country-Land C

ANTWORT UMSEITIG.
Bitte sehr deutlich schreiben.

Final Words

Handwritten Red Cross
25-word transmission
from Eric to Florence
AUGUST 24, 1944

COMMUNICATIONS

Approved by the Commandant

FROM
(Name in full) Eric Henry Liddell.
(Nationality) British.
(Address) 23,8. Civil Assembly Centre. No.3,88.
Weihsien Shantung
China.

TO
(Name in full) Florence Jean Liddell. (Mrs).
(Nationality) British.
(Address) c/o Rev W. Toulston.
United Church of Canada.
South Bank
Chungking. China.

MESSAGE

Was carrying too much responsibility. Slight nervous
breakdown. Am much better after month's rest in
hospital. Doctor suggests changing my work / giving
up teaching and athletics and taking on physical
work like baking. A good change. So glad to get your
letter of July. Mrs Longman is much better. Dean
and Helma making preparations for marriage on April 18.
Will send particulars later. Wish you could enter into
the celebrations. Joyce Stranks has been a great help
to me in hospital, keeping me in touch with the news.
Enjoying comfort parcels. Special love to yourself
and children.

Date Feb. 21st 1945. Signature Eric Henry Liddell.

Final message from
Eric Liddell, received
by Florence after
hearing of his death
FEBRUARY 21, 1945

nowhere near the physical shape of Eric. Transitioning from Tientsin to Siaochang would be demanding, requiring a robust constitution. Sending Eric and his family to Siaochang would alleviate the financial predicament at the college.

Eric could not argue that the plan had merit and seemed to provide a workable solution . . . *if* he was willing to move his young family. The conveniences and amenities that Florence and Eric enjoyed in the large and prestigious port city of Tientsin would not at all be found in Siaochang. Rearing children would be significantly more difficult in such a rural setting and with a smaller social network.

As painful as the decision was, Eric knew that the rural areas of China were no place for his wife and children. Banditry, political fighting, violence, and human depravity were part of daily life. He decided that he would go to Siaochang alone and would visit with Florence and his girls only a few days each month.

Every moment of his life—the early years of being apart from his family, save Rob, and both his athletic and spiritual training—had prepared him for all that awaited him within the next few years.

He simply didn't know it yet.

CHAPTER 16

A PROPHET IN HIS HOMETOWN

*In your hearts revere Christ as Lord. Always be
prepared to give an answer to everyone who asks
you to give the reason for the hope that you have.
But do this with gentleness and respect.*

1 Peter 3:15, NIV

Late 1930s

He missed his family. But the longer Eric spent on the mission
field in Siaochang, the more he knew that he and Florence had
made the right choice when they'd decided he would go
it alone.

Months had passed. Months of work.

But every chance he could, he returned to Tientsin to Flossie
and his little girls. Often when he returned, he managed to make
it early enough to put them to bed but not always. On this particular night, when the moon had risen hours earlier and now shone
down full and brilliant on their home, Eric paused in front of the
house, looking up, scanning the windows for any sign of life.
Seeing none, he tapped on the door. Seconds later, it creaked
open to reveal Yu Kwan, the houseman who had worked for Eric's
mother since his birth and who had continued to serve Eric and
Florence since their wedding. "Mister Eric," he whispered.

Eric put a finger to his lips and shushed as he walked through the door. "Has Mrs. Liddell gone to bed?"

"Just now," Yu Kwan said. "Probably still awake."

Eric rushed to the bedroom he shared with his wife to find her sitting at her dressing table, pulling a brush through her auburn hair. "Hey, Flossie."

She spun around gasping, then stood and crossed the room, rushing into his arms.

The next morning, as the sun's light replaced the moon's glow, a tiny Heather crawled into her parents' bed, waking them. Eric blinked as he reached to stroke her soft, dark hair, willing himself to wake fully.

Heather jumped, then looked at her mother. "Who's this?" she asked, her large eyes staring at Eric. "The cook?"

Eric raised himself up on his elbows and gaped at his wife. "I knew we were friendly with the cook, but I didn't know it had come to this!" Then he wrapped his arms around them both and drew them to his chest, which rumbled with laughter.

THE WEEDS OF THE WORLD had grown tall and unpruned, casting a vast shade of darkness not seen around the globe for a long time. Japan, among other notorious powers, had lurked in the shadow of these stalks for years with the poise and patience of a cat, ready to pounce on its victim. In July of 1937, Japan finally seized its moment and lunged toward its chosen prey—China.

China, weakened by drought, regional floods, and the distractions of its own civil and political strife, was at its most vulnerable point. The people of the Middle Kingdom had been more than ready for a hopeful ray of light to burst through and bring new joy over their dim horizon. But the Land of the Rising Sun was not what they had in mind.

A unified Japan had in relative ease sacked the major Chinese cities of the east coast and taken control of all the shipping ports. On July 30, 1937, while Florence and the girls were in Pei Tai Ho, Eric watched Tientsin fall to the Japanese. Only days earlier, when the fighting had begun, Eric—along with Carl Longman and Dr. E. J. Stuckey—had gone to the roof of MacKenzie Hospital to observe. The sounds of gunfire and the cries of the people, as well as the feelings of panic and desperation, reminded Eric of what he had experienced as a child in England as World War I took place in his backyard.

Daily, Eric busied himself helping the Chinese refugees who poured into the school and hospital seeking safety. Within a couple of weeks, however, the Chinese returned to their homes, and Eric found that—especially for foreigners—life returned to as normal as possible under Japanese control.

For two months—September and October—Eric returned to teaching by day and enjoying his family at night and on weekends. But in November, a desperate letter arrived in Tientsin from Will Rowlands, changing everything.

Siaochang, he reported, had been cut off from the missionaries in Tientsin by the flooding, leaving him isolated as the lone missionary at the outpost. Information came at a minimum. Nearly everything there had been destroyed. He needed help, most especially from Dr. Rob Liddell.

The LMS decided that Eric and Rob would venture to Siaochang to assist and restart their service, although they were uncertain of what to fully expect. After a rough start and restart, the brothers left Tientsin on November 29 and journeyed mostly by way of riverboat through the perilous countryside.

Eric and Rob had to keep their wits about them, navigating through Japanese invaders, the Communist troops, and the national armies, as well as guerilla forces and thieving bandits who took advantage of the country's volatility. Eric learned the hard way that he should keep his money hidden in his shoes.

After walking the final ten miles of the journey, the Liddell brothers arrived at Siaochang to find Will Rowlands in reasonable condition and thoroughly appreciative to see his colleagues. Among their first duties was to reassess the quaint Siaochang mission, which consisted of four houses, a hospital, a women's dorm, a church, and a boarding school.

The flooding had indeed taken its toll. Repairs were needed. The three men discussed and evaluated a strategy for future mission work. Roughly eighty people lived in the compound. Some were strong, confessing Christians. Others, not so much. For the people's spiritual rebuilding, Eric, Rob, and Will aimed the gospel at the center of their group and slowly worked their way out.

The consensus was that their mission work would be conducted with the understanding that China would win the war against the Japanese—eventually; that surely, with enough persistence, China's slow waiting-game approach of guerilla warfare would pay off. Their sheer size and volume of people had brought them victory time and again throughout history. China possessed so much land and contained vastly superior population numbers compared to Japan. Surely, the proverbial tortoise of China's battle approach versus the hare of the Japanese would ultimately carry the day. It would only be a matter of time. How much time, no one could predict. There remained only one certain fact for Eric and Rob, as well as for the other missionaries and the Chinese people: as extreme atrocities of war brought sickening report after sickening report, life in China would be unstable for a good long while.

Early 1938 brought Eric Liddell a new season of work—village ministry. Technically Eric carried the title of "Hospital Superintendent" of the mission, a slightly comical position in that Eric had no prior medical training. There was method to the madness, however, as the title credentialed Eric in a valuable way to the myriad warring factions swarming the area.

Each day Eric pedaled off on his bicycle with a mounted cart in tow and a Red Cross armband securely pinned to his upper sleeve. He artfully balanced the peaceful solitary bicycle rides through the serenity of the country trails with the harrowing strategy of avoiding military forces. Despite his best efforts, Eric could not always evade being detained, searched, or interrogated. These were the times when the armband came in handy, and Eric wore it boldly.

The Red Cross armband signaled to any hostile group that might seize him for questioning that he and his work fell under the auspices of the hospital mission. Eric was quickly recognized as someone who could help others, particularly soldiers who likely would be in medical need . . . if not at that moment, soon enough.

Some interactions were more stressful than others, but Eric genuinely exuded a love for humanity like no other, a trait that transcended culture. He possessed a strong sense of the nearness of God no matter the circumstances. Because of this strong assurance, he did not become rattled when grilled for information. Instead he always managed to parlay pardon from his captors, conveyed through a smile, a shared family photograph, or gentle laughter. In this way, Eric mastered the missionary tactic of being "wise as serpents and innocent as doves" (Matthew 10:16).

One of Eric's strengths was his ability to quickly relate to others, even those perceived as enemies. His sincerity toward the locals was authentic and convincing.

Eric wrote to D. P. Thomson, sharing with him some of the experiences he described as the most joyful and freedom-filled work of his time in China, even though he missed Florence and his daughters terribly.

The floods have caused much havoc, but the loss sustained
by them forms only a small part of the sorrows of the people.
Fear reigns in all their hearts. Bands of irregular soldiers,

bandits, etc., are all over the countryside. They settle on a village and live off it and the surrounding villages. Repeated demands are made to the villagers to supply grain, money, rifles, and food and they must supply these as best they can. Fear reigns everywhere and the bitterest thing of all is to think that this trouble comes to them from their own people in the midst of a great national tragedy. No year would have given me a better chance than this one in the country "to sit where they sit till their sorrows become my sorrows."[1]

No matter the task and no matter how long he was kept away from his family, Eric did not complain. He simply didn't allow a spirit of negativity to overcome him in his new work environment. Instead, he sought the positive with extraordinary skill and used it to his advantage.

Because many of the villagers reverently remembered Eric's father, James, and his work among them, Eric endeared himself to the Chinese people in Siaochang's surrounding villages with a certain indigenous quality no one else could bring. Some even remembered Eric and Rob as young boys. Just as he had been called Liddell ii back in his days at school in England, Eric now went by the local moniker *Li Mu Shi*—Pastor Liddell—the very title his father had been called so many years before. For Eric, this seemed another subtle wink from God, underscoring that in leaving the classroom for the countryside, he had made the right decision.

By June, Dr. Rob Liddell—now the chief surgeon of Siaochang—felt more than ready for his furlough. He headed back to Scotland for a year with his wife, Ria. The two eagerly anticipated being with both of their children and reconnecting with their British relatives and friends.

On the heels of Rob's departure, Eric took a brief hiatus with his family during the month of July. Pei Tai Ho always did wonders for his soul. Dashing down the shoreline after Patricia and soaking in the ocean waters were great ways to burn off the energy of his two little girls before lunch and naptime.

But not nearly enough time had passed before Eric had to head back to his work. Nurse Annie Buchan had returned to the hospital in Siaochang to help pick up the slack Rob's absence had caused, but even still, Eric knew full well that with his brother gone, more would be asked of him. Not that he wouldn't readily accept the job and perform the tasks well, because with God's help, he would.

•　•　•

The severity of the war worsened, but Eric whistled, hummed, or sang his way through the trials, sowing seeds of joy wherever disharmony clanged. The dangers were quite sobering and real. The noise of bombs, explosions, and machine-gun fire rose as common background noise to Eric's work, both on the mission compound and in the field.

At the close of 1938, Eric wrote Florence and their daughters a final letter for the year.

Dear family,

I am writing this after an eventful few days. Last Sunday we had planned to hold a big baptismal service for several nearby villages but, already the day before, we heard heavy gunfire in the distance and by breakfast time a scouting plane was circling overhead. So many from the outlying villages didn't turn up, rightly fearing that an attack was about to start. As I addressed those receiving baptism two shells exploded outside with a terrific noise and there was silence for a moment before we were able to continue. I don't think any who were baptised that day will easily forget what happened. No one left after the service was over, so we just continued with hymns and witness to keep up our spirits.

As there were no opposition forces here, truckloads of Japanese soldiers soon hurtled through the village gates and they searched every building in the place. Though they came into the church they left without causing any real damage, but in the evening, when everyone had gone home and was too frightened to come to evening service, the church door opened and in came the man who used to be the local opium-addict, thanking and praising God. It seems that, having reached a living faith in Christ, he had then been arrested on a trumped-up charge but, unlike many others, he had been acquitted. Hurrying home he had come to church straight away to give thanks for his deliverance, unaware of the terror we had all known earlier in the day. Feeling I had been given a congregation, I got on with the service! . . .

Often now when I'm cycling from village to village, what with the frozen ground and the ruts, I have great difficulty in staying on the bicycle and I've a splendid collection of bruises. Nearly everyone is afraid to speak to me in public, but going into their homes, telling them how so many others are in a similar situation, and getting them to sing hymns, has a wonderfully restorative effect—especially when I sing in English—which makes everyone roar with laughter, even though they don't have much to be cheerful about. . . .

Now, with so many homes vandalised by visiting troops, most people are living crowded together, hungry and prey to disease. At least since the National govern-ment outlawed footbinding the women and girls are

spared that agonising pain and deformity, but in places
where Jesus is scarcely known you find next to nothing is
done to help the weak and distressed, especially children
and, more especially girls. Do you remember that little
girl, frostbitten as the result of neglect, whose feet had
to be taken off, though with care she did grow well and
strong? Well, I found out quite recently that she married
and that her children taught how love can help and heal.
We must never forget that Jesus means us to pass on
to others His love in deeds of kind thought, remember
that what is done for one of His little ones is done for
Him. . . .

But goodness knows where it will all end. What with
the Japanese, local warlords and increasingly poor living
conditions the situation here is growing worse each day.
I wonder what has gone wrong with the world.[2]

By summer 1939, Eric and Florence were relieved to depart
China for the respite of Canada. Initially Eric offered to delay their
trip, but his superiors insisted that he take the time to rest up so he
could return refreshed and ready to work hard again.

Florence grew excited to show off their two little ones to her
family in Toronto and looked forward to generally enjoying life in
Canada again before moving on to Britain.

Before leaving China, Eric wrote to D. P. Thomson,

I cannot close without a witness to the goodness of God, as
a sense of his presence and protection has been constantly
with me. It would be untrue to say that the year has brought
no danger, but he who said "Lo, I am with you always," has
been true to his promise. . . . The flag is still flying so don't
get depressed. There is still plenty to thank God for.[3]

• • •

The Liddells traveled to Toronto full of anticipation and glee and in search of peace. On their voyage they often stood on the ship's deck to watch the sun rise in the mornings and then set again in the evenings. But as they enjoyed the warm summer breeze on their faces, a flame of fear had begun to spread, eventually catching fire throughout Europe.

And a German firebrand by the name of Adolf Hitler stood poised and ready to douse the blaze with gasoline.

CHAPTER 17

AN ISLAND
OF PEACE

A time to love, and a time to hate;
a time for war, and a time for peace.
Ecclesiastes 3:8

September 1939

Eric sat in an armchair, a cup of tea resting on the piecrust table next to him, a Canadian newspaper spread between his extended arms. He frowned at what he read, knowing full well that the headlines affected not only the world at large but also him and his family in particular.

Greatly.

A shuffling in front of him caused him to bring the top of the paper down. "Flossie," he said.

She carried her own cup of tea and wore a smile that faded as soon as she read his expression. "What is it?"

"A German U-boat off the coast of Ireland fired a torpedo at the SS *Athenia*."

Florence eased into a nearby chair. "Did anyone—"

"They're dead. Nearly 120 of them."

His wife nodded. She understood his dilemma without his

even having to speak it. "I think I know what you're about to say next."

Eric frowned as he folded the paper and placed it next to the now-tepid cup of tea beside him. "Let's see what the next few days bring, shall we? Before we make any decisions of our own."

MERE DAYS AFTER the Liddells arrived in Toronto, in September 1939, war escalated from a possibility to a reality. After the SS *Athenia* sank, Germany invaded Poland. France and Britain declared war days later.

World War II was in active theater.

Eric and Florence planned to stay in Toronto for a month and then take the girls to Scotland. As much as they had looked forward to showing Patricia and Heather to Florence's family in Canada, they were equally eager for Eric's family to meet their daughters. But if Eric had learned nothing else in his time as a missionary, it was that best-laid plans are rarely realized. Since it was no longer considered safe for civilians to travel across the Atlantic, Eric and Florence were forced to make quick decisions. Eric had never been one to shirk his duties, but he had also—as best he could—kept his wife and daughters out of the line of fire. He certainly had not come halfway around the world to put them in danger.

Eric wrote to LMS Foreign Secretary Cocker-Brown and explained that he did not want to risk traveling with his family through the ominous ocean waters and suggested he could take their furlough in Toronto for the year. This would ensure their safety while they rested up. Considering the situation, it seemed like a more than reasonable request.

Cocker-Brown wrote back on behalf of the LMS stating they had strongly hoped and planned for Eric to be in Britain for the year. They needed him for deputation speaking engagements in order to raise support for the ongoing mission work. The war, they reminded him, greatly inhibited the potential availability of money people might be able to give in support.

Eric was displeased but understood the London Missionary Society's response. His obedience to and respect for authority kicked in. Certainly, he reasoned, if he had been brave enough to work in the midst of war in northern China, he could do the same in the present situation, crossing the perilous Atlantic to furlough in Britain. Surely any other man would not acquiesce so obligingly, given the circumstances. But Eric once again demonstrated loyalty to his God, his family, *and* his employers by sacrificially making a difficult decision. He put everyone else first and in the best position possible while placing himself—and his own personal interests—last.

Eric ultimately decided to traverse to Britain alone, a decision that would keep his family protected in Toronto.

After so much intermittent time on the mission field, Florence had looked forward to spending the year with Eric and their young children together. Spending much of the furlough separated had not been a part of her careful plans nor was it in her interests. But after tense negotiating between husband and wife—both missionaries to China—his reasoning won out. They rented a house in Toronto, where Florence and the girls could live for the remainder of their furlough.

Again, Eric wrote to the LMS. He stated that he would come to England alone, but it would be at great personal financial cost. He hoped the LMS could help alleviate the burden of having to essentially double their cost of living during the yearlong furlough.

Letters crisscrossed, the final two missing each other. As Eric sailed the Atlantic unscathed and without incident, a letter from Cocker-Brown arrived at the Toronto address ultimately allowing Eric to decide his own path forward.

• • •

Britain had somewhat forgotten one of her favorite sons. Even still, one of its November newspapers boldly commented on Eric's return, saying,

Mr. Eric Liddell, has arrived after a second period of seven years missionary labours. A son of the late Rev. J. D. Liddell, Edinburgh, he became science master in the Anglo-Chinese College in Tientsin 14 years ago, and since 1937 he has been carrying on evangelistic work in that area under the direction of the Chinese mobile unit. He and his wife are both in excellent health. Mrs. Liddell, who is the daughter of the Rev. Hugh MacKenzie of the Church of Canada Mission, is meanwhile remaining in Canada.[1]

The famed runner-turned-missionary's return did not garnish quite the fanfare as his first furlough seven years prior, which was fine by Eric. But the LMS had hoped for a more favorable splash what with World War II suffocating all the remaining oxygen out of Britain's discussions.

Mary Liddell's home had been lonely and quiet since James's death, and she rejoiced to welcome Eric in for the year. Rob's family had been back for a while by then, Jenny stayed busy with her family at their estate in Carcant, and Ernest now trained as a lieutenant of the Royal Artillery.

The threatening nearness of war loomed over the British Isles. Eric, swept up in patriotism and seemingly on a whim, applied with the Royal Air Force, offering his services as a pilot. Not that he knew anything about flying, but the thought of doing all he could to defend Britain, his home, his culture, and his family was certainly enough for him. Moreover, he had served alongside his elder brother,

Rob, in the mission field. The possibility of serving his country with his younger brother, Ernest, felt right.

Eric becoming an aviator in his own Spitfire, warding off the German Luftwaffe, would have been enough to get any British journalist's blood pumping, and the cartoonists would have had plenty of fodder for conjuring the most dominant image yet of the Flying Scotsman. But the vision of Eric Liddell—British icon and Olympic champion—joining aerial formation with the winged squadrons of the skies was not to be.

Eric had been regarded as a national treasure. The thought of frivolously losing him on the front lines of battle possibly played a role in the RAF's decision making. Eric had been considered many things, but expendable was not one of them. And so, in a letter of declination, the British Royal Air Force deemed Eric, at thirty-seven, too old to enlist, though they did offer him a safer desk job.

* * *

With his immediate family in Canada and himself in England, Eric now understood better how his old flatmate, Gerald Luxon, had felt as a grass widower. He told the deputation committee to feel free to set up a rigorous travel and speaking schedule for him. While he was a bachelor for the year, he said, they may as well use him as best they could, for the betterment of the mission and to keep his own mind off Florence, Patricia, and Heather.

During his time in England, an obvious visit Eric planned to make was to see D. P. Thomson, who at forty-three had tied the knot for the first time. As a wedding gift, Eric gave them a watercolor painting created by Li Hsin Sheng, a man in Siaochang whose life Eric had saved. After presenting D. P. and his wife, Mary, with the gift, he shared how he had come to purchase it.

Months earlier, while transporting an ill Chinese man to the hospital in Siaochang via mule and cart, Eric heard of another man in nearby Pang Chuang who was barely clinging to life. Although by any standards it was a dangerous mission to try to rescue the second man, Eric felt compelled to try nonetheless.

Eric found the man with a deep gash in his neck. He and five others had been taken out by the Japanese and then forced to kneel in the dirt. Using a saber, a Japanese officer beheaded each victim. But the sixth man—the man who had painted the wedding gift Eric now offered to D. P. and his bride—had somehow survived for several days, lying in a temple.

Eric found the man, then managed to get him into the cart with his other wounded passenger. Painstakingly, he carried the two over a nearly twenty-mile journey of bumpy roads and fields to the hospital in Siaochang.

The first man died. But when the second man recovered, he became a Christian and, soon thereafter, painted a peony rose with a Chinese caption that read, "The peony rose is the most beautiful in China. Her modesty and manner come from God."

Eric had the painting copied to lithographs, brought several with him to England, and gifted one to the Thomsons.

The story of the painting's origin hit its mark with D. P. Soon preachers and speakers told the story of the work from pulpits all over Scotland. Copies of the lithograph were recreated and sold, the money going to the LMS work in China.

* * *

Eric made his deputation rounds throughout the region, speaking in churches, schools, town halls, and rotary clubs.

A popular Congregationalist minister who had gone to a few of Eric's speaking engagements captured the mood in a later written report, saying,

There is one characteristic of Mr. Liddell, which impressed me very deeply on the two or three occasions of my meeting him. . . . I well remember the address he gave at "Swanwick-At-Home" in Manchester, which I chaired, during his last furlough. It was just a simple portrait gallery, in words, of some of his Chinese friends and contacts. The audience, at first, was obviously puzzled by its extreme simplicity, for it was the first time most of them had heard this famous Eric Liddell, and they had come expecting rhetorical fireworks. But as the address proceeded, the audience became profoundly attentive. Those Chinese were with the speaker in the room.

This simplicity of his was, in truth, that rare gift of the childlike spirit which the Kingdom consists, and before the address ended, the audience was aware of it. As I remember it, Eric did not say a great deal about the more adventurous side of life in Siaochang, but rather spoke as though Japanese armies, Chinese armies (whether Government or Communist), and bandits, were the normal background of the day's work.[2]

Eric gave another talk in which he spoke effortlessly of invading soldiers, threats on the roadways, and the starvation of countless Chinese. His method of delivery and calmness of voice gave the impression that—despite the topic—all was well in Siaochang. Only later did another report reveal to those who'd heard Eric's speech the truth behind the difficulties he and the other missionaries had endured.

Eric's God-centered spirit had been the calm of the mission work's everyday storm, and he insisted that all people—whether Japanese or Chinese or British—be treated *not* as Japanese or Chinese or British, but as God's children.

Near the end of February 1940, with the United States naval presence aiding in perceived protection, people began to regard the Atlantic as safer than previously suspected. With this news, Florence—missing her husband more than she could bear—begged Eric to let her and the girls cross over to be with him. At the same time, the LMS informed Eric they wanted him to stay in England longer than previously expected. This meant he would not see his family for an extended period *and* that Florence would soon have to decide about her lodging.

After much consideration and prayer, Florence and Eric determined it was high time the girls came to Scotland.

In March, Florence and the girls crossed the Atlantic without episode in a ship nearly without passengers. When Patricia and Heather pressed her with questions about the oddness of it all, Florence simply stated, "God is in control; everything will be fine."

Because Eric was speaking in Ireland when they docked in Liverpool, Florence, Patricia, and Heather maneuvered their own way from the dock to the train station. A serious accident occurred during the train ride from England to Edinburgh. Even though dozens of passengers were injured, Eric's family survived with only a few bruises.

Ria Liddell and Charlie Somerville met Florence and their nieces at Waverley Station, then drove them to Mary Liddell's home, where they waited a few more days for Eric to return. Once he did, the family of four held each other tightly and breathed each other in, making it difficult to know for sure who was most excited to see whom.

Mary Liddell was more than willing to watch the girls, who enjoyed playing with Jenny's daughters. It provided Eric and Flo much-needed time to steal away for dinner or a film or simply to talk without interruption. The streets of Edinburgh were darkened due to fear of air raid bombings. But for the two lovers desperate to reconnect, the necessities of war provided an oddly romantic backdrop.

Sooner than either he or Florence liked, Eric had to return to his speaking schedule, but he managed to ease the pace a bit with his family near him. Flo spent her time away from her husband looking after the girls and following up on correspondence. Her letters revealed that not every relationship within the Camelot of the Liddells' castle was without differences. In a letter she wrote to her sister Margaret, she penned,

> Mrs. Liddell is fine and we get along very well together. She has failed a lot since we saw her ten years ago but she is really very energetic. She thinks I underclothe the children but we haven't come to blows yet!! . . .
>
> Eric goes away again this Sat. and then I'll try and get some work done!! The children will hardly let Eric out of their sight. We're all having the time of our lives and enjoying life immensely. . . .
>
> Cheery-bye for now. Try and find a minute to send me a scratch.
>
> Your ever loving sister, Flo.[3]

CHAPTER 18

KEEP CALM AND CARRY ON

God is our refuge and strength,
a very present help in trouble.
Psalm 46:1

May 1940

Eric strolled behind his daughters, who skipped along the stone fencing in the estate belonging to his sister and her husband, drinking in the hills and glens around him—the bleating of sheep, the morning songs and twittering of birds, and the giggles of his girls.

They'd so needed this time, he and Florence. He and Florence, Tricia and Heather. When Jenny had suggested that his family come to Carcant—when she'd boasted of the thousand acres and the small family cottage perfect for respite—he'd not hesitated for a moment to say yes.

Every day, the girls ran wild through the green countryside, laughing and playing with their extended family. If he only gave them this time and nothing more during their furlough in England, he hoped it would be enough—enough to last them a lifetime.

A sudden stop in their playing drew his attention to a tiny

creature a few yards away, bunny ears up, nose quivering. Tricia turned to him and whispered, "Daddy . . . a rabbit . . ."

A rabbit indeed. And that meant rabbit stew.

Like a flash Eric bolted, as did the rabbit, scurrying along the line of the fence. But Eric was faster, and within seconds he had the furry bunny clasped in his hands. "Daddy, you caught it!" he heard as one hand gripped its neck to snap it.

He hadn't thought. He hadn't anticipated what little girls might think of such an act. They didn't mind eating meat, but they'd never seen it before it was butchered.

His head spun to meet their horrified gazes.

"Daddy!" Tricia cried. "You killed it!"

"Now, girls," Eric said, struggling to find a way to ease their upset, "you should know that if you sprinkle a little salt on a rabbit's tail, it slows them down, and you can catch them."

Patricia turned to Heather with a start. "Hurry!" she squealed, turning back toward the house. "Let's go get some saltshakers!"

DURING THESE WARM and lazy days, as Eric and his family enjoyed the sheer beauty of life together, Rob Liddell worked on a personal conundrum of his own. Young James Ralph's health issues continued. For Rob, the thought of leaving his children again, one of whom suffered physically, was a tough call. World War II and the precarious situation in the Far East did not settle him or Ria. With remorse and exhaustion, Rob reached out to the London Missionary Society, asking for a quiet release from his duties. The LMS understood the difficult circumstances and reluctantly granted his request.

After returning to Edinburgh, Eric and Florence absorbed the unanticipated news. Eric lamented the impending result of his brother's decision but could not argue with his reasoning.

Eric continued his deputation speeches on behalf of the LMS as his deadline to return to China approached.

At one such meeting, Eric clearly laid out the situation in China:

Even before the war, there was a considerable amount of illicit trade between Manchuria and North China. I have watched heroin runners in operation, not even challenged on the railways because of a desire not to give offence. Now that the Chinese Customs are controlled by the invaders, the cities are being flooded with Japanese goods at prices which no other nation can compete with.

When it comes to education, the Japanese have come to the conclusion that from education we will achieve the greatest sense of patriotism, which is something new in China. The Chinese give their loyalty to family rather than country. . . .

The Japanese feel that they must control the schools, while the universities suffered much worse. I, myself, saw one bombed to bits in Tientsin two and a half years ago.

We see a good deal of guerilla warfare along the railway lines. One day, a band of roving Chinese removed a few rails from the tracks—they believe they will win the war this way. The Japanese promptly replaced them and immediately sacked the adjacent village. Over such an extended territory there could be up to 100 fights like this every single day.

In Siaochang we gave the combatants medical aid, but refused it to neither side. Those villagers still have their land and we, at the mission, help them to plant crops there.

Please understand, our area near Siaochang has not been attacked so much as other areas. We have the constant guerilla warfare, yes. But through the grace of God, we have been able to carry on our work in China.[1]

Despite the challenges of ministry in China, Eric loved his heritage, his father, and everything for which he stood. But pondering the astonishing reality that he was the last of Liddell missionaries in China came as a dramatic weight. Rob easily utilized his medical skills for the British war efforts, and young Ernest had now been stationed for artillery duty. Even with danger in the air, Eric wondered how he could possibly stay in what felt a much-safer place. The Liddell legacy along with his call from God beckoned him in every fiber of his being.

Eric and Flo knew World War II had only started to heat up, and it did not appear it would slow down anytime soon. Hitler had just begun to flex Germany's muscles throughout Europe.

Eric and Florence, however, had a call from God to serve in China, period. Keeping themselves protected was not their sole objective. They trusted the will of God. If he had called them there—even amid danger—there could be no better place to dwell. The fear of bombing attacks on Britain or an invasion of Britain was imminent. Would they not be just as safe—if not safer—in China?

After much prayer and discussion, they made their decision: come August, they and their children would head back to China. They said their painful good-byes to their dear ones and boarded a steamer to begin their travels across the Atlantic to spend time with Florence's family and then on to the Far East.

Eric gazed back at his special country. This would be the last time he would set eyes on his beloved Britain.

• • •

Unlike during the trip from Canada to England, drama and turmoil filled the trip from England to Canada.

When their ship arrived in Nova Scotia, Eric found the time to send off a few details to his mother:

We went on board at the scheduled time. There was a good bit of inspection. Cameras were taken from us and will be returned on landing. The boat has a number of children on board. I don't know how many, but I should say that at least half are children. It's a small boat, with a complement of 300 passengers and crew. There are a few even younger than Heather.

We were in convoy and had an escort. The convoy is a delightful sight. Can you imagine 50 ships, all going along together, not of course in single file, but in about five lines. It is magnificent. Most of the ships are cargo ones; any passenger ships are in the centre for greater protection.

It wasn't until we were off the Irish Coast that the real excitement started. It was 8.30 at night, when the children were asleep. We were hit by a torpedo. Whether it was a "dud" and only the cap exploded, or whether it had expended its energy, having been fired from too great a distance, or had exploded right below us, we are not sure. I would say that we were actually hit, and that only the cap exploded, judging from the feel in our cabin. No alarm was given for us to go to the boats, but the signal for all boats to zigzag was given by ours.

The next night we lost one of our ships at the back of the convoy. The sea was choppy—a very difficult one to spot submarines in. The escort left us the next day. This was the hardest of all days. About 10 a.m. a small boat about a quarter of a mile from us was torpedoed, blew up, and sank in two minutes; they must have hit the engine boiler. We were on deck ready for boats, and everyone zigzagged. About noon the "all clear" went and we turned to dinner. We had just started, and were half-way through the first course, when the alarm went again. Another boat torpedoed. It didn't sink. We heard later that it was able to get along. Whether it turned back or tried to carry on, I don't know.[2]

Eric's letter went on to explain more of the harrowing consequences of traveling from Europe to North America during the war but ended with "Both kids are well, except that 'Tricia has developed a cough these last two days. They weren't scared at all, for they didn't really know what it all meant."[3]

During their time on deck, Eric had kept his children occupied with games, even as little Tricia declared to her father, "Daddy, that boat went down." Eric knew the danger he and his family steered through, but he made certain his young daughters kept their childhood intact, even as he allowed God to still his concerns. He'd watched five of the fifty ships go down and heard the estimated loss of life calculated to be eighty souls.

From Nova Scotia, Eric wrote another letter to his mother, telling her of an onboard desire for a Sunday service, complete with thanksgiving for their safe arrival. Word leaked aboard the steamer that Eric was a minister, so naturally he had been asked to lead the service—an opportunity he happily accepted.

As much of a joy as it was to celebrate with the people, to sing and praise God in thankfulness, Eric and Florence's concern fell to Patricia and Heather, both of whom had contracted German measles. This brought new concerns for their parents who knew what passenger illness meant when it came to leaving the ship. But the authorities gave a green light for travel when they heard that Eric and Florence, along with their two ill daughters, only had two hundred miles to go before reaching their destination.

Eric and Florence found all the hotels filled in Nova Scotia, but they did not dismay—the Red Cross had a place nearby that supplied tea and milk as well as beds for children. Eric sent his family for a little rest while he took care of the pressing business of retrieving their luggage.

Still at the station, Eric loaded their luggage—the heavier pieces for Vancouver and the rest for Toronto. The clock struck midnight, and Eric found a ready taxi to take them back to the ship in hopes of bunking there. But as soon as they arrived, a shipmate informed them that "all the beds have been stripped, sir."

Bone-weary, Eric, Florence, and the girls slept in their traveling clothes on top of bare mattresses.

Ten days later, after spending time with family in Toronto, a long train through Canada forged the Liddells across North America. Their visit with the family had been wonderful but not long enough.

Never long enough.

Another long but considerably less terrifying voyage across the Pacific to China awaited them. Finally, after a little over a year abroad, they arrived back in Tientsin in late October 1940 and began to prepare for a move to Siaochang.

Eric and Florence had spent many hours during their trans-Atlantic and trans-Pacific journeys discussing the possibility of moving the family to Siaochang. Perhaps it might be different this time, they reasoned. Perhaps it would be safer and their family could stay together rather than having only the snippets of time together that Eric's solitary work afforded them.

But their expectations were not matched with the current developments in Asia. Siaochang—and the rest of China—had changed a lot during their time away, and not for the better.

Quiet murmurs buzzed that there was a possibility of all foreigners being sent out of China—or detained. Eric and Florence immediately felt the shattering of their hopes of staying together. Florence and the girls moved back into their house in Tientsin while Eric headed out for Siaochang.

But when Eric arrived there, he found the village garrisoned and its south side surrounded by a high wall. Land had been requisitioned without compensation. Graveyards had been desecrated, and the mission had been closed. Because of its value to the Japanese, the compound had also been turned into an impromptu Japanese base camp, although the hospital stayed operational. Dr. Ken McAll and Nurse Annie Buchan worked under that stress and were overjoyed when Eric arrived.

Eric stayed with area missionaries and traveled around the region on his bicycle.

His muscles reminded him his first week back that he had not pedaled for a year on the cumbersome trails of the northern China backcountry. He powered through it in his signature style, popping in on various churches. He concentrated on the many new villages in the southern territories of Siaochang that he had not visited much, if at all, in the past, and he realized that in the midst of fears and alarms, the world and life goes on.

Eric did his best to spread hope by speaking, teaching, and always thinking about how to make a contribution to ensure a better world. Eric described his work as "giving, giving, all the time, and trying to get to know the people, and trying to leave them a message of encouragement and peace in a time when there is no external peace at all."[4]

Dr. Ken McAll, a bit of a neophyte to the rural missionary setting he had been called to, offered a portrait of Siaochang life at that time:

> In the hospital we have been able to help the wounded of
> four armies, the Japanese, the Chinese Central Army, the
> Eight Route Army, and the Chinese Army that is helping
> itself under the Japanese. The local people are not unanimous
> as to which of the first three types of armies they prefer,
> as most people think of their own money and food before
> their country. . . . We have had many visits from troops as
> they have passed through or used our Mission as a base for
> operations. . . . With these visits we usually have a huge

rush of refugees from the village. We take all the women
and children into the Church. It shows that in their mind
we stand for a safe refuge, unbroken by the worldly warring
outside.

Our peaceful state is, some of us think, due to an early
attitude that Eric Liddell helped us to; one of treating all
these soldiers as children of God whom he cares for; and
that it was for us, as we showed these over the premises to
witness to them, explain why we were here, and try to help
them as we ourselves have been helped by the Almighty. To
this end, Eric spent most of one day with the Japanese in our
Hsien city, and I think those who listened certainly caught
some of his idea, for the next time they came they were full
of questions, and one Japanese spent an hour with me in my
room in hospital.

It is possible that there was room for doubt as to the
genuine spirit of this Japanese response. But there can be
none as to the eager sincerity of Eric Liddell's desire for
them.[5]

Despite the obvious and constant challenges, Eric shared a unique
perspective of seeing avenues for the gospel of Jesus in unobvious
ways, ways the average person would not see. He wanted to help
others see the beneficial effect beyond the naked action of the service
itself. Even the smallest labor of love mattered. Eric believed that
through service to others, God is there—hidden and helping through
the hands of the helper.

• • •

LMS missionaries to China felt a most difficult sting. Months went
by without letters from England. For those whose children went to

school there, the agony of not knowing how their loved ones were faring during the war was nearly unbearable. Eric and Florence had not heard from family since their return either.

Even as the usual joy of Christmas wove its way in, Eric watched Chinese men—miserable and dispirited—forced to work for the Japanese. He was more than ready to return to Florence and his girls in Tientsin.

The menacing murmurs of foreigners being made to leave had graduated to an indisputable cry of inevitability. Eric's call was his call, though. The perplexing role of a servant of the Lord is the dichotomy of battling weariness in ministry while never feeling worthy enough to rest for too long. After two weeks with his family over the holidays, he headed back to Siaochang.

Nurse Annie endorsed that one could hardly argue with the value of his unique skill set and ministry. "Eric's methods in systematically visiting the churches," she wrote years later,

> preparing plans, drawing maps, and holding regular
> conferences with the Chinese preachers, were never
> complicated, but simple, clear and direct, like his own
> character. In preaching he never expounded elaborate
> theories, but suggested the possibility of a "way of life"
> lived on a higher plane, to use his favorite expression,
> A God controlled life. In Siaochang, our preachers,
> nurses, and students hung on his words, and
> the common people heard him gladly.[6]

When speaking of Eric, Dr. Ken McAll recalled,

> He would just shoot off on bicycle and go anywhere and
> everywhere, all over the countryside. He was an evangelist to
> the villages. He didn't stay put. He was out most of the time,

very rarely was he staying with us in our houses. And he kept his wife and babies in Tientsin where they were safer because it really was dangerous. We were constantly being shot at or locked up by the communists for identification.

He was an extraordinary fearless person, he had this awareness of Jesus being with him all the time. If you ever asked him a question of should we do this or that, he would lower his head, and say, "Yes. Well, just be quiet for a little while," then would raise his head come out smiling. . . . He gave me a new discipline, because I had someone to check things with.[7]

Eric often thought of subtle ways he could assist the local Chinese pastors, more than through one-on-one interactions. He began to develop structured ideas for writing his own devotional book during the long intervillage bicycle rides. He thought the work would ideally be for young Christians but could also serve as a tool for area pastors.

In March, during another Tientsin pop-in with Florence, Eric shared his writing ideas and thoughts. Florence was excited for him, but she had an announcement that she thought might trump his news. They would have another baby soon.

The great news of a third child also brought more serious discussions of what their life together would and should look like. The violence of the war had escalated. Eric had been shot at on more than one occasion. Foreigners returned home for fear of detainment or of being forced out of their work. The missionary community had shrunk and continued to grow smaller. Even Tientsin was no longer considered safe for raising little ones, let alone the most suitable place to bring another tender soul into the world. Many missionary families around them were sorting out their own judgments and priorities of what to do.

The time had come for Eric and Florence to face a major life decision. Unlike the choice of whether or not to run on a Sunday, this one demanded to be wrestled with.

CHAPTER 19

TOGETHER APART

The LORD *watch between you and me,*
when we are out of one another's sight.
Genesis 31:49

Spring 1941

As they had so often done, Eric and Florence put their daughters to bed at night, then stole away to their own room to talk. There never seemed to be any other time. The days were spent with work or with family and friends. And Tricia and Heather, of course, were always keen to hear.

Some things were best left out of a child's equation, like war and the decisions it forced upon the adults who weighed its consequences.

As soon as the door closed behind him, Eric crossed to the dressing table, removed his watch, and laid it next to his wife's hand mirror. His fingers traced the scrolled gilded outlines of the mirror. "Oh, Flossie," he sighed.

"Should I make us some tea?"

He looked at her. She rested, her shoulders against the panels of the door and her feet crossed at the ankles. Eric couldn't help but wonder whether she was too tired to walk the rest of the way into the room, or too afraid. "No. I'm fine." He sat in the nearby chair and removed his shoes. "We've got to make these decisions, my girl."

Florence sat on the bed, curling one foot behind her knee. "What do you think best, Eric?"

"We could stay here. Together. All of us. Keep up the work."

"Or we could call our work here done," she countered. "And go home to England or to Canada."

"Or . . ." Eric raked his teeth over his bottom lip. Their third option was one he didn't want to consider.

"Don't say it, Eric."

"I have to." He looked at her fully. "You could return to Canada, and I can stay. Finish what needs to be finished." He blinked. "Not forever. Just for a season."

Florence shook her head. "I can't think about it right now."

Eric scooted up to rest his elbows on his knees. "I have to think about it, Flossie. Keeping you and the girls safe is the most important thing right now."

And in the end—with God's help—he knew the bulk of the decision rested on his shoulders. His alone.

But could they live with the consequences of that decision?

AS THEIR WORLD CHANGED DAILY, Eric feared that his family might be kidnapped. With his wife expecting their third child, and as a dedicated family man, he prayed harder and more fervently.

One question overshadowed all others: Could Eric put off making up his mind? With every day—and every moment of the day—that passed, he knew time was most surely of the essence.

The London Missionary Society had often functioned as a bureaucratic quartermaster for its deployed families. Unexpectedly, they demonstrated an open approach for how to handle the increasingly chaotic world stage. Instead of mandating what all missionaries must do, they allowed each to discern matters on their own and determine what would be best for each family. Some elected to stay, some to go, and others to separate. This was an emotional season for all, sorting out priorities, responsibilities, and the call of God, while watching their precious relationships with family, friends, and colleagues sever one by one.

Daily life moved forward, despite sociopolitical pressure. A father-daughter relay race against some of Patricia's classmates in Tientsin had come upon Eric and his family. Naturally, "Team Liddell" was the odds-on favorite. As the first leg of the relay, Patricia had delighted in holding her father's undivided attention during the "handoff." In lieu of a brisk exchange, she opted to run around with the relay handkerchief in her hand, playing chase rather than keeping her father's esteemed track record intact. This may have been Eric Liddell's only DNF (Did Not Finish), and the afternoon ended with a brief chiding of Patricia. "Now, Patricia," he said, "remember, we always want to do our best in everything."

Eric always aspired to do his best—in *everything*. If he contained a shred of hubris, it may have asserted itself in his insistent perfectionism, which could and did rub certain people the wrong way. This characteristic would often rear its head during his decision-making process. The selfish route versus the selfless route had often been employed for major life decisions, particularly for ministry-minded people like himself. But delineating between the two motives was never easy.

After a decade and a half of service, Eric was one of the elder statesmen of the Tientsin missionary community. He did not want to completely carry his witness for Christ out of China, particularly at a time he believed it was most needed. He felt very strongly about that, and Florence agreed.

The godlier, selfless Christian path would be for Eric to serve

God and stay in China alone. Or was that the selfish path? Did his roles as missionary and pastor trump his roles as husband and father? Sending his family to Toronto alone would put added stress on Florence, leaving her to raise three little ones on her own. Yet even in China, they were so often separated.

Still . . .

Eric and Flo ultimately decided that he would stay serving in China, and she and the girls would return to Toronto. Eric would remain for only one year—two at most, he assured her. They were both young and strong. Soon enough, they'd reunite, either in China to continue the work or in Toronto to determine what lay in store for them during their next season of life.

Either way, they'd be together.

Temporary separation had always been understood as a potential reality within the realm of missionary work. By staying, Eric could focus on gospel proclamation exclusively.

A lovely sunny day in May 1941 cast a shadow upon Eric's family as they said their final farewells. Eric insisted that Flo and the girls make their voyage on a Japanese vessel, which they agreed would be the safest transport, so they made their way to Kobe, Japan, where the female Liddells had tickets to board the *Nita Maru*.

The day of departure, while Eric helped his family to their cabin, Florence kept her hand on her rounding belly. She didn't feel well, but whether it was her pregnancy or the thought of leaving her husband behind in a war-torn country, she couldn't be sure. Heather skipped about on deck, content with the lollipop her father had given her. Patricia, equally delighted with her treat, received special instructions from her father.

He sat the girls down next to their mother and whispered in Patricia's ear, "Tricia, I want you to look after your mother, and I want you to look after Heather, and help with this new baby that's coming, and I want you to do this—promise me that you will until I return."

"I will, Daddy. I promise," she replied.

Eric kissed them all, and after final, loving embraces, he made his way off the ship. Moments later, he turned to see his family waving madly at him from the upper deck.

"Good-bye, Daddy!" the girls shouted.

Eric waved back.

"I love you! I love you! Come home soon!"

PART THREE

The Third 100

Faith in the Day of Hardship

CHAPTER 20

AN UNEXPECTED OPPORTUNITY

*These have been written so that you
may believe that Jesus is the Christ,
the Son of God; and that believing
you may have life in His name.*

John 20:31, NASB

May 1941

Those who love God never meet for the last time.

The words his mother had spoken to him so long ago jarred
Eric from his work, and he looked up. Where had they come
from?

Surely, soon enough, he would see Flossie and Tricia and
Heather and the little one yet to be born. Surely he and the love
of his life would watch their daughters blossom and grow. Then,
one day, he'd set his brow and stare down his nose—teasing,
taunting—at the young men who came to call. Then, as Hugh
MacKenzie had done, Eric would walk each one down an aisle
toward a man who would adore her as he adored their mother.

Surely.

And then he and Flossie would grow old together. They'd
gather the grandchildren and unfathomable joy would fill
their home. They'd grow old together, sitting in front porch

rockers—perhaps in Carcant with Jenny and Charles—and watch the sheep graze along the hillsides of Scotland.

Their parting only a few days earlier had not been their last time together.

Surely not.

ERIC HAD SOBERLY RETURNED to his work, never imagining how quickly it would evaporate before him. The hospital in Siaochang closed for good, which forced the missionaries to make yet another move.

Nurse Annie, who had long observed the handwriting on the wall, initially went to work at MacKenzie Hospital alongside Dr. Geoff Milledge. In time, however, she angled for a nursing reassignment to the Peking Union Memorial Hospital, most notably to enable her to care for a sick friend who lived in the city. Her persistent politicking paid off. After showing up at the Japanese district office in Tientsin every day for a week, she wore the commander down. He gave her his official approval, provided she never came back. Annie assured him she would not and went on her way. She figured the longer she was in a position of value, the safer she could be while still accomplishing her work.

During the summer months, Eric ventured to Pei Tai Ho as he had done for many years, but he found it nearly devoid of the vacationers who had once enjoyed it. These were lonelier days than he had known before, especially with his girls so far away. Japan's presence in China had changed so much—in both large and small ways. Even the senior MacKenzies, who might have provided Eric some comfort, were no longer in China. Instead, they enjoyed a furlough in Canada, sharing a home with Eric's wife and daughters.

As seemed to have been true for so much of his life, Eric was alone.

On the first day of September 1941, Eric returned to Tientsin.

He moved in with A. P. Cullen, who had also sent his family to safer grounds and who had a flat in the French concession. The two men thought it quite something that at one time A. P. had been Eric's teacher, then his missionary colleague, and now also his roommate. Above all, they were brothers in the Lord. And they were friends.

Each afternoon they enjoyed long walks together—a time when they could discuss the world's situation at large and, more intimately, how it affected them personally. Eric also continued to ponder a book on discipleship he hoped to write—one that would one day serve Chinese pastors.

Together the two men celebrated life's accomplishments—the birthdays of family members separated from them—with a cup of tea at the Cosy Club or an economical meal out at the Europa Café. And, with each passing day, Cullen noticed that the joy of the Lord never left Eric's face.

That exuberance was most noticeable in mid-September when Eric received a cable from Canada telling him that Nancy Maureen Liddell had entered the world.

He quickly sent a cable back to Canada: "Wonderful news!"[1]

Eric remained busy by continuing in the work God had called him to. He bicycled around and preached, led Bible studies, and encouraged those he met along the way. But he could not help but notice that opportunities and freedoms lessened and stalled. He kept at it as best he could, eventually noting that—for the first time in perhaps his whole life—he had more time on his hands than he knew what to do with.

Weeks grew into months as communication slowed to a snail's pace. Because of the increasingly unpredictable and intermittent postal service, news from "home" became feast or famine. At times, those in China felt relieved to get a single letter. At other times, they were astonished to receive over thirty letters in a single day.

Eric's hunger for contact with loved ones living on the other side of the world grew.

.   .   .

Years later, A. P. Cullen noted that the one area of Eric's life that fascinated him most was the rate at which Eric's spiritual life developed, most especially in the face of war. This was fascinating to him, but not confusing. While no one could quite understand how Eric had been able to accomplish his feats in sports, Cullen knew *exactly* the formula for his spiritual medals. Years after Eric's death, Cullen noted,

> [Eric] had as a foundation the inestimable advantage of truly Christian inheritance and truly Christian parents, and he would be the first to acknowledge how much he owed to them. On this foundation, from the time he began to think for himself, he steadily and painstakingly built up that Christian character for which we honor him today.
>
> Very early in his life he began to reveal that strength of determination and firmness of purpose which was such a marked feature of his character. . . . Since he came to China in 1925, I have been watching his progress. At first, while he was adjusting himself to his new work, there appeared to be nothing remarkable in that progress, but as the years have rolled by, the momentum has steadily increased; indeed, the growth of his spiritual life affords a remarkable parallel to his methods of running a race, for one of the astonishing things in his victories on the track, as we have already heard, was that he was always a bit slow in getting off the mark, mainly, I am convinced, because his fine conscience would never allow him to "beat the gun."[2]

Cullen went on to describe Eric's "conscientious thoroughness, attention to accuracy and detail," which, he said, showed up in all of Eric's work. Eric gave the greatest care and attention to everything he put his hands to. "Given these two qualities—an unflinching purpose and a finely sensitive conscience—add to them an ideal of a life completely dedicated to the service of God and men—and you have the secret of Eric Liddell's career."[3]

Whether Cullen realized it or not, in a few sentences he gave the world a glimpse into Eric Liddell's greatness. A. P. Cullen—teacher, friend, co-missionary—answered the "why" for anyone who might wonder that generations come and go and people still say, "Eric Liddell's life fascinates me."

But Cullen was also quick to share that Eric was not superhuman:

Let no one think that he did not have his temptations, just as we have, temptations to indolence, slackness, compromise, and what not. But he won his way through, by persistent study, regular times of devotion, constant meditation, insistent prayer, getting up early in the morning and spending one hour—two hours—in a concentrated search for God's will as revealed in the teaching of Jesus and the Bible generally.[4]

During the time he lived with Cullen, Eric worked on the devotional book he'd had in mind by poring over the writings he had come to treasure, the ones that drew his heart and spirit closer to the heart and Spirit of God. The one-on-one ministerial interaction he experienced as he pedaled from village to village continued to inspire him as he inspired others, but he could not stop thinking about and hoping for a discipleship program that would continue after he left one village and cycled into the next.

Something effective he could leave behind.

While Eric and Cullen continued with the good work in China,

Hugh MacKenzie made a declaration in Canada. With a fervent belief that his colleagues in China needed him more than ever, Hugh informed his wife and other family members that he wanted to return to his work in the Far East. Based on all he knew, Tientsin was in crisis. With his connections and ministry worth, he could better serve God and others *there* than at home. He packed his bags, including a recently taken photo of Florence and her three daughters—a gift from a loving wife to her heartsick husband.

Hugh kissed his family good-bye and made his way to San Francisco, where he planned to board a ship for China. But in the early morning hours of December 7, as fog along the dock wrapped around his body, a car struck him and rendered him unconscious.

After a quick trip to the hospital and being given the okay to leave shortly thereafter, Hugh once again attempted to reach the San Francisco docks. Again, he was stopped—this time by the news of a Japanese attack on the US naval base at Pearl Harbor in Hawaii.

The United States had officially entered the war, and Hugh MacKenzie returned to Canada, never to set foot in China again.

•   •   •

The news of the attack on Pearl Harbor reached Tientsin in the early-morning hours of December 8 (the attack had taken place while Eric and Cullen slept). Before most were awake, Japanese soldiers wrapped Tientsin in barbed wire and closed the gates between the British and French concessions. Chinese soldiers gave up and gave in.

Japan now had control over China.

Three days later, the students at TACC were sent home and the school was closed. The residence where Eric and Cullen lived was searched and a radio was confiscated.

Eric and Cullen were ordered to the Japanese military headquarters to register as British nationals. There they answered questions about themselves and reported all personal property and financial holdings. They were placed under house arrest.

The remainder of the month inched by with little news from the outside and no movement between the French and British concessions. Christmas was celebrated, but not in the same spirit as it had been before.

Never one to waste precious moments, Eric used this time to undertake the arduous task of writing the manuscript that had so often tickled his mind but had yet to make it to paper. He approached the process with his typical gusto. Ironically, while others may have bemoaned living in lockdown, house arrest became the perfect season in Eric's life to accomplish his unfinished dream. An inordinate amount of time needed to be filled during the day, and it was nice to have Cullen—a fellow theologian—as a constant spiritual wall of wisdom to bounce his thoughts off. And Cullen continued to be inspired and awed by the man he'd watched grow from a young boy into a ministry colleague.

Eric eventually titled his work *The Disciplines of the Christian Life*, which contains a foundation of Eric's Scottish Congregationalist–instilled principles as well as eclectic additions from the Oxford Group, other theological writings he studied, and experiences from his missionary work and ministry. Eric's unique voice provides fresh insights on Christian doctrine.

Like a theologian taking a page from the Protestant reformers of centuries prior, Eric sat at his desk, Bible open, and wrestled with, sorted out, and defined Christian doctrine as he saw it. He read, reread, and edited through what he wanted to retain and what he might dismiss. In doing so, he meticulously sifted until what was left was sound biblical theology on subjects such as "The Life of Jesus," "The Character of Jesus," "The Holy Spirit," "The Kingdom of God," "God's Moral Law," and "The Life of Paul." Within the pages of his book, Eric shared what he had come to realize about baptism, Communion, and what he titled "The Three Great Festivals of the Church—Christmas, Easter, Pentecost."

As we know it today, Eric's discipleship book contains much of the doctrine outlining his unique spiritual path, and it encourages those who read it in following that same path.

Eric's Congregationalist upbringing had anchored him in a bold, resolute local autonomy and allowed him the freedom to adopt other strains of theological wisdom. His church in Scotland and those throughout Britain had done the same from their vantage points. In time, much of Scottish Congregationalist church doctrine would progress in a different direction from where Eric had set his course of faith to sail.

Eric had lived most of his adult life in China, away from Britain and Congregationalist leadership. Initially varying a degree or two theologically due to context, their bearings would ultimately drift further apart over time. It is not surprising that a missionary and sending church body, with the underlying open principles of the Scottish Congregationalist Church, would vary on understandings of faith, given their different locations, customs, and experiences. Eric's mother ship of Scottish Congregationalism back home would, in time, take on waters of progressive thinking, which eventually submerged it in pluralistic Unitarianism. Eric's religious compass landed him on a figurative island, theologically distinct and somewhat separated from his Congregationalist brethren back home.

Eric's dogmatic writing has built a lighthouse for disciples who feel cast about or as if they are treading water in open seas of spiritual turbulence. Written during a time of political fear and a personal time of separation from his most cherished loved ones, Eric's manuscript spotlights grace and truth. In essence, he encourages readers to put on a life preserver of faith in Jesus Christ and outlines the routine and discipline of being fed by the Word of Christ to demonstrate grace in everyday living.

Years later, after the release of Eric's book, D. P. Thomson described it, saying, "It includes, amongst other things, nearly 60 pages devoted to Bible readings, with comments for every day of the year. It is a work which involved immense labour and unremitting care, and it is the fruit of those long hours he spent in meditation and prayer."[5]

Eric Liddell's time of study and growth, which became *The Disciplines of the Christian Life*, was his last great gift to anyone who reads it. Although written from a tiny corner of the world—a mere dot on the map—its ripples spread far beyond what he could have ever imagined.

CHAPTER 21

DETAINMENT

Therefore, my dear brothers and sisters, stand firm.
Let nothing move you. Always give yourselves fully
to the work of the Lord, because you know that
your labor in the Lord is not in vain.

1 Corinthians 15:58, NIV

January 1942

"The Japanese have ordered all British and American nationals living here in Tientsin to pack up their belongings."

Eric sat at his desk working on his manuscript when Cullen came to the door with the news. At that, Eric closed the Bible that rested open near his elbow, then turned back to his roommate. "What do we have to do?"

Cullen's face remained steadfast in the wake of change. "We have to find a new place to live, I'm afraid. Within the British concession."

Mere days later, bitter cold cut through Eric's clothing and nipped at his fingers and face as he moved what meager possessions he could into the home of Howard Smith, who lived with his family at the Methodist Mission Compound. Another LMS missionary, Gwen Morris, along with Gerald Luxon and his family, also took refuge with the Smiths.

"Tighter fit than we had before," Gerald quipped to Eric.

"You mean back when we were flatmates?" That seemed a lifetime ago.

The unrest of the past few months cast a shadow over Gerald's face. "Who would have ever imagined this, Eric? Would you?"

Eric willed his eyes not to drop to the floor. One day at a time meant one day closer to reuniting with his wife and children. "No," he said. Then he held out his hand palm up. "But God has us, Gerald. I have no doubt."

Gerald nodded. "Where did Cullen go?"

"A family—friends of his who live near Union Church—offered him a room."

"And the Longmans?"

"They're with the Earls."

"I see." Gerald started out of the room, his shoes scuffling along on the hardwood floor, all the while muttering, "Who would have imagined this . . ."

WITH THE FRENCH CONCESSION—including MacKenzie Hospital—now evacuated, the Japanese required foreigners to wear armbands that designated their nationality. Whenever they left home, Eric and the others from LMS slipped on a red band with the word *YING* (for *Ying Kuo*, which means "England") stitched in black. While they were free to move about in the concession, the Japanese required that they bow to the sentries who stood guard at the checkpoints. Eric never made a fuss; he respected others and in turn received the same respect.

The Japanese sealed the French concession with an electric fence. This meant that the missionaries were effectively kept not only from their homes but also from their work. Not that this created idle time for Eric. He may not have been allowed into the rural areas for ministry, but that didn't keep him from organizing prayer meetings.

This proved to be tricky, though, because the Japanese—in an effort to discourage uprisings—forbade large gatherings of ten or more within the foreign community, whether inside or outside of homes or other buildings.

Essentially, meeting for worship became illegal.

However, family clusters could continue to meet within houses, and the LMS ladies could still organize afternoon teas. Eric suggested that each pastor write a sermon for Sunday and allow the tea party rotations to use their time together to present God's Word. In this way, everyone stayed busy and spiritually fed, and fellowship morale remained high.

Eric spent a good deal of his time meeting and praying with individuals as well as completing his book on discipleship. He also worked on another short devotional, *Prayers for Daily Use*, which he penned specifically for the congregants of Union Church. "I have tried to bring before you certain thoughts which I have found helpful in the Christian Life," Eric wrote in the preface. "The aim is that we should be like Jesus, thoughtful, kind, generous, true, pure and depending entirely on God's help, seeking to be the kind of man or woman He desires us to be: seeking, in all things, to do His Will and to please Him."[1]

Eric wrote feverishly during this time. He enjoyed it, and it served a greater purpose than passing the time, although such an effort could hardly go unrecognized. At home, when he wasn't writing, he did his part by teaching cricket to the Smiths' sons and tennis to their daughters.

While her children enjoyed living with and being taught by an Olympic gold medalist, Mrs. Smith discovered new challenges. With so many people under one roof, getting enough bread for their meals became nearly impossible.

"By the time I get to the bakery," she told the adults in the house, "the bread is gone."

Eric cleared his throat discreetly. "I'll go," he said. "I can get up early enough to be there by five o'clock each morning."

And so he did.

Mrs. Smith also discovered that Eric knew his way around a broom. During the year that Eric lived with the Smiths, one of North China's famous dust storms blew over Tientsin. Even with the doors and windows tightly shut, dust crept into the house and settled on the furniture, shelves, and tables.

Mrs. Smith sighed over the enormity of the task in front of her. "I'll take care of it first thing tomorrow," she told her husband the evening after the storm had passed. "Before everyone comes down for breakfast."

But the next morning when Mrs. Smith crept down the stairs at six o'clock, she found Eric quietly finishing up with the cleaning. He'd risen at four thirty and, without waking a soul inside the house, cleaned the house thoroughly.

Many years later, Rev. Smith said of Eric,

> For a year we had the privilege of his sharing our home.
> I never saw Eric angry. I never heard him say a cross or
> unkind word. He just "went about doing good," and he did
> so unobtrusively, so self-effacingly, and so naturally that one
> just took it for granted that Eric was just like that, because
> day by day he kept an early morning tryst with his Lord.
> The pattern of his daily living was so little marred by faults
> because he offered up, quite simply, each smallest thing to
> Christ. He was Christ's man.[2]

The buds of spring finally bloomed, bringing with them the celebration of Christ's resurrection. Remarkably, on Good Friday, an assembled choir performed at Union Church to a standing-room-only crowd. Two days later, the people returned for the Easter service.

Eric continued the work he'd found to do, his writing, and the long walks with Cullen. The two men talked openly about their wives and children, sometimes repeating the same stories they had told the day before because news from England and Canada came so rarely. By this point, Cullen had not seen his family for two years and at times wondered if he ever would again.

As Eric explored the theme of surrender to God, which impacted his humble approach to the rest of the world, he returned to his writing desk:

> When surrender is being made, whether alone or with another person, the mind should not be focused only on our act, but also on God's forgiveness. *The Cross, and what has been done for us by God, is far greater than anything we are doing.* We are saved by grace and by grace alone. Surrender means the end of the great rebellion of our wills. We capitulate; God can act.[3]

In August, as the time came to let the LMS know whether he intended to stay or go, Eric received an invitation to come to Canada after the war, where the offer to take up a rural pastorate awaited him. He wrote to Florence, asking for her thoughts, and saying that even though he knew the work would be difficult—and of course they must consider the children—he thought it sounded like the best thing for them to do. He also let her know how the writing of his "manual" was coming along.

About this same time, Florence received a letter from LMS Foreign Secretary Cocker-Brown asking if she thought Eric, once he was able, would go to Canada or the UK for repatriation. For a moment, Florence wondered if Eric might—indeed at *that* moment—be on his way back to Canada. But she guarded her heart against that hope.

In October, Eric again wrote to his wife, telling her of the books he'd been reading to better grasp and understand the mentality of war, books such as *The Grapes of Wrath*, *All Quiet on the Western Front*, and *Journey's End*. But, he told her, he had also read a book on the life of George H. C. Macgregor, which he had chosen to keep his reading material balanced. This was a book, he told her, about "one of those men whose work is finished at 36, but who, by that time, are ready to join the Choir Invisible."[4]

In a letter dated November 5, 1942, Eric wrote to Florence again, telling her more about the book he'd worked so diligently on, the one filled with daily Bible readings: "If it never comes to anything it will have been useful for my own thinking. And to me will always be a companion booklet to the Daily Prayers which I got out. It would be so easy to let this time go by with nothing done; nothing really constructive, and so have the days frittered away."[5]

In Canada, the MacKenzie and Liddell families moved into a house at 21 Gloucester Street in Toronto. At night Florence and her girls sang songs, then ended their day with a prayer for all those they loved and who now served in the war.

Then, each night before lights-out, the girls whispered into the night air as their father began a new day in China. "And help Daddy to come home soon."

• • •

As was true for everyone in China, little was certain for the LMS missionaries who lived there. No one was sure how long they would remain in reasonable living conditions. Word on the street had been that the foreigners would soon be moved to an internment camp. They were told by the Japanese not to be concerned, that they would have all the amenities they had been accustomed to in Tientsin. But only the foolish believed that. Eric, who'd been made a representative for the missionaries to the Japanese officials and vice versa, decided it would be better to prepare for the worst and hope for the best.

On March 12, 1943, he called a meeting and relayed the news everyone had dreaded. All foreign nationals—British, Americans, Dutch, and Belgians—would be interned four hundred miles away at Weihsien, in the Shantung Province, which had, at one time, been an American Presbyterian mission. The location was isolated, yes, but those interned there would experience "minimum force."

Those about to be interned were told they could send ahead four pieces of luggage per person—one to be bedding and the other three trunks or boxes. They would be allowed to carry two suitcases by hand. Great speculation arose as to what might be deemed of absolute necessity. Blankets? Books? Perishables? What about pots and pans? Should doctors and nurses carry medical supplies? It was certain they would need eating utensils, one plate and one cup per person.

Reducing one's life and household to a few bags seemed an impossible task. Salvation Army Officer Brigadier Ken Stranks urged anyone with a musical instrument to bring it along because, when times got bad—as surely they would—at least they would be able to make music.

The four pieces per person were scheduled to be sent to Weihsien on March 26, 1943. The new internees they belonged to were sent by train in three shifts—the first on March 23, the second on March 28, and the third on March 30.

Both Eric and fellow missionary Carl Longman took the third train.

In describing those days, Rev. Longman wrote,

Arrangements for the rail journey of over 400 miles were splendidly carried out. We assembled at 7.30 p.m. on March 30th and had our luggage inspected by Japanese guards— our first contact with them. We moved off at 9 p.m., marching along the streets lined by sympathetic, silent crowds of many nationalities, the majority, of course, being Chinese. Third class carriages—very crude compared with British "Thirds" were provided, and we took our allotted places in them. We moved out of the railway station at 11.40 p.m. and sat up all night.[6]

At ten o'clock the next morning, the third shift of internees changed trains at Tainan, then arrived at Weihsien at three forty that afternoon. After reaching the camp, they walked beneath iron gates where, many years before their arrival, "Courtyard of the Happy Way" had been carved in Chinese within the arch.

The new internees were eagerly greeted by those who had arrived previously. Eric and his fellow inmates gathered on the athletic ground, where they received preliminary instructions and were then led to their living quarters. Single men and women filed into dorms. Married couples and those with families were sent to thirteen-by-nine-foot rooms.

Initially, Eric shared a room such as this with Rev. Edwin Davies (called Bear) and Rev. J. A. McChesney Clark (called Josh). Gone for them were spacious rooms and rambling streets. Gone were cafés and restaurants. Gone were the everyday comforts of private baths and uninfested bedding on which to sleep. With only a little space for three grown men, Eric felt as though he had somehow been transported back to boarding school.

More than 1,800 people lived indefinitely inside the mission, walled off by an electrified barbed-wire fence where watchtowers rose from stone perimeters. Armed guards and Alsatian police dogs marched along the walls, and every day the detainees woke to roll calls, bayonet drills, and hunger.

Early on, Eric discovered that his group from Tientsin had not been the only detainment of foreigners. Other segments from around China had also been transported to Weihsien. Numerous new faces made Eric and the others intrigued yet anxious as they quickly realized how tight their living conditions would be. Filtering into cramped quarters solely with familiar faces would have been much easier than doing so with a large group of strangers. "First come, first served" had not been the most hospitable greeting they could have hoped for but had been the general sentiment.

As cumbersome and complex as settling had been, another train soon arrived with more foreigners from Peking, among them Nurse Annie Buchan. She was relieved to see Eric and Cullen, just as they were to see her.

The weather did not and would not work in their favor. The spring and autumn climates were tolerable, but the summer brought sweltering heat to that area of China. In late August, when the rainy season began, roads washed out, walls collapsed, and roofs leaked. The winter blasted the internees with arctic chills, so much so that blankets became precious commodities.

Sanitation, or the lack thereof, also became an issue. With only twenty-three latrines for 1,800 men, women, and children, lines— especially first thing in the morning—were exceedingly long. The plumbing, due to limited water supply, did not work, which meant a backup of excrement onto the floors of the bathrooms.

But the biggest mess they had to deal with in the camp would be of their own creation.

CHAPTER 22

INCURVATUS IN SE

*I know how to be brought low, and I know
how to abound. In any and every circumstance,
I have learned the secret of facing plenty and
hunger, abundance and need.*

Philippians 4:12

Early April 1943

"We have to organize," Eric said to the men who had gathered outside the dorm room he shared with Josh and Bear. "And we have to be logical." He placed his hands on his hips, splaying his fingers. "We don't know exactly how long this could go on—how long before we return home."

"What are you saying, Liddell?" one of the younger men asked him, a man Eric recognized as Langdon Gilkey.

Eric raised his chin ever so slightly. Gilkey came from solid—though certainly liberal—theological stock. But he had barely crawled into his twenties when he arrived in China as a missionary, shortly before being interned.

"Call me Eric. And what I'm saying—" Eric glanced around the small crowd and then beyond to make certain none of the Japanese were nearby. "What I'm saying to all of you is that we're here. That much we can know for sure. And this place used to be a mission compound, so we've got, at the very least, the buildings we need. We have doctors here. We have nurses—like Annie—and an old hospital."

"Gutted," someone reminded him.

"But it's there." Eric refused to be dissuaded and looked to his friend Cullen for support. "We have teachers—men like you, Cullen. And me. We can organize. How many children do you suppose they've brought in from the boarding schools or with their parents?"

"Too many," Gilkey replied, his voice tinged with bitterness. "And I've heard more are arriving from the Chefoo School."

"Do you know when?" Bear asked him.

"No."

"Could be a while," Cullen said with authority. "Could be tomorrow. The way things have been . . . who knows."

"Whenever they arrive, they and the children already here will need continued education," Eric replied. "And sports. They must be kept active." He looked at Cullen again. "Especially those who've already made it to adolescence."

Cullen groaned in agreement.

"We can do this," Eric said, the confidence rising in his voice. "If we put our minds and hands together, we can."

"And what do you propose for schoolbooks?" Gilkey asked. "What will you teach them with?"

Eric had already given that question to God. He prayed that the teachers from Chefoo would bring textbooks with them, but until then . . . "I've taken that to the Lord, and God has provided an answer. My knowledge of science doesn't reside in a schoolbook. My knowledge resides here," he said, pointing to his head. "Give me paper and ink. With God's help, I'll write the books myself."

WEIHSIEN BOASTED ONLY four showers and little water. That meant that most of the internees bathed using water caught in buckets.

Men were allowed daily showers. Women could bathe only three times a week. Often the icy water stored in buckets for early-morning face washing had to be broken apart before it could be splashed.

The Weihsien internees were not mandated to perform slave labor. They did not endure the dehumanizing sufferings that would later haunt the world in reports from the concentration camps of Nazi Germany. It became evident soon enough that the internees' biggest adversary was not the war, the forces of nature, or even their Japanese captors. Their biggest enemy was the slow and painful truth *incurvatus in se*—each one's selfish desire to curve inward and live for his or her own exclusive interests. This ugly reality unfolded quite rapidly, especially in a setting where sharing and working together seemed to be the only option and resources were scant. Those who doled out half cups of watered-down stew often took the brunt end of fury from the hungry being served. Exhausted women often threw dirty dishwater on those who worked beside them. And British secretaries who had been housed with older female missionaries found themselves at odds to the point of the freshly formed Camp Housing Committee having to referee their squabbles.

Most of the foreigners had come from white-collar backgrounds— businessmen, educators, lawyers, and engineers—most with their children in tow, as well as a large contingency of Catholic priests and nuns and the large missionary community. Almost everyone in the camp was used to employing the Chinese to perform all the difficult daily physical work for them. Cooking, cleaning, plumbing, maintenance, and the like had not been their practice or their forte.

The finer, nobler pursuits in life had always come at the price of the common man grinding out the raw work of life via blood and sweat. Now a group of people almost completely unprepared for the task was left to fend for themselves. As if the challenge were not complicated enough, eleven nationalities were represented within the large group. Learning by the minute how to coexist became a psychological chess match, calculating each minuscule move to conquer a new small space. But coexist they must. The internees quickly realized the need to work together if they wanted to survive at all. They organized a hospital, formed kitchens, and determined schedules for menial tasks such as potato peeling and latrine scrubbing.

Daily roll call formed at 7:30 a.m. and again in the evening, and each call took enough time for all the prisoners to reach their "roll call district," followed by strict lineups. Prisoners wore their numbers pinned to their chests, and after they were numbered off, they remained in line until the guards tallied the counts from each of the six districts. Between roll calls, however, the men, women, and children of Weihsien were free to do as they pleased. This meant organized school for the children, but for the adults it meant something even more detailed.

The question of a democratic election process had been debated, but the lack of who's-who knowledge and communication complicated the endeavor. A management committee for the camp was finally appointed under the direction of the Japanese commandant, a civil officer, and the military police. The established departments were discipline, education, entertainment and athletics, employment, engineering and repairs, finance, general affairs, medical, quarters and accommodation, and supplies.

Individuals who were physically able had assignments during the day with a rotation of responsibilities. Much like the apostle Paul, Eric possessed the rare ability to remain content in all situations. His assignments were half-time teacher of mathematics and half-time director of athletics. He was also considered "warden" of blocks 23 and 24, two large buildings housing some 230 people. Eric served as a tremendous impromptu mediator between the Japanese guards and several of the hotheaded internees, often using humor to defuse tension.

Two weeks after his arrival at Weihsien, Eric sent a twenty-five-word letter to Florence via the Red Cross, which stated, "Simple hardy life under primitive conditions. Living with Josh and Bear in small room. Good fellowship, good games. Teaching in school, food sufficient, boundless love."[1]

The Catholic clergy quickly became cherished members of the Weihsien camp as they were the only ones brave and willing enough to deal with the overflowing latrine situation. Armed with shovels, mops, and face masks, they went to work. Members of the engineering and repairs department were then able to develop a rigged system of decent plumbing that alleviated the maddening demand.

Unless an individual possessed a clearly specialized and necessary practical skill, creative solutions were employed. Lawyers baked, businessmen cleaned, and missionaries washed. Annie Buchan served with the medical personnel and brought the hospital back into decent shape. Eric and Cullen established a school and a Sunday school, and Eric managed to develop an active athletic community and Bible study groups. Eric naturally sought to establish rapport with the youth in the camp amid a climate of constant irritation, menial tasks, and general insufficiency. When he wasn't working with the younger children on their math and science or coaching sports, he aided the young men and women who had completed high school and needed to prepare for university.

The persistent wear and tear on the people showed on their quickly soiled and worn-down outerwear. Such was their adjustment to prison-camp life. Years later, a fellow internee stated in a letter to D. P. Thomson that

> I was trudging wearily, laden with two heavy suitcases and feeling desperately hungry and tired after two bad days on a Chinese coastal steamer, down the rough path within the Japanese Internment Camp in Weihsien, North China. We were being shown our dormitory, an empty, barn-like room,

and were feeling utterly miserable. Suddenly the person who was helping me along whispered, "Don't stare now, but the man coming towards you is Eric Liddell."

I was too limp to connect the oncoming stranger with the "well-known" Olympic athlete of some years before, but I glanced aside to note the man on the path. He was not very tall, rather thin, very bronzed with sun and air. He was wearing the most comical shirt I had ever seen, though I was to get quite accustomed to similar garments in that place. It was made, I learned later, from a pair of Mrs. Liddell's curtains. But what struck me most about him was his very ordinary appearance. He didn't look like a famous athlete, or rather he didn't look as if he thought of himself as one. That, I came to know in time, was one of the secrets of his amazing way. He was surely the most modest man who ever breathed.[2]

Langdon Gilkey had a keen eye for observing human behavior. He wrote years later,

In such a situation, the more basic human virtues suddenly claimed their rightful place. A man's excellence was revealed by his willingness to work, his skill at his job, his fundamental cheerfulness. On a kitchen shift or kneading dough in the bakery, any sane man would rather have next to him an efficient hard worker who could laugh and be warmly tolerant of his fellows, than to have there the most wealthy and sophisticated slacker or grumbler. After working or living beside a man for months, who cared— or even remembered—whether he was Belgian, British, or Parsee? Thus in a very short time people became to us personalities, pleasant or unpleasant, hard working or lazy, rather than the British, Eurasians, or Americans that they were when we first met them.[3]

Disenchanted by the missionary community in the camp, Gilkey also cited Bertolt Brecht, from *The Threepenny Opera*: "For even saintly folk will act like sinners, unless they have their customary dinners."[4] It was painfully obvious to Gilkey that even Christian missionaries were sinners. They struggled at times even more glaringly than numerous others in the daily grind of the camp.

Apathy toward religion spread quickly when it was realized that the Christian missionaries were complaining noticeably louder than the nonbelieving community and that they were occasionally more obstinate toward adaptation.

Eric Liddell, however, didn't fit in with that crowd.

Mary Taylor Previte, the great-granddaughter of J. Hudson Taylor (who founded the China Inland Mission), had been only nine when the Japanese rounded up her siblings, her teachers, and herself from their boarding school in Chefoo. In her writings about her time in Weihsien, she fondly remembers "Uncle Eric," saying,

> Almost everyone in camp had heard of Eric Liddell. The folklore about him seemed almost bigger than life. . . . But Uncle Eric wasn't a Big Deal type; he never sought the spotlight. Instead, he made his niche by doing little things other people hardly noticed. You had to do a lot of imagining to think that Liddell had grabbed world headlines almost 20 years earlier, an international star in track and rugby.
>
> When we had a hockey stick that needed mending, Uncle Eric would truss it almost as good as new with strips ripped from his sheets. When the teenagers got bored with the deadening monotony of prison life and

turned for relief to the temptations of clandestine sex, he and some missionary teachers organized an evening game room. When the Tientsin boys and girls were struggling with their schoolwork, Uncle Eric coached them in science. And when Kitchen Number One competed in races in the inter-kitchen rivalry, well, who could lose with Eric Liddell on our team?[5]

Eric was gentle above all else. He looked for opportunities to serve others within the camp, often ignoring his own needs for the sake of others. As one of his fellow detainees said of him years later, "He lived a far better life than his preaching."[6]

• • •

Rooming in Weihsien brought its own varied issues. Two men who had not gotten along outside of the camp were placed together—and who knew for how long? They found a quick and courteous solution: they hadn't spoken to each other *before* Weihsien; they'd simply continue along that same path *inside* the camp.

When it came to lights out, Cullen found himself in a new and different place. The men in his dorm—once asleep—snored and issued other loud grunts and groans. He found it difficult to fall asleep until he discovered a new method—he got into bed, closed his eyes, and imagined driving down his favorite roads in England.

Young and inexperienced Langdon Gilkey found himself in another quandary. As a member of the housing committee, he was called one evening to deal with a squabble in one of the ladies' dorms. There he found older missionary women in a standoff with younger British secretaries.

"What seems to be the problem here?" Gilkey asked, noting the cuts and scrapes the women had inflicted on one another.

"We're tired of hearing of their prayers," one of the younger women barked.

"And we're tired of hearing of your previous sexual escapades," an older woman responded.

The conflict restarted, with Gilkey unsure how to respond. Finally, he raised his hands and said, "I'll have the committee examine this issue."

The looks on the women's faces indicated he would next wear the results of their fury, so he quickly turned and left the premises.

But not everyone found discontent. Those who had had enough foresight to bring flower and vegetable seeds from home shared with those who had not. Soon enough, prison neighbors dug into the earth alongside each other, planting seeds. Over time, with proper watering and tending, the blooms of flowers and vegetables brought color—and food—to Weihsien.

• • •

Queries of what—if any—practical purpose religion served rose in different pockets and corridors of the camp. After the behavior of some of the missionaries, the relevance of faith had been the subject of fervent debate.

Not that this was anything new. The value of religion in the secular world had always been a controversial subject. A growing mass within the camp seemed open to the idea that religion in the arduous environment of the camp should remain an afterthought, especially when life-essential work had to be done.

Eric knew the pressure of the situation was building and that certainly faith in Christ was *the* essential need in life. Instilling heavenly thinking in an earthly context had always been the trick.

After the Chefoo children arrived, Eric stepped into the ministry that would prove to be his last. Although he could not be with his own children, he now supervised the younger children's dormitory. This required him to move from the room he shared with Bear and Josh into a larger dorm that housed four missionaries, two missionaries' sons, and six businessmen altogether.

Eric received two notable letters from Florence after he entered Weihsien. The first was long and detailed. In it, Flo described the living room she sat in with all the well-wishers cheering Eric to come home soon and the fun antics and intricacies of living with extended family.

Toward the end of her correspondence, Florence came to the meat of her missive:

> Well honey, I suppose you might be interested in hearing about your own family! They are growing like weeds and it gives me a queer feeling to realize they really belong to me. Patricia is quite the young lady and is so pleased with herself because she has learned to swim—roller-skate and ride a bicycle this summer. Heather still likes to keep her toe on the ground when she swims. Tricia's hair is still short and curly and she has a lovely little figure and she is as quick as ever on her feet. So is Heather. Her hair is as straight as ever. . . . She is far more inquisitive than Tricia and is most interested in the why and wherefore of everything—on the whole they are angelic and are a great help with Maureen.
>
> Maureen is a wee minx and is a great joy to us all. She carries herself very straight and has such a determined walk. She is as happy as ever. I wish you could see her trying to make herself heard above the babel of the older children. . . . The children miss you so and are always talking about when you come home.[7]

Florence concluded with an endearing personal note for her husband:

> Oh Eric, my thoughts and prayers are ever with you and I long for the time when we'll be able to live as a family again. But as I said before, I'm sure we have both learned a great deal and had a lot of experiences that we would not have missed for anything. We will appreciate our life together all the more and in the meantime, we have some wonderful memories to live on. . . . Yours, forever and a day, Florence.[8]

Eric would read and reread the letter as if it were treasured Scripture. Then he would see the bleak camp, which beset him on all sides. He kept Florence's letter tucked into his pocket, as close to his heart as possible.

Toward the end of 1943, Eric received a twenty-five-word Red Cross note from his wife. "Daddy died peacefully Nov 13th," it read. "Failing since pneumonia summer. Margaret, Finlay, Louise here. Overwhelmed kindness friends, relatives. Mother magnificent—continuing here—all well. Dearest Love."[9]

The pain of Flossie's words gripped him. She'd lost her father; he'd lost his friend.

Worse still, he had not and could not be there to hold and comfort his dearest love.

CHAPTER 23

DISCIPLESHIP

*In everything set them an example by doing what
is good. In your teaching show integrity, seriousness
and soundness of speech that cannot be condemned,
so that those who oppose you may be ashamed because
they have nothing bad to say about us.*

Titus 2:7-8, NIV

Early Winter 1943

Eric grinned in spite of the meaning behind the words the children sang—a song he knew they'd composed to help them deal with the facts of their lives.

"We might have been shipped to Timbuktu," the song repeated into its second round.

"We might have been shipped to Kalamazoo. It's not repatriation . . . nor is it yet stagnation . . . it's only concentration . . . in Chefoo!"

They're so young, he thought. Too young to spend their days of now-lost innocence within the electric fence of an internment camp. To go to bed and wake up hungry. To be forced to wear the threadbare hand-me-downs of the clothes the other students had outgrown.

Running barefoot over the dusty streets of Weihsien during

the summer months was one thing, but seeing their feet red and swollen in the bitter chill of winter was another.

"My feet are so cold, Uncle Eric," Sarah, a pretty girl in her mid-teens, had said to him. "Do you think they'll ever be warm again?"

He assured her that they would, even as he thanked God he'd put his own children on a ship sailing away from Asia and toward North America. This was precisely the reason why. They were without their father, yes, but they went to bed with full stomachs. Their feet were never cold. Not like this.

Sarah pulled at her blouse. "And look, Uncle Eric. I'm sixteen years old, and I'm wearing an old tablecloth when I should be in a pretty frock," she said. "How depressing."

True. Sixteen and wearing a tablecloth could certainly be considered an awful fate. But it didn't have to be. Eric stretched the hem of his shirt toward her. "My wife's curtains," he told her, smiling.

The words brought the relief he'd hoped for. The girl laughed with a merriment that, despite her circumstances, reached her eyes.

The children's song changed, and Eric watched the line of them as they marched back to their barracks under the watchful eyes of their teachers, who reminded Eric of his old boarding school masters. The teachers at Weihsien would instruct the students to "sit up straight" and "eat with proper manners"; "being in prison doesn't mean a loss of etiquette." They would also say, "There aren't two sets of rules, children—one for the outside world and one for in here. Learn this, and it will serve you well years from now."

Eric shook his head as the children bellowed a new song. "God is still on the throne," they sang. "And he will remember his own. . . . His promise is true. . . . He will not forget you. . . . God is still on the throne."

ERIC TOOK TO THE ROUTINE of jogging around the camp's perimeter—not only to keep in physical shape but also as a time to pray for the growing concerns of the people in Weihsien. As one of the "ambassadors of faith" within the camp, he continued to offer his best in the give-and-take of tough times. But complaints, low morale, and apathy constantly challenged his message of peace, hope, and the love of Christ.

In the face of antagonism, Eric perpetually pointed out some amusing incident to be happy about. He organized sporting events and competitions, wrote textbooks by hand (his self-created science book was titled *The Bones of Inorganic Chemistry*), and helped establish games to keep the children entertained and their minds focused not on the negatives of internment but on more positive things.

With an overabundance of rats in the camp, the adults fashioned a game to see who could kill the most. An infestation of bedbugs meant another contest to see who could kill the most.

But vermin and biting insects weren't the only concerns. When they weren't dealing with rats, bedbugs, or hunger, Eric and the other internees kept a watchful eye on the weather. Some days were excruciatingly hot, but—as Eric quickly pointed out—the weather *would* cool again. And when bitter cold nearly froze them to death and the detainees wondered if they'd ever feel the warmth of the sun on their skin again, Eric reminded them that, soon enough, they'd once again complain about the heat.

The hot weather meant more than being miserable; it brought dysentery and typhoid. And the cold weather meant more than the difficulty of keeping warm; with the chill came pneumonia and frostbite. Additionally, every morning in winter, when Eric and his fellow "campers" woke, they found the water in the wash buckets had frozen . . . but at least they could break the solid surface, wash up, and remind themselves that, come summer, they'd *wish* for a little ice.

To create a sense of community, the streets were given the names of well-known places such as Park Avenue and Wall Street. Then there was the dining room. If ever a location existed where the worst in human behavior could be observed, it was the kitchen and dining hall. The work was difficult. Often the cooks, once they received meat (some of which they couldn't identify), had to cut around maggot-infested, rotting flesh. With barely enough food to go around, those standing in long lines with empty plates and bowls grew dismayed when the growl of their stomachs met the small portions doled out. So, to ease the tension, the Weihsien residents gave the same old meals of hot porridge for breakfast, stew for lunch, and watered-down stew for dinner names of culinary delights—Coq Au Vin and Quiche Lorraine.

Anything to ease the mounting tension.

For a while, a forty-year-old Australian-born Trappist monk, worried more for the children than for his own safety, used a drainage tunnel as a means of smuggling food into Weihsien—that is, until one of his lookouts became preoccupied by a female internee. A Japanese guard caught Father Patrick Scanlan in the act and sent him to a cell within the Japanese side of the camp.

But the monk was not discouraged. Instead of bemoaning his fate, when night cloaked the prison, he bellowed songs as loudly and as off-key as possible until finally the guards—who had been unable to catch so much as a wink of sleep—told him if he would only stop the noise, they would release him from his sentence early.

He did . . . and they did. And when he returned to the internees, everyone—including Eric—gave him a hero's welcome.

But at the end of the day, the incomparable Eric Liddell was human. While some of his fellow internees were not even aware that he had a family in Canada (he always seemed more interested in the families of others than in talking about himself), in his most quiet times, he worried about Florence and his girls. He wondered when he would hold them and kiss them again.

And he wondered when he would finally meet his little Maureen.

• • •

The Japanese enforced strict rules on the camp, but they did allow the internees to worship freely. Catholic mass was held regularly for the high volume of Catholic priests and nuns in the camp (although they were moved to Peking at summer's end 1943—a sad day forthe entire camp). Sunday school and Protestant services were held in the Weihsien Union Church building located to the right of the camp's gates. Evenings brought the opportunity for hymn-sings and concerts. The Salvation Army band performed public meetings on Thursday nights and provided an hour of song in the open square on Sunday mornings.

Eric knew that healthy religion produced healthy citizens—for *any* society. Daily, he set out in his typically quiet example, authentically demonstrating this point, despite the loudening drumbeat of sentiment to the contrary. Every morning he and dorm mate Joe Cotterill rose long before the sun, lit a peanut-oil lamp, and—using Eric's book of daily Bible readings—studied the Word together. They discussed what they'd read, prayed together, and then set off for their individual tasks, each day more bonded than the day before. And while these moments of Bible reading and prayer would forever shape Joe's spiritual life, he was also one of the few to ever see Eric truly angry.

Eric helped organize game nights for the youth to keep their minds off things of a more carnal nature. Both Eric and Joe were among the volunteer chaperones, ensuring that the games played were appropriate—such as checkers or chess.

One evening when Joe failed to show up for his turn at chaperoning, Eric dropped in and found the games without adult supervision. When Eric found Cotterill, he issued an adamant reprimand. "We have to be the adults here, Joe!" he said to his stunned roommate. "These young people are finding life difficult enough right now, and it's our role to keep them in line."

In addition to teaching, coaching, and other various duties, Eric had been elected as one of the twenty members of the Weihsien Christian Fellowship General Committee and was given charge of the youth department. Subsequently he seemed always surrounded by children and teens. Eric recognized the vital importance of the responsibility.

Many of the youth flocked to Scotland's greatest athlete, not for his fame but because of his genuine care and interest in them. Besides helping with their schoolwork, Eric established a rapport and played games with them. Often he came up with clever ways to celebrate life's events with them, since these events were usually overshadowed by other concerns. In his trademark style, he created greeting cards accentuated with puns or told the children innocent inside jokes. As the children became aware of their circumstances—as they watched grown men and women dwindle down to unlivable weights and attended the funerals of those too sick to survive—Eric's genuine and persistent assurance of God took effect on their often-damp spirits.

But when they asked Eric to play games on Sundays, the answer was a firm no.

In the late 1960s, a man then in his midforties sent a letter to D. P. Thomson to share his memories of Eric. In it he wrote,

> I met Eric for the first time in Weihsien Internment Camp in 1943 when I was 18 years of age. At a special evangelism rally he spoke on the story of the rich young ruler, showing us in a way I shall never forget the cost of Christian discipleship. I was immediately impressed by his humility and directness of speech. This was apparent not only at a religious meeting but also as a coach or referee on the playing field or in the lecture hall.
>
> Together with other young people I had the great privilege of listening to Eric, as a private tutor, lecture on

Physics and Chemistry. As I recall his painstaking teaching methods, and his patience with me who was always slow to grasp mathematical formulae, I am amazed and grateful for this example of a superb teacher.[1]

How thrilled many of Eric's pupils felt when, years after detainment, the schooling they received in the camp was deemed acceptable at top universities.

●　　●　　●

Eric's disciplined and methodical approach to life, with his solemn religious routines, soon became apparent not just to the youth but to the numerous adults as well. The beauty of Eric's style was that he would inevitably pique the interest of others. Eric had never been one to force his faith on anyone, but once invited to chat about it, Eric's faith never failed to roar with fervor. And prison life had not weakened Eric's beliefs but rather had strengthened them.

Eric's demeanor was one of quiet power, something more than the poise acquired from a trained mind or the knowledge that he had been and still was considered one of the world's great athletes. Those who watched him within the camp understood that he viewed God as Father, Christ as Savior, and the Holy Spirit as Guide. Being in the internment camp had not changed that belief.

Eric's faith and the way it played out in his efforts for the camp made a marked difference in camp conditions. Even the ever-recalcitrant Langdon Gilkey over time recognized a warming in the people, and not just from the weather. He wrote,

With the advent of spring, a marked change came over the face of the camp. Where there had been rubble and dirt, there were now bright patches of color in the gardens and neat patios. These were only the physical evidences of a change that also occurred on a deeper level. Within a few months this poorly prepared and, indeed, almost desperate group had transformed itself into a coherent civilization, able to cope with its basic material problems and day by day raising the level of its life on all fronts. The food was almost palatable, the baseball league enthralled everyone; and the evenings were now warm enough for a stroll with a girl friend. The camp was almost becoming a pleasant place in which to live.[2]

Almost. But without anyone's knowledge, it would too soon become a pleasant place to die.

CHAPTER 24

ERIC IS IN

*Do not forget to do good and
to share with others, for with
such sacrifices God is pleased.*

Hebrews 13:16, NIV

Early Summer 1944

On a too-warm afternoon, Eric ambled toward his dorm to retrieve
a book he hoped to share with a student that evening after
supper. The scent of food cooking in the kitchen—bitter and strong—
and the muck of the latrines wafted across the camp, and he
wrinkled his nose. Not even his earliest years of boarding school
had fully prepared him for this odor.

As he turned a dusty corner, he noticed one of the Russian
prostitutes in the camp leaning seductively against a wall, talking to a man who bristled with intentions. As soon as the woman
spotted Eric, she righted herself, blushed, and nodded. The man
turned and, seeing Eric, mumbled an embarrassed "G'day." Eric
did the same, then smiled as the two went their separate
ways. Perhaps he couldn't stop all the sin in the camp, but his
unexpected presence had at least postponed one act.

Eric no sooner came into eyeshot of his dorm than he noticed a sign nailed to the red-paneled door leading to his room. Closer inspection revealed three words: Eric Is Out.

He unhooked the sign and immediately noticed writing on the reverse side: Eric Is In.

"Ah, there you are," Joe Cotterill said from behind him.

"What's this?" Eric asked, holding up the sign.

Joe slipped the sign from Eric's fingers to rehang it, this time with Eric Is In facing forward. "You have so many of the young people knocking on the door when you aren't here, we thought we'd make it easier for them . . . not to mention easier for those of us who have to keep answering the door."

Eric laughed as he flipped the sign back to Eric Is Out. "I'm only here to pick up a book," he said with a wink. "Not to hold counseling sessions."

THE WEEKS AND MONTHS found a rhythm. Eric's workload left little time for idleness and worry. In the near-century that has passed since his time in Weihsien, Eric has been remembered as *the* person in highest demand in the camp. He carried fifty-pound Red Cross parcels from the church to the homes of those too old or too ill to come fetch them. He hauled buckets loaded with coal dust and chips for making briquettes up and down the camp's roads. He stood in the queue to draw the fuel ration for the elderly and sick and for those whose duties prevented them from doing it for themselves. He tore his wife's sheets he'd brought from Tientsin to mend hockey sticks for the youth teams. And in the moments between all this . . . and the teaching . . . and the coaching . . . and preparing young minds for God's Word, Eric stood as a listening ear to anyone who needed him.

Eric still had his regular workload assignments to accomplish, which he shared and rotated with his dorm mates. Carrying fresh water for drinking, bathing, or cleaning, as well as carrying away garbage, easily kept his muscles toned. The challenge of motivating people to carry their fair share of the work remained a delicate battle. The general perception was that there always seemed to be too many people riding in the proverbial wagon and not enough people pushing and pulling. Queuing up for meals, which everyone had to do and which took precious time, remained a cleverly placed and convenient break for many.

As the internees saw the beginning of their second year in Weihsien, Eric savored another chance to record his affections to his family. In a postcard dated March 27, 1944, he penned, "You seem very near today, it is the 10th anniversary of our wedding. Happy loving remembrances; we must celebrate it together next year."[1]

Eric chose to delight in and teach the young people in his charge the joyous treasures that God has hidden in each day and the freedom of understanding the grace of God. During a prayer session—which often felt more like gripe sessions—one of the teenage girls broke down.

"Lord," Kari Torjesen prayed, "I am willing to stay in this prison for the rest of my life if I can only know you." Years later, Kari said, "I'd planned to go to college. Instead I went to prison . . . [but after that prayer] I was free! It was as if the gates had been opened. I was released in my spirit."[2]

Steadily, as Eric had observed throughout his life, God produced more and more fruit when Eric diligently attended to ministry. But the question of how long until the war would end and they could go free persisted.

Eric's subtle but constant reassurances of the faithfulness of Christ made him an example of character, integrity, and hope to the internees, no matter the situation. He refused to focus on the despair of uncertainty and took every opportunity to turn despair into hope. He shared the love of Jesus with those who felt bound, physically or even spiritually, despite their active imaginations for rescue.

There has been some recent speculation that one such freedom fantasy did come true for Eric. Recently it has been claimed that Winston Churchill arranged with the Japanese government for a prisoner exchange for the peaceful release of Eric Liddell. Upon hearing the news, Eric offered to allow an expectant mother—one of the prostitutes in the camp—to take his place. This is an exquisite story of sacrifice, and one consistent with Eric's typically selfless nature, but the factuality of the event remains uncertain.

A fellow missionary recounted a tale of the powerful effect Eric's presence had on depressed people in the camp. A businessman who had been brought up by parents who were strict Brethren found himself unable to reconcile himself to the narrow attitudes they adopted. But his association with Eric at Weihsien turned his skepticism into a personal faith in Christ, which led him to seek baptism while in internment.

Eric Liddell's theology of feeling unrestricted within the controlled hands of Christ became increasingly evident and manifested itself one day in a startling way. In a remarkable illustration of his faith journey since the Olympics, Eric amazingly broke his long-standing rule of no sports on the Sabbath.

Initially when asked about playing any sport on a Sunday, Eric gave his expected no. But winter provided a bleaker challenge than the warmer months. The action of hockey in the arctic air got the youth out of the dorms and kept them warm at the same time. And, of course, Eric loved to play with them—save on Sundays.

On Sundays the youth played without Eric's supervision or participation, and brutal conflict ensued, becoming a weekly issue. The problem of the youth fighting on the sports field persisted for over a month. Any other day, Eric would have been in their midst, monitoring their athletic activity in some way. But the lack of "Uncle Eric" did not dissuade the youth from seeking to kill their boredom. Sunday after Sunday, the pent-up youth went out.

Eric evidently recognized the bomb about to explode and defused it. In what can only be described as a massive shift from his earlier legalistic approach—one that made him more famous than a gold medal ever could—Eric agreed to come out to the sports field. "I won't play; I will only referee," he said. Eric reasoned that drilling a positive example for the youth and establishing order, even at the expense of keeping his untarnished Sabbath record intact, was for the greater good.

Eric's reputation extended far beyond the sports field, the classroom, or the Sunday school class. During their time in Weihsien, Helena Campbell approached Eric, asking if he would baptize her daughter, Eileen. Helena had heard the gospel message Eric continued to preach in word and in action and had come to believe that she should have her daughter baptized. That day the camp's kitchen sink became the font of baptism.[3]

In his book *Disciplines of the Christian Life*, Eric articulates his own views on baptism:

> In the Epistles baptism is regarded as the sacrament by which people entered into the new life which Paul describes as "in Christ." . . .
>
> The apostles are told to baptize "in" or "into the name of the Father, and of the Son, and of the Holy Ghost." These words, *into the Name*, are of great significance. . . .
>
> Christian baptism thus becomes not only the representation of the spiritual cleansing that God gives to us in Jesus Christ, but also the means by which that blessing is conveyed to us in response to our profession of faith.[4]

Eric's writings make clear that he believed and instructed *teaching toward baptizing* (sharing the faith with adults, leading to baptism) as well as *baptizing toward teaching* (baptizing an infant and raising them up in the faith). He also connected salvation to baptism in his specificity of infant baptism:

> The practice of infant baptism rests also upon the revelation of God given us in Jesus Christ. That revelation makes clear to us that, *in the matter of our salvation, God always acts first.* God does not wait for our repentance; he sends his Son to bring about that repentance. He comes to meet us, and our experience of his love creates the spirit of new obedience. *Everywhere and always it is God who takes the initiative.*[5]

And so it was that one more heart—that of Eileen Campbell—was kindled to faith.

While the heart of one mother in the camp rejoiced, another's was torn in half. Separated from her husband during the war, a mother and her teenage son stood in their usual lines at roll call. The teenager discussed with another boy whether the perimeter fence was indeed electrified. To prove he was right, the teenager grabbed the fence and was electrocuted in front of everyone, including his horrified mother. Eric ministered to the heartbroken woman as best he could.

Later, the mother said of Eric,

> I recollect the comfort he brought to me in one of our meetings, when he taught us that lovely hymn—

> *Be still my soul; the Lord is on thy side;*
> *Bear patiently the cross of grief or pain;*
> *Leave to thy God to order and provide;*
> *In every change He faithful will remain.*
> *Be still, my soul, thy best, thy Heavenly Friend*
> *Through thorny ways leads to a joyful end.*

Then again, as he spoke from the text, "Be ye reconciled to God," he questioned if we were reconciled to God in all His dealings with us—not only in the initial step of salvation, but day by day in our sorrows and trials were we reconciled to God. So my memories of Eric are of one who was quietly and victoriously reconciled to God.[6]

Eric's head ached over tragic events such as these, as anyone's would. For a while, he chalked up his dull but constant headaches to the gloomy circumstances they all faced together. Grief, depression, and malnutrition tag-teamed, preying on the minds of many. But for some reason, Eric's headaches kept worsening—more than normal annoyances.

Something, he feared, was just not right.

CHAPTER 25

GOOD NIGHT, SWEET PRINCE

Come to me, all who labor and are
heavy laden, and I will give you rest.
Matthew 11:28

Early Winter 1944

Temperatures dropped dramatically within the camp as Christmas loomed, the camp half in anticipation, half in dread. One more week and Eric and his fellow detainees would celebrate yet another holiday within the interior of a barbed-wire prison camp.

Or was Christmas two weeks away? Eric couldn't remember.

It seemed lately that the days—holy or not—slipped one into the other, each arriving with a deeper level of pain behind his eyes. He could do only half the work he had typically accomplished, and his precious time in God's Word each morning had become difficult. Lines of Scripture blurred on the pages or made little sense at all.

On some mornings, he managed to open his eyes—blessedly—to no headache at all. Or, at the very least, to only a mild one. Other mornings, however, the pain was agonizing, penetrating to the back of his head. He tried to ignore it, but those days made the denial impossible.

He had told Nurse Annie—and only her—that he feared something was wrong inside his head. But maybe, he hoped—he prayed—the headaches were the result of too little nutrition. Too much physical labor. Too much hot and too much cold. Too much time behind prison walls.

Earlier that morning he'd woken somewhere in between. Not quite miserable. Not quite pain-free. He rose, had his morning devotions with Joe, then set about his chores. But by early afternoon, the throbbing had returned, and he retreated to his bunk, lay flat on his back, and attempted to sleep.

Or to dream of his reunion with Flossie and the girls.

Only moments after he closed his eyes—or had it been hours?—the door opened quietly, and the sound of shuffling feet near his bed roused him. Whoever had come in moved about the room quietly. Eric attempted to open his eyes to see which of his roommates had joined him, but the light became a piercing sword.

The whiff of something putrid reached his nostrils. "What is that smell?" he asked without moving, then winced. His words had been too harsh—something his roommate didn't deserve.

"Eric?" Joe Cotterill's voice eased across the room, questioning the tone.

"Are you . . . cooking something?" Eric asked, attempting to smooth out his voice.

"I'm frying bread in a little peanut oil," Joe answered. "Nothing different than usual."

But it was different. Horribly different. Why couldn't Joe detect that? "Whatever it is," he mumbled, "it smells terrible."

Eric's harsher-than-intended confrontation of his roommate lay between them, unmentioned, for days until Eric—feeling better than he had in weeks—spotted Joe along the dusty streets of Weihsien. He called out, crossed over, and immediately apologized for his previous behavior. "I've had the most awful headaches lately," he told Joe. "When they come on, I just need a quiet place to rest."

"Probably just fatigue," Joe said, which would make sense to anyone within the camp. Eric did the work of three men, counseled and coached the youth, and taught school from complex books he had personally written.

The two men smiled in reconciliation, shook hands, and then Eric went on to his next assignment. But Joe watched Eric as he ambled away. There was something odd in his gait. The usual pep was missing. He didn't walk; he plodded.

IN JANUARY 1945, Eric—along with many others—came down with the flu and a painful case of sinusitis. Although treatment brought relief to the rest, Eric didn't seem to improve.

Still, he continued without complaining, although he spent hours in bed with a cool cloth over his eyes and often missed roll call. Finally, his headaches plagued him so much that he again sought out Annie, who insisted he check himself into the camp hospital.

Eric was miserable, but he patiently endured while he rested. Fellow detainees grew more and more concerned as the days passed without seeing Eric exuberantly strolling out and about, holding class, or attending prayer meetings. Out of the approximate fifteen hundred prisoners, this one man's light shone so brightly that when it dimmed, the entire camp felt the effects. While Eric suffered, Weihsien camp was put to one of its greatest tests.

•   •   •

One snowy day in mid-January, as eighteen-year-old internee Norman Cliff stood in filthy overalls working in Kitchen I, a young American rushed in and said to him and the others who stood at their assigned cauldrons, "Come have a look at what's coming through the prison gates!"

Norman and the kitchen workers rushed out, following the

American to the main road in time to witness countless donkeys pulling carts stacked high with boxes marked "American Red Cross."

As the internees followed the caravan to the church, visions of the treasures inside danced like the sugarplums they'd dreamed of only a month earlier at Christmastime. During a holiday when, before internment, they had celebrated with more than enough delicacies and joyous celebrations around roaring fires, the past December had seen the prisoners with meager rations and only a few festivities. The winter weather, with its dramatically dropping temperatures, had been met without the coal dust necessary to make briquettes for burning. The prisoners were starving and freezing.

But now . . . who could begin to imagine what lay nestled within those boxes! Since the day the gates closed behind them years earlier—and especially since Father Scanlan's arrest—the internees had not tasted sugar or milk, fruit or butter. Their clothes became more threadbare, they walked in shoes without soles, and children—in need of more calcium than egg shells could provide—grew teeth without enamel. With the war raging across the globe, supplies became scarcer, and severe malnutrition knocked at every door. Whatever lay within the boxes was nothing short of a godsend.

When the cart wheels rolled to a stop, the prisoners of Weihsien camp swallowed hard, wide-eyed in anticipation. A crew of men unloaded the carts, carrying the boxes into the church where they would be inspected and counted by the Japanese. Two hours later, a man with a tally sheet emerged and announced that there were more than enough for each person in the camp to receive one box each.

Joy on top of joy!

But the next morning a jagged shard deflated the enthusiasm when one of the Japanese officers posted a notice informing the prisoners that a group of Americans had decided that because the *American* Red Cross had sent the supplies, the provisions should go to their countrymen only. At that time, a mere two hundred

Americans dwelled in the camp. Based on their reasoning, that ratio said that each American should receive seven and a half parcels and everyone else none.

Arguing commenced, not only within the rest of the camp but between the ranks of the Americans as well, specifically some who argued that, in the Spirit of Christ, the bounty should be shared with all. But others, despite being missionaries, declared it *immoral* to segment the boxes if they had been intended *only* for the Americans.

The Japanese, perplexed by the attitudes and apparent civil war, posted a sign for all to see:

DUE TO PROTESTS FROM THE AMERICAN COMMUNITY, THE PARCELS WILL NOT BE DISTRIBUTED TODAY AS ANNOUNCED.
THE COMMANDANT

The Japanese continued to stand guard over the boxes, which remained stacked in the church where they'd been unloaded. Meanwhile, the commandant contacted his superiors for direction. As he waited, the Americans came back with a new idea: Everyone in the camp gets a box, they proposed. The total would cover one and a half boxes for each American, with the other internees receiving the leftovers.

But the Japanese said no. They would wait to hear from headquarters.

Finally, Tokyo wired back, stating that each internee was to receive one parcel. What was left over was to be sent to other camps. The greed of a few meant that the extra provisions would now go somewhere else. This was a hard lesson for the Weihsien camp but a blessing for those who suffered elsewhere.

Two weeks after the boxes had arrived, the Japanese set a date for distribution. After roll call and breakfast, the internees lined up, skinny arms stretched outward. Then, loaded down with a three-foot by one-foot by one-and-a-half-foot box, they stumbled back to their individual rooms to open their belated Christmas gifts.

The boxes all had "four small sections, each with powdered milk, cigarettes, tinned butter, spam, cheese, concentrated chocolate, sugar, coffee, jam, salmon and raisins."[1]

Meals could now be followed by desserts. Tea, formerly drunk only black, could now be enjoyed with sugar and milk. Bread could be slathered with jam or butter or sandwiched with Spam and cheese.

As the camp set up a system of exchange—a pack of cigarettes for two bars of chocolate; two tins of Spam for one of coffee—adults calculated how to make the provisions last as long as possible. According to Norman Cliff, once these packages were distributed, "physical hunger and exhaustion were less acute, and with this the general morale was clearly lifted."[2]

And a great lesson had been learned. As Langdon Gilkey later wrote in his book, "The irony of this was not lost on the gleeful camp: the demand by the Americans for seven and one-half parcels had effected in the end the loss to each of them of an extra half parcel! Thus, as Stan and I grimly agreed, even an enemy authority can mediate the divine justice in human affairs."[3]

Perhaps a larger life lesson came from the two South Africans who were also detained at Weihsien.

When the parcels were finally distributed, the people discovered that two hundred pairs of boots from the South African Red Cross had been included. Upon this discovery, the two men posted the following notice:

DUE TO THE PRECEDENT THAT HAS BEEN SET, THE SOUTH AFRICAN COMMUNITY IS LAYING CLAIM TO ALL 200 OF THE BOOTS DONATED BY THEIR RED CROSS. WE SHALL WEAR EACH PAIR

FOR THREE DAYS TO SIGNAL OUR RIGHT TO
WHAT IS OUR OWN PROPERTY, AND THEN SHALL
BE GLAD TO LEND SOME OUT WHEN NOT IN USE
TO ANY NON-SOUTH AFRICANS WHO REQUEST
OUR GENEROUS HELP.[4]

Perhaps their morality play helped ease the tensions. Perhaps their post brought laughter and healing. Either way, Eric had not been engrossed in any of this drama. Eric's light, which had shone so brilliantly in the camp, grew dimmer by the hour. The strain of missing his family began to show in Eric's demeanor as he grew weaker. Eric's deepening depression did not escape Annie's acute eyes or ears. One afternoon he said to her, "My biggest worry, Annie, is that I didn't give Flo enough of my time."

Annie assured him that Florence, the daughter of a missionary, understood their time apart better than most women might. "And remember, the reason you were separated was your work for God."

Initially, doctors diagnosed Eric's condition as a "nervous breakdown," brought about by his intense workload coupled with his deepening need to see his family again. This news distressed Eric greatly.

"There is one thing that bothers me," he told a China Inland Mission missionary couple who lived on the top floor of the hospital. "I should have been able to cast all this on the Lord and not buckled down under it."[5]

●   ●   ●

Those closest to Eric knew something was more seriously wrong with him than a weakened body brought about by camp-life stressors. Eric had grown quieter—revealing less of his typical wit and regular repartee—and his speech became slower.

Both youth and adults visited Eric whenever he felt up to the visits. One day, in the earliest days of February, eighteen-year-old Stephen Metcalf, who had shown signs of being a good runner, stopped by.

"Steve," Eric said, looking toward the young man's feet, "I see your shoes are worn out. It's winter now and . . ." Eric pressed his running shoes, held together by string and strips of linen, into Stephen's hands.

He gave Stephen a nod and, with a pat on the hand, released his shoes to the much younger runner.

"It wasn't until much later," Stephen said in remembering Eric, "that I realized that those shoes had meant something to him and that he had gone to a lot of work to patch them up for me."[6]

Better than the gift of a pair of ratty running shoes, however, were the lessons Eric had taught Stephen and the young people who lived alongside him in Weihsien. "Love your enemies," he'd told them. "Pray for the Japanese guards . . . pray for them who persecute you."

Stephen Metcalf would later become a lifelong missionary to Japan and would never forget the gift of Eric Liddell's running shoes or his lessons of "the baton of forgiveness."[7]

On Sunday, February 11, 1945, Eric suffered a mild stroke. He fought to rally back to health, even to the point of walking with aid up and down the hospital corridors. Annie Buchan fought for her patient to get undisturbed rest, but his loved ones always managed to sneak in to see him . . . or he snuck out. He even managed to climb four flights of stairs to the little room where the CIM missionary couple lived to enjoy afternoon tea with them.

Annie and the doctors began to speculate that their initial diagnosis of a nervous breakdown had been incorrect and that Eric was suffering from an inoperable brain tumor. They knew there was little they could do about it, even without the privations of the internment camp.

Still, Eric held out optimism, especially for the youth who came to see him.

One of the young girls, Joyce Stranks, often popped in to visit, to wish him well, and to continue to learn what "Uncle Eric" had to teach. Those sessions—with Joyce and the other young people— took a great amount of energy, but Eric couldn't resist. Nurse Annie, however, always knew when to shoo the youth away.

On Sunday, February 18, the Salvation Army Band, which included Norman Cliff and Peter Bazire, who played trumpet, gathered on the hospital grounds as they did each Sunday and Wednesday afternoon to play for the sick inside the infirmary. After playing a few favorite hymns, a note came to the band leader from Nurse Annie.

"Eric Liddell is dying," it read. "He would like it if you played 'Finlandia' / 'Be Still, My Soul.'" The ragtag band somberly collected themselves, and the melancholy melody soon floated through the windows of the hospital.

In the morning hours of Wednesday, February 21, Eric climbed the stairs again to visit with the missionaries who lived there.

After returning a plate they had used to send some treat to Eric the day before, he smiled and then told the couple he felt much better. Later in the day, he managed to write a short note to Florence with the desire to get it to the post that day.

Somehow, he managed.

While walking back to the hospital, Eric ran into the wife of a missionary he had worked with in Tientsin.

"Have you heard from Flo?" she asked him, thrilled to see that he appeared his old self.

"Oh, yes," he said. "I got one of her letters recently." And then, though his words were slower than usual, he told the missionary's wife the news Florence had sent his way.

The woman, concerned that Eric had been out too long, encouraged him to return to the hospital so he could rest.

"Oh, no," he said. "I must just get my walking legs again."

It was now three thirty in the afternoon; the missionary's wife walked with him to the hospital door so he would arrive in time for tea.

Later, Joyce Stranks came in to visit with "Uncle Eric." One of Eric's favorite topics for the youth was surrender to Christ, which he shared again with Joyce. The teenager listened intently as he spoke until, lost in thought of this complete and absolute surrender to Christ, Eric began to have a seizure. Joyce ran out of the room, calling for Nurse Annie, who reprimanded the teen for tiring her patient, and then drew the curtains around his bed.

As Annie tended to Eric, he managed to breathe out his last words. "Annie," he said, "it's complete surrender to God . . ."

With that, Eric Liddell faded from consciousness.

Joyce stood on the other side of the curtain, sobbing until someone escorted her out of the room.

Later that night, twenty minutes after the clock struck nine, Scotland's greatest athlete crossed the finish line of his earthly life and into his heavenly home.

He had completed the race.

CHAPTER 26

ERIC IS OUT

I am the resurrection and the life.
Whoever believes in me, though he die,
yet shall he live, and everyone who
lives and believes in me shall never die.
Do you believe this?
John 11:25-26

ON FEBRUARY 22, 1945, silent snow descended from the heavens. Nature's halfhearted attempt to blanket the internees with a pure facade brought no warming comfort. There was no coal to burn for a fire anyhow. Chilling news began to spread as internees fussed to seek warmth. "Eric Liddell died last night." The bitter words were repeated over and over that day, seemingly growing more dominant each time. The Eric Is In / Eric Is Out sign, which hung on Eric's dormitory door, proved to be too painful to any who came to seek solace from Eric's peers regarding his absence. The sign soon came down.

Everyone struggled to process the grief or find words to make the emptiness subside. Young Beryl (Goodland) Welch, the fourteen-year-old daughter of a Chefoo teacher, managed to scratch in her diary that day, "Dear (Old) Uncle Eric died last night. It was so sudden. He wrote a letter to his wife just that day. Everyone was greatly impressed. I feel so sorry for her. Most people thought he was the best man in the camp. What a loss!"[1]

So many of the youth close to Eric felt as though the light had left the camp. But they were not alone. Grown men who would otherwise never cry in public broke down unashamedly at the news.

An autopsy, in which Joe Cotterill aided, was performed on Eric's body the following day. The doctors confirmed that an inoperable brain tumor had grown to the point that Eric's surrender to that infuriating outcome was the sole remaining option. His death could not have been prevented medically. Even if Eric had been in the finest of facilities and under the best of care, it would have taken a miracle to guide Eric unscathed through that surgery to health again.

Funeral arrangements began to take shape. Rev. Arnold Bryson, senior missionary of the London Missionary Society, would conduct the service, though many others would voice their endearing thoughts. On Saturday, February 24, Eric's fellow internees—who together represented twenty-one nationalities—poured into a Weihsien church built to hold 350 people. When all the seats had been taken, the remainder of the mourners gathered outside in the bitter cold and swirling snow, unaffected by dropping temperatures or their hunger, to pay their respects to a man who had been the "finest example of Christ"[2] many of them had ever known.

Rev. Bryson began the service with the same triune invocation Eric's father had spoken over him in his baptism: "In the name of the Father, and of the Son, and of the Holy Spirit . . ."

Rev. Bryson continued,

It is fitting that the predominant notes of this service
should be praise and thanksgiving to God for all that Eric
Liddell has done and all that so many of us owe to him.
To most in the camp who heard on Thursday morning

that he had suddenly passed away after a relapse on the previous night, the news came as a great shock, and to a large number, with a sense of personal loss. For he was an outstanding figure in our community, known to all and respected by everybody.

From his humble and modest demeanor, no one could have guessed that here was a man with an international reputation on the running track and football field.

The sudden removal of such a man in the prime of his life, and at the peak of his powers, inevitably raises questions in our hearts. Why did God take him from a world in which such men are so sorely needed today? But God makes no mistakes. His thoughts are not our thoughts, neither are his ways our ways. Perhaps in God's loving purpose, by Eric's early promotion to higher service he was spared years of acute suffering, and we can only bow to God's will.

Yesterday a man said to me, "Of all the men I have known, Eric Liddell was the one in whose character and life the spirit of Jesus Christ was preeminently manifested." And all of us who were privileged to know him with any intimacy echo this judgment. What was the secret of his consecrated life and far-reaching influence? Absolute surrender to God's will as revealed in Jesus Christ. His was a God-controlled life and he followed his Master and Lord with a devotion that never flagged and with an intensity of purpose that made men see both the reality and power of true religion. With St. Paul, Eric could say, "I live, yet not I, but Christ liveth in me." If anyone was ready for his Master's call, it was our friend, whose happy, radiant face we shall see no more on earth, but his influence will surely live on in the hearts and lives of all who knew him.

Rev. Edwin Davies gave a final prayer. The congregation sang "For All the Saints Who from Their Labors Rest," then recited the Lord's Prayer.

Eight men, one being Stephen Metcalf, raised the fragile casket carrying Eric's earthly body onto their shoulders. Gingerly they walked out of the church toward a small cemetery adjacent to the Japanese garrison officer's residence. Behind them, the youth and children of Chefoo marched as the honor guard.

As they walked along, the wind slicing through their thin clothing, Stephen glanced at his newly received track spikes that had been so lovingly given to him only weeks earlier by his hero. *Is this all that happens to honor such a great man? Is this it?*

When they arrived at the burial site, the eight men lowered the casket into the grave, then—along with the five hundred who had followed them—recited the Beatitudes and wept.

Even the handful of Japanese guards in the cluster removed their caps.

On March 3, A. P. Cullen hosted a special memorial service for many of the people who still grieved. Eight hundred people attended. Annie Buchan, Carl Longman, and numerous friends and colleagues spoke.

At the end of the service, Cullen shared the thoughts that had gripped his heart for more than a week:

> Death has been very busy in our ranks the last few months, and now it has stricken down in the very prime of manhood, and almost without warning, one of the best known and most deservedly popular of our number. To our eyes there is something tragic and almost unbearably poignant in the sudden blow that has shocked the whole camp, the swift passing of one whose life, with its many contacts, was so valuable, so worthy of the highest praise. But this afternoon

we are not here to dwell on the apparent tragedy nor yet upon the sense of irreparable loss. We are here, first and foremost, in this Memorial service, to give thanks to God for the life so finely lived, the fight so nobly fought, the race so cleanly run, and to find renewed inspiration for ourselves in the example that Eric Liddell left us. To him those stirring words of Bunyan may be as fittingly applied as they were to Mr. Valiant-for-truth: "So he passed over, and all the trumpets sounded for him on the other side.'"

The congregation sang a few hymns, including "Be Still, My Soul," and read from one of Eric's favorite passages on love, 1 Corinthians 13. Mere human words could not take away the pain and sadness, but the words of Scripture, and the promise of the resurrection of the body and the life everlasting, would and did begin the healing process.

Cullen wrapped up his thoughts for the group.

Why is it that Eric was one of the best-known, most popular and respected persons in camp? Why is it that in a camp like this, where criticism is so rife that hardly anyone in the public eye is immune from it, why is it that no one ever seems to have a word to say in criticism of Eric—always the reverse? Something, of course, has to be allowed for his renown as an international athlete. But at the bottom the answer to each of these and similar questions would be found to have its basis in one fundamental cause—Eric's Christian character.

Mr. P. A. Bruce, Headmaster of the China Inland Mission School at Chefoo, gave the final address. After several minutes of relaying what he knew of and about Eric Liddell, he paused, drew in a breath, and said,

One word more. What is to be the effect of this life upon us here? Why did he live the life he lived? Why did he become a missionary? Because he felt he could do no other. On the one hand, he strove to live a life well-pleasing to God at all times. And on the other hand, to commend the gospel of God to all whom he met. What effect has his life here amongst us made upon you?

After the service, friends hovered together, sharing fond memories of the man they had loved so much. A prostitute in the camp confided special insight of her own about when Eric had helped her with a shelving unit. "He was the first man to help me without asking for a favor in return." The quiet chatter soon turned to cautious but contagious laughter—the predictably muted joy which so often happens at funerals when loved ones exchange untold tales.

Years later, Mary Taylor Previte penned, "There, a little bit of Scotland was tucked sadly away in Chinese soil."[3]

Eric Liddell's influence would live on because Eric Liddell's legacy and impact would remain with the people in the camp. One day, they would be free, and for days and years thereafter, for the rest of their lives, they would tell their stories of Uncle Eric.

•　•　•

In amazing tragedy, the news from that horrible week remained contained within the walls of Weihsien.

On May 1, 1945, Mr. Cocker-Brown at the London Missionary Society received an envelope from the British undersecretary on a day when excitement buzzed in the air. Word of Adolf Hitler's death had begun to spread. The atrocities of war were about to end. Surely this day—and this envelope—could contain only good news.

Full of optimism and vigor, he tore into the letter.

Sir, AZAS

I am directed by Mr. Winston Churchill to inform you with regret that the Swiss representative at Shanghai has reported by telegraph that the Reverend Eric Henry Liddell died at Weihsien on the 21st February, 1945. The cause of death is not stated.

I am, Sir,

Your obedient Servant,

I. W. O. Davidson.[4]

In utter shock, Cocker-Brown called Rob Liddell immediately. Rob had been working at a hospital in Edinburgh. The men decided as the heartbreaking conversation unfolded that LMS headquarters would relay the news to Florence in Toronto and that Rob would share the sad tidings with the remaining Liddell family in Scotland.

Jenny took the news exceptionally hard. Mary Liddell had passed away only months earlier. However, with the resurgence of new grief, Jenny could at least trust that Eric had never had to bear the loss of their beloved mother. Now James, Mary, and Eric celebrated eternal life on streets of gold.

On May 2, more than two months after Eric's passing, Rev. A. E. Armstrong and Rev. George King knocked on Florence Liddell's door. It was a day she would never forget. Her heart shattered as the news set in. She dropped to the stairwell and sobbed uncontrollably with her mother. Maureen and Heather followed the sounds of sadness.

"What's wrong?" the girls asked.

"Daddy is in heaven with Bumpa," Florence said past her sobs.

That afternoon, Patricia came home, anxious to tell her mother that she had won first place at a school track meet. But her fleeting joy evaporated. Together with her mother and sisters, she would learn a new kind of endurance.

On May 5, 1945, Toronto honored Eric with a memorial service at Carlton Street United Church. The next two days culminated with a global celebration of victory in Europe (V-E Day), which only added irony to the injury suffered by the Liddell/MacKenzie family. Their hope for the resolution of war for so long, and its fulfillment, seemed forever spoiled by irreplaceable loss.

On May 27, 1945, Morningside Congregational Church in Edinburgh, Scotland, observed a memorial for Eric. There, his Scottish siblings, extended relatives, and friends lamented together in loving remembrance. More than one thousand people attended, packing the church to overflowing.

D. P. Thomson attended the service, later commenting,

The details of the last few years of his life are not yet known to us, but we can be certain that under the most severe of all trials, he exhibited just those qualities which he showed in his sporting life. His was perhaps a short one; but his work, as he clearly saw it, and, as we believe divinely inspired, carried out away from the applause of the crowd, will remain an inspiration to many. In these days of exaggerated hero worship and publicity for sporting champions, Eric Liddell's example reminds us to put things in their proper perspective. Sport to him was sport—not the be-all and end-all—and success in it did not prevent him from picking out the things spiritual from the things temporal. He was an example which must have helped others to make a similar choice.[5]

All of Scotland mourned in a Saltire salute for their beloved son. The Scottish flag hung at half-mast for a good while in honor of Scotland's national treasure. England's Union Jack followed suit.

•　　•　　•

It is interesting to note that the Scottish Saltire flag bears St. Andrew's cross—a white X-shaped cross across a blue field, which honors the stylistic martyrdom of St. Andrew. The beaches of St. Andrews, Scotland, later became the iconic backdrop of the 1981 blockbuster film *Chariots of Fire*, immortalizing Eric Liddell, running in all his glory among the legendary 1924 Olympians.

To those who miss him, or any faithful loved one in death, Eric left a bit of comfort behind in his theological writing about Holy Communion with the saints, those on earth with those in heaven. During the sacrament of Holy Communion, it is as if the skies are ripped open, uniting believers in the world with Christ and the saints who have fallen asleep in him.

Eric wrote,

> Many have found the act of communion the means of grace by which they are best able to realize this great truth of our abiding in Christ, and Christ's abiding in us. . . .
>
> The sacrament also has its social aspect. From the beginning the disciples used to meet together for a service in memory of our Lord which they called the Breaking of the Bread. At first it was an ordinary meal (called the Love Feast) and ended with the Lord's Supper being observed. In this way it was a reminder that Christian discipleship is not a solitary life, but a life in which we are united together in a great fellowship because of our common relationship to Jesus Christ. Our fellowship with Christ finds expression in

a spirit of brotherhood and sisterhood in our attitudes to, and conduct with, one another. . . .

The fellowship of those we have known and loved is never more real than when we join with others in the act of communion with our Lord and Savior. We are part of— and in fellowship with—those who have gone before, who by faith subdued kingdoms, wrought righteousness, lived lovingly; who by patiently enduring, suffering, and serving have worked for his kingdom on earth.[6]

Those who miss the faithful departed need only look to Christ and the Holy Sacrament of Communion that he freely offers, connecting the two.

CHAPTER 27

A LIDDELL EPILOGUE

I know that my Redeemer lives, and
at the last he will stand upon the earth.
And after my skin has been thus
destroyed, yet in my flesh I shall see God.
Job 19:25-26

A WEEK INTO HER KNOWN WIDOWHOOD, Florence summoned
the strength to write back to the London Missionary Society. She
knew she had to move forward. She had three precious little ones to
consider, and she knew what Eric would have expected of her. She
wrote to Mr. Cocker-Brown:

Dear Mr. Cocker-Brown:
    It is over a week since Dr. Armstrong and Mr. King came
to break the news to me that you had sent by cable. I wanted
to write before this to thank you for your sympathy and that
of the L.M.S. Fellowship which you also extended to me in
that cable.
    It was a stunning blow and I still can hardly believe it,
but I have been very conscious of the prayers and thoughts

of countless friends over in England and Scotland and here too.

My first reaction was, "That is why he has been so near me lately." I have dreamt more about Eric in the last few weeks than I have all the rest of the time I have been home. Every time (in the dreams) he was here we were all terribly happy and everything was so vivid. My reaction was "That is just wishful thinking getting the better of you."

Then in making plans for the summer and autumn I seemed to come up against a stone wall. Plans that seemed excellent at first seemed to get blocked. I don't know when I have been so conscious of a restraining hand and I simply couldn't understand it. I felt sure there was going to be some change in plans but I couldn't see what.

The thought flashed into my mind, "Could it be that Eric is really coming home and we may have to go over to England to meet him? No that's wishful thinking again." Never once did I have any premonition of this and even after I knew I was so vividly conscious of Eric being happy. I could just see his sunny smile and twinkling eyes.

It has been a strange and wonderful experience. At times I have been numbed and overwhelmed by a sense of unreality—of pain—of fear for the future and then there has come welling up from within that power of faith which has carried me through. My faith has been wonderfully strengthened. In looking back I have so much to be thankful for. God has provided so wonderfully—we have been so happy and I know that He is working out his purpose and that good can come out of even this.

I have been overwhelmed by the kindness and thoughtfulness of my own immediate family—relations, friends, China friends, and people I don't even know.

My heart aches for Jenny, Rob, and Ernest. I wish they could have been at the Memorial Service that we had last Saturday. Beautiful, sincere tributes were paid to Eric by Mr. King who was repatriated from Weihsien and by Mr. Faichney who was the Minister in Union Church, Tientsin, for five years and was a great friend of ours.

I have just been hearing today of tributes paid to Eric's memory in several of the churches here on Sunday.

Please forgive me for rambling on like this. I have never had the pleasure of meeting you but I always remember how highly Eric spoke of you and how he enjoyed his visit in your home in June '40 while on deputation in the South of England.

I just wanted you and the other friends to know that I have been very conscious of your prayers and sympathies but you must not grieve for us.

I feel that Eric and I had as much happiness in our few short years together as many couples have in a whole lifetime and I thank God for the privilege of being Eric's wife.

I only hope that the children (they have been perfectly sweet and such a comfort to me) will take after Eric and follow in their Master's Footsteps.

Yours sincerely,

Florence Liddell [1]

By autumn of 1945—mere months after Eric's fellow prisoners at Weihsien had been liberated by American allies—Florence had begun to move confidently in Christ, following in her "Master's Footsteps." Eric's life insurance policies and his LMS pensions had been sorted out. Florence set her eyes toward nursing again, determined to be the best mother she could be for her and Eric's three daughters.

At that time, when multitudes of women in North America were busy greeting their husbands, now home from the war, Florence received one last envelope from the Canadian Red Cross Society. A chill came over her as she gathered the strength to open it. She knew it would most likely be the last communiqué she would receive from her beloved Eric.

Her intuition was correct.

Dear Mrs. Liddell,

We are enclosing three Red Cross messages, which have just been received in this office.

We felt sure that you would want to have these messages in spite of the distress they would cause you.

Yours sincerely,

Miss M. E. Breckenridge[2]

Enclosed were Eric's final three communications to Florence. Trembling, she found her favorite chair, then sat to examine them.

AUGUST 24TH, 1944

Large airy room with eleven others. Healthy, enjoying some reading. Constantly remember and picture you all. Dearest love to all, everything sufficient. Longing for you, love.

Eric.[3]

Florence placed the first one to the side, then opened the second.

AUGUST 27TH, 1944

I have received some of your letters and have news up to January. The hot summer is over, we are enjoying the cooler autumn already. I constantly picture you all. This may reach you at or near the anniversary of your father's death. You will know that my thoughts and prayers will be with you—and especially with Mother. Give her my special love. I see Tricia, cycling, swimming and skating, and Heather following fast in her footsteps. I wish I could hear them read to me! Maureen,—I long to see her—She looks fine in the snaps. I long for you Dearest—and the time when we shall start a home together again. May it be soon!

Love, Eric.[4]

Then, finally, she began to read the post Eric had painstakingly managed to get to her the day he passed from life to glory.

FEBRUARY 21ST, 1945

Was carrying too much responsibility. Slight nervous breakdown. Am much better after month's rest in hospital. Doctor suggests changing my work. Giving up teaching and athletics and taking on physical work like baking. A good change. So glad to get your letter of July. Mrs. Longman is much better. Bear and Nelma making preparations for marriage on April 18. Will send particulars later. Wish you could enter into the celebrations. Joyce Stranks has been a great help to me in hospital, keeping me in touch with the news. Enjoying comfort parcels. Special love to yourself and children.

Eric Henry Liddell.[5]

Florence couldn't help but see that the last bit of correspondence had been dated the very day Eric entered eternal rest, the day he had somehow found the strength to walk to the post.

She reread the final correspondences from her husband, imagining him as he penned them, wrapped in the hope of their seeing each other again.

And so they would.

She slipped the letters back into the envelope they'd come in, then sat back in her chair and pondered the intimacies of the Master they shared.

And his promises. Each and every one.

THE FINAL 100:
THE RACE BEFORE US

WHILE SERVING AS A MISSIONARY, Eric received a letter from a friend in Britain inquiring what type of books he would like to be sent for him to read. Eric responded, "The kind of books I would like most would be, biographical. There are a lot of small books like that, biographies about great men. I think that kind of book always helps one most to do better."

What Eric couldn't have realized at the time was that he was becoming one of those "great men" or that his story would inspire countless others to indeed "do better"—to run the final race in such a way as to win a much greater prize.

Many have been inspired by Eric's captivating life and ministry— including me. As an eight-year-old Christian possessing the same first name as that of the Flying Scotsman and sharing a zeal for running, I became an instant fanatic of Eric Liddell by watching *Chariots of Fire*. I thought the parallels ended there, yet at that time my race had barely begun. Amazingly enough, I also happened to run collegiately. I served in my church's youth ministry, and I served as a missionary in China, where, like Eric, I met my wife. I went on to study theology and ultimately became a pastor and a writer.

As such, it has been one of the absolute highlights of my life to meet and communicate with some of Eric Liddell's family, including his three daughters. I will never forget trading stories with them over lunch while looking into their eyes, which had once looked into his. Because I believe we need more people in the world who value the level of sacrifice, humility, integrity, and general churchmanship that Eric Liddell possessed, carrying the torch of his story is a particularly important leg of my race. His life pointed to Christ in a steady, unique, and powerful way, and perhaps, somewhere, there is another eight-year-old who needs to learn that.

The legacy of Eric Liddell is the legacy of all Christians—to run their own race of faith and to share that faith as best they can, passing the burning torch to the next runner. Each runner from generation to generation runs in his or her own way, as each Christian faces a unique set of circumstances.

Our final race is before us with a great prize realized within the forgiveness of sins and eternal life that abounds for all through the death and resurrection of Christ. The cost counted through the race of faith is entirely worth it, if for no other reason than to see a glimpse of the multitude of lives that are eternally saved by grace as a result along the way. Yet there are many hurdles we face and obstacles we need to train for, just as Eric did.

Eric Liddell's many challenges would have been much more difficult had he not prepared for them. His early life in boarding school apart from his family prepared him for his missionary years separated from his wife and children. His reluctance to embrace fame enabled him to endure solitude on the mission field. His openness to other strains of Christian thought, particularly of the Oxford Group, gifted him with flexibility to loosen his rigid grip on legalism and ease tension in the internment camp. Eric didn't always know how his decisions of the moment would impact the race he ran, but in each moment, by seeking to live a "God-controlled life," he was able to run well even when he was surrounded by trouble and uncertainty.

Eric's obedient witness of Christ's grace serves as a reminder to us when we face our own times of increasing trouble and uncertainty. Through the strengthening of faith in Christ, we too are able to build our stamina and run with purpose toward the finish line of our own races. Every race demands training, and the race of our lives is no different. As the apostle Paul reminds us, "Every athlete exercises self-control in all things. They do it to receive a perishable wreath, but we an imperishable. So I do not run aimlessly" (1 Corinthians 9:25-26). An imperishable prize awaits those who run well. So just as Eric prepared—even without realizing it, by being fed in the faith and through his continual acts of faithfulness—let us "press on toward the goal for the prize of the upward call of God in Christ Jesus" (Philippians 3:14).

And the man who ran so well and revered the Lord's Sabbath rests with one last treasure of truth for us—the eternal eighth day Sabbath, which helps us prepare in our own race and keep our eyes on the ultimate prize amid the unique challenges we face in such times as we are called.

In the book of Genesis, the description of the first six days of Creation is completed in the saying, "There was evening and there was morning." Yet on the seventh day, a Saturday—the *Sabbath* day—this phrase is not used. There is morning, but there is no mention of evening. God begins resting, and the reader is left in suspense. The seventh-day Sabbath's rest is only fulfilled much later—when Christ himself rested in the tomb. Jesus Christ, who takes the place of all sinful mankind from the first Adam, becomes the second Adam. Christ died on a Friday, the sixth day; he rested in the tomb on the seventh day; and he rose again on Easter Sunday, completing the seventh day, thereby beginning an eternal "eighth day." Sunday the eighth day becomes a new Sabbath day for worship in which we await Christ's ultimate return—a day that will have no end.

Some today have called Eric Liddell a martyr, yet that designation isn't quite accurate. While no one would dispute Eric's character or that he died during his missionary work, Eric Liddell succumbed to natural causes, not hostile forces ending his life because of his Christian faith.

Besides, Eric was never one for noble titles.

Martyr or not, Eric Liddell is at rest, but his race goes on. The Christian message and the missionary legacy he carried was handed off to him by previous runners. He ran with it well, then faithfully passed the baton, inspiring countless other saints to do the same.

Eric Liddell's God and Master, Jesus Christ, is the firstborn of the dead, and he will deliver this same promise of a resurrection and everlasting life to all who believe and rest in him upon his final return. This is the hope in which Eric spent his life. A hope he confessed in the creeds tens of thousands of times throughout his life and taught in innumerable ways to any and all who would listen.

He who has ears, let him hear.

Rev. Eric Eichinger

AFTERWORD

*When you speak of me, give the glory
to my master, Jesus Christ.*

Eric Liddell

Eric Liddell touched and inspired many people throughout his life, and he continues to do so. Eric's life was a race, and though it concluded all too soon, his message of Christ's love and grace was passed on to more people than he could have possibly imagined. The legacy he carried did not die, for it was not his alone; it had been passed down to him. He merely offered his best, sprinted forward full tilt with it, and handed off the relay baton to the next waiting runner to carry on. In 1981 the incredible bombshell film *Chariots of Fire* was nominated for seven Oscars and won four of them, including Best Picture and Best Original Score. It thrust Eric Liddell back into circles of relevance and influence in dramatic form. Today, he and Florence—both with the Lord—have three children, nine grandchildren, and fifteen great-grandchildren.

Florence Liddell took several years with her three daughters in Toronto, Canada, slowly and steadily trying to heal from the tragic loss of their beloved Eric. She continued working as a nurse. Eventually she remarried, to Murray Hall, a widower himself. Their marriage produced another daughter, Jeannie. Murray died in 1969, leaving Florence with feelings of loneliness once again, yet Eric remained in her heart. Florence made a few visits back to Scotland to see Eric's relatives. She died at peace in 1984.

Rob Liddell continued as a surgeon in Scotland with Ria and their children, James Ralph and Peggy. Both children became doctors as well. Rob was naturally well-liked and successful in his professional life in Scotland, but in 1958, Rob and Ria moved to Australia, where James Ralph was working in medicine. Peggy remained in Scotland and proved to be instrumental and supportive with assisting the start of the Eric Liddell Centre.

Jenny Liddell Somerville and Ernest Liddell both remained in Edinburgh all their days. Jenny happily married and had two daughters, Rosemary and Joan, in addition to her stepchildren. Her daughter Joan has said that her mother was always very supportive of her famous brother's running, and it bothered her how she was portrayed in *Chariots of Fire*. Ernest endured a head injury during World War II. Though it plagued him the rest of his life, he did marry and had a daughter, Susan, who lives in Edinburgh.

Patricia, Heather, and Maureen Liddell, the three daughters of Eric and Florence Liddell, continue to reside in the surrounding metropolitan area of Toronto, Canada. They all unitedly and yet uniquely testify of their parents' special love for each other as well as of Eric's exuberant charm and missional heart for people. During their early years, they experienced understandable grief over the absence of their father. While they were delighted about the surprise success of *Chariots of Fire*, they would have gladly traded it for a childhood spent with their loving father. One by one, as they heard some of the amazing stories of how he touched the lives of so many youth from the Weihsien camp, they grew to understand his being there. In time, they received the opportunity, through a Day of Discovery documentary trip back to China hosted by historical author David McCasland, to walk in the very footsteps of their parents. The documentary film inadvertently brought great peace and healing.

David Patrick Thomson retired from full-time ministry in 1966. The General Assembly of the Church of Scotland remembers him as "one of the outstanding leaders of the Church in this generation." D. P. authored many books, two specifically about Eric. He died in 1974 and is still regarded as Scotland's Evangelist.

Professor A. P. Cullen, worn down by age and general camp life, made his way home to his family in England after the war. He led a mostly peaceful life, enjoying quiet times with his Lord, his loved ones, and his studies. He got a dog, and from time to time was known to speak Latin to him. He named the dog "Fido" from the Latin *fide*, "faithful."

Dr. Kenneth McAll fondly remembers many quiet mornings of prayer shared with Eric Liddell. Those regular devotions were "the key to everything," he was quoted as saying. In time he returned to England and began a practice with his wife. They lived quietly and peacefully, yet Kenneth could not seem to shake his fascination with the events he had observed in China regarding the intersection of medicine and spirituality. This fascination led him to further study psychology, and ultimately he authored the book *Healing the Family Tree*. His objective remained to help people get in touch with God and to learn to live completely under his direction.

Nurse Annie Buchan returned to Scotland in poor health around Christmas 1945, after her release from Weihsien. Annie was set on going back to China, and although she wasn't able to settle in northern

China, she became matron of the Union Hospital in Hankow. She returned to Scotland for good in 1950. She was matron at the Colony for Epileptics near Glasgow until 1955. She helped to form a local committee in Peterhead for World Refugee Year (1959–1960).

Stephen Metcalf was strongly influenced by Eric and committed himself to serve as a missionary to the Japanese. Metcalf arrived in Japan in November 1952 and entered the OMF International Language School and ultimately ended up planting new churches. He happily married and had five children. He and his family were responsible for the successful establishment and consolidation of new churches in several towns. All his years Stephen treasured the running spikes Eric gave him.

On Valentine's Day 2002, Eric Liddell's roommate **Joe Cotterill** married his second wife, fellow Weihsien detainee **Joyce Stranks**, who had been with Eric at the time of his final seizure. Joe married his first wife, the late Jeanne Hills, while the couple was still interned by the Japanese. In March 2017, Cotterill and Stranks celebrated Joe's one hundredth birthday with a cake, a toast, origami peace cranes, a card from Britain's Queen Elizabeth (whom Cotterill had met years earlier), and a special trumpet solo of "Finlandia" by **Peter Bazire**, who had played outside Eric's hospital.

Rev. Dr. Norman Howard Cliff earned an MPhil at Open University in Buckinghamshire and a PhD at Buckingham University. At his latter graduation, he was capped by Margaret Thatcher. Rev. Dr. Cliff went on to write seven books and a thesis titled "A History of the Protestant Movement in Shandong Province—1859–1951."

The Weihsien prison camp internees were released from their Japanese captivity in August 1945. United States B-29 Liberators flew overhead, and paratroopers floated down in dramatic fashion. It took months for many of the Chefoo students to be reunited with their parents, some of whom had left China and returned to England, not knowing the fate of their children. Others took trains and carts pulled by mules and walked across mud-slick China to reunite with parents that many of them had not seen in five years or more. The vast majority of those interned at Weihsien would never forget the way Eric Liddell inspired them in his own unique yet powerful way.

ACKNOWLEDGMENTS

I WOULD BE GRAVELY REMISS if I did not thank Patricia, Heather, and Maureen (Liddell). It has been one of the absolute biggest privileges of my life getting to know each of you through this endeavor. Your willingness with time and resources has been as comforting as it has been thrilling. Thank you from the depths of my heart for your enthusiasm and patience.

More thanks to Eva Marie Everson—for adjusting to my alliteration, tossing out all of my grammatical garbage, and neatly folding all of my linguistic laundry, and for your—ahem—dedication.

Thanks to:

Rebeca Seitz (SON Studios)—for the appreciation of chasing after big vision, the ability to see potential, and the courage to take a chance.

Jonathan Clements (Wheelhouse Literary Group)—the consummate advocate.

Jon Farrar and the team at Tyndale House Publishers—for your devotion to your craft, professionalism, and attention to detail.

Howie Klausner—for asking me, "*Why* do you want to write?"

Jeannie Hughes—for eleventh-hour photo scans, "urgent" e-mail correspondence, and daily laughs.

The saints at Zion Lutheran Church, Kalamazoo, Michigan, for providing me with a firm foundation.

The saints at Bethel Lutheran Church, Clearwater, Florida, who have created an oasis of a working environment for me.

David McCasland, a historian of historians, and all those like him who have planted a literary garden from which to pluck.

Major thanks to all of my family and friends who have endured me and encouraged me through this process.

And to Jesus—who makes all this possible.

Rev. Eric Eichinger

NOTES

CHAPTER 3: THE STARTER'S PISTOL

1. *The Glasgow Herald*, August 11, 1921, as quoted in David McCasland, *Eric Liddell: Pure Gold: A New Biography of the Olympic Champion Who Inspired Chariots of Fire* (Grand Rapids, MI: Discovery House, 2001), 56.
2. D. P. Thomson, *Scotland's Greatest Athlete: The Eric Liddell Story* (Barnoak, Crieff, Perthshire, Scotland: Research Unit, 1970), 34.
3. Ibid, 28–29.
4. Ibid, 38.

CHAPTER 4: MUSCULAR CHRISTIANITY

1. David McCasland, *Eric Liddell: Pure Gold: A New Biography of the Olympic Champion Who Inspired Chariots of Fire* (Grand Rapids, MI: Discovery House, 2001), 71.
2. D. P. Thomson, *Scotland's Greatest Athlete: The Eric Liddell Story* (Barnoak, Crieff, Perthshire, Scotland: Research Unit, 1970), 44.

CHAPTER 5: OLYMPIC MIND GAMES

1. D. P. Thomson, *Scotland's Greatest Athlete: The Eric Liddell Story* (Barnoak, Crieff, Perthshire, Scotland: Research Unit, 1970), 53.
2. Ibid, 50.
3. Ibid, 29.
4. Ibid, 42.

CHAPTER 6: INTO BATTLE

1. D. P. Thomson, *Scotland's Greatest Athlete: The Eric Liddell Story* (Barnoak, Crieff, Perthshire, Scotland: Research Unit, 1970), 59–60.

CHAPTER 7: A VICTORY LAP

1. D. P. Thomson, *Scotland's Greatest Athlete: The Eric Liddell Story* (Barnoak, Crieff, Perthshire, Scotland: Research Unit, 1970), 68.
2. Ibid.

3. Edward S. Seares, *Running through the Ages* (Jefferson, NC: McFarland & Company, 2015), 168.

4. Russell W. Ramsey, *God's Joyful Runner* (South Plainfield, NJ: Bridge, 1987), 53.

5. Ibid., 73.

6. D. P. Thomson, *Scotland's Greatest Athlete: The Eric Liddell Story* (Barnoak, Crieff, Perthshire, Scotland: Research Unit, 1970), 70.

7. Ibid, 72.

8. Ibid.

9. Ibid., 73.

10. David McCasland, *Eric Liddell: Pure Gold: A New Biography of the Olympic Champion Who Inspired Chariots of Fire* (Grand Rapids, MI: Discovery House, 2001), 103.

11. Ibid.

12. D. P. Thomson, *Scotland's Greatest Athlete: The Eric Liddell Story* (Barnoak, Crieff, Perthshire, Scotland: Research Unit, 1970), 74.

CHAPTER 8: DOCTRINAL DISCERNMENT

1. D. P. Thomson, *Scotland's Greatest Athlete: The Eric Liddell Story* (Barnoak, Crieff, Perthshire, Scotland: Research Unit, 1970), 75.

2. Ibid., 74.

3. Eric Liddell, *The Disciplines of the Christian Life* (New York: Ballantine Books, 1985), 61.

4. David McCasland, *Eric Liddell: Pure Gold: A New Biography of the Olympic Champion Who Inspired Chariots of Fire* (Grand Rapids, MI: Discovery House, 2001), 115–16.

5. Ibid, 111.

6. Ibid.

7. D. P. Thomson, *Scotland's Greatest Athlete: The Eric Liddell Story* (Barnoak, Crieff, Perthshire, Scotland: Research Unit, 1970), 81–82.

8. Ellen Caughey, *Run to Glory: The Story of Eric Liddell* (Uhrichsville, OH: Barbour, 2017), e-book.

9. David McCasland, *Eric Liddell: Pure Gold: A New Biography of the Olympic Champion Who Inspired Chariots of Fire* (Grand Rapids, MI: Discovery House, 2001), 119.

CHAPTER 9: A SORT OF HOMECOMING

1. David McCasland, *Eric Liddell: Pure Gold: A New Biography of the Olympic Champion Who Inspired Chariots of Fire* (Grand Rapids, MI: Discovery House, 2001), 125–26.

2. Eric Liddell to Effie Hardie, February 19, 1926, Eric Liddell Centre, accessed September 21, 2017, http://www.ericliddell.org/about-us/eric-liddell/personal -correspondence-of-eric-liddell/.

CHAPTER 10: A SLOW BLOOM

1. Russell W. Ramsey, *God's Joyful Runner* (South Plainfield, NJ: Bridge, 1987).

2. Eric Liddell, circular letter, 1928, Eric Liddell Centre, accessed September 19, 2017, http://www.ericliddell.org/about-us/eric-liddell/personal-correspondence -of-eric-liddell/.

3. Eric Liddell to Effie Hardie, February 19, 1929, Eric Liddell Centre, accessed September 19, 2017, http://ericliddell.org/about-us/ericliddell/personal -correspondence-of-eric-liddell/.

CHAPTER 11: ORDINARY TIME, EXTRAORDINARY DAYS

1. Ellen Caughey, *Run to Glory: The Story of Eric Liddell* (Uhrichsville, OH: Barbour, 2017), e-book.
2. Eric Liddell, circular letter, 1928, Eric Liddell Centre, accessed September 19, 2017, http://www.ericliddell.org/about-us/eric-liddell/personal-correspondence-of-eric-liddell/.
3. David McCasland, *Eric Liddell: Pure Gold: A New Biography of the Olympic Champion Who Inspired Chariots of Fire* (Grand Rapids, MI: Discovery House, 2001), 149.
4. Ibid.

CHAPTER 12: ONWARD AND UPWARD

1. Eric Liddell to Effie Hardie, January 31, 1930, Eric Liddell Centre, accessed September 21, 2017, http://ericliddell.org/about-us/ericliddell/personal-correspondence-of-eric-liddell/.
2. Eric Liddell to Effie Hardie, February 19, 1929, Eric Liddell Centre, accessed November 15, 2017, http://www.ericliddell.org/about-us/eric-liddell/personal-correspondence-of-eric-liddell/.
3. David McCasland, *Eric Liddell: Pure Gold: A New Biography of the Olympic Champion Who Inspired Chariots of Fire* (Grand Rapids, MI: Discovery House, 2001), 155.
4. Ibid., 157–58.

CHAPTER 13: A GAZE INTO THE LOOKING GLASS

1. D. P. Thomson, *Scotland's Greatest Athlete: The Eric Liddell Story* (Barnoak, Crieff, Perthshire, Scotland: Research Unit, 1970), 121.
2. Ibid.
3. David McCasland, *Eric Liddell: Pure Gold: A New Biography of the Olympic Champion Who Inspired Chariots of Fire* (Grand Rapids, MI: Discovery House, 2001), 163.
4. Ibid., 164.
5. "Stuart Sanderson (1887–1971)," Initiatives of Change, January 14, 2014, http://uk.iofc.org/stuart-sanderson-1887-1971.
6. Ibid.
7. D. P. Thomson, *Scotland's Greatest Athlete: The Eric Liddell Story* (Barnoak, Crieff, Perthshire, Scotland: Research Unit, 1970), 126.

CHAPTER 14: PATIENCE AND TACT

1. Russell W. Ramsey, *God's Joyful Runner* (South Plainfield, NJ: Bridge, 1987), 180.
2. David McCasland, *Eric Liddell: Pure Gold: A New Biography of the Olympic Champion Who Inspired Chariots of Fire* (Grand Rapids, MI: Discovery House, 2001), 174.
3. Ibid.
4. Ibid., 176.

CHAPTER 15: STEADFAST WEDLOCK

1. D. P. Thomson, *Scotland's Greatest Athlete: The Eric Liddell Story* (Barnoak, Crieff, Perthshire, Scotland: Research Unit, 1970), 105.
2. Ibid., 138.

3. David McCasland, *Eric Liddell: Pure Gold: A New Biography of the Olympic Champion Who Inspired Chariots of Fire* (Grand Rapids, MI: Discovery House, 2001), 183.
4. Ibid.
5. Ibid.

CHAPTER 16: A PROPHET IN HIS HOMETOWN
1. David McCasland, *Eric Liddell: Pure Gold: A New Biography of the Olympic Champion Who Inspired Chariots of Fire* (Grand Rapids, MI: Discovery House, 2001), 204–5.
2. Eric Liddell to his family, December 1938, Eric Liddell Centre, accessed September 19, 2017, http://www.ericliddell.org/about-us/eric-liddell/personal-correspondence-of-eric-liddell/.
3. D. P. Thomson, *Scotland's Greatest Athlete: The Eric Liddell Story* (Barnoak, Crieff, Perthshire, Scotland: Research Unit, 1970), 162.

CHAPTER 17: AN ISLAND OF PEACE
1. D. P. Thomson, *Scotland's Greatest Athlete: The Eric Liddell Story* (Barnoak, Crieff, Perthshire, Scotland: Research Unit, 1970), 163.
2. Ibid., 168.
3. Ibid., 217.

CHAPTER 18: KEEP CALM AND CARRY ON
1. D. P. Thomson, *Scotland's Greatest Athlete: The Eric Liddell Story* (Barnoak, Crieff, Perthshire, Scotland: Research Unit, 1970), 166–7.
2. Ibid., 170–1.
3. Ibid.
4. David McCasland, *Eric Liddell: Pure Gold: A New Biography of the Olympic Champion Who Inspired Chariots of Fire* (Grand Rapids, MI: Discovery House, 2001), 223.
5. D. P. Thomson, *Scotland's Greatest Athlete: The Eric Liddell Story* (Barnoak, Crieff, Perthshire, Scotland: Research Unit, 1970), 168–9.
6. Ibid., 148.
7. "The Story of Eric Liddell: Olympic Champion—Man of Courage," *Day of Discovery*, season 32, episode 22, aired December 5, 1999 (Grand Rapids, MI: Day of Discovery, 2008), DVD.

CHAPTER 20: AN UNEXPECTED OPPORTUNITY
1. Duncan Hamilton, *For the Glory: Eric Liddell's Journey from Olympic Champion to Modern Martyr* (New York: Penguin, 2016), 241.
2. D. P. Thomson, *Scotland's Greatest Athlete: The Eric Liddell Story* (Barnoak, Crieff, Perthshire, Scotland: Research Unit, 1970), 176.
3. Ibid., 176–77.
4. Ibid., 177.
5. Ibid., 178.

CHAPTER 21: DETAINMENT
1. David McCasland, *Eric Liddell: Pure Gold: A New Biography of the Olympic Champion Who Inspired Chariots of Fire* (Grand Rapids, MI: Discovery House, 2001), 241.

2. D. P. Thomson, *Scotland's Greatest Athlete: The Eric Liddell Story* (Barnoak, Crieff, Perthshire, Scotland: Research Unit, 1970), 179.

3. Eric Liddell, *The Disciplines of the Christian Life* (New York: Ballantine Books, 1985), 10–11.

4. D. P. Thomson, *Scotland's Greatest Athlete: The Eric Liddell Story* (Barnoak, Crieff, Perthshire, Scotland: Research Unit, 1970), 182.

5. David McCasland, *Eric Liddell: Pure Gold: A New Biography of the Olympic Champion Who Inspired Chariots of Fire* (Grand Rapids, MI: Discovery House, 2001), 247.

6. D. P. Thomson, *Scotland's Greatest Athlete: The Eric Liddell Story* (Barnoak, Crieff, Perthshire, Scotland: Research Unit, 1970), 185.

CHAPTER 22: *INCURVATUS IN SE*

1. "The Story of Eric Liddell: Olympic Champion—Man of Courage," *Day of Discovery*, season 32, episode 22, aired December 5, 1999 (Grand Rapids, MI: Day of Discovery, 2008), DVD.

2. D. P. Thomson, *Scotland's Greatest Athlete: The Eric Liddell Story* (Barnoak, Crieff, Perthshire, Scotland: Research Unit, 1970), 192.

3. Langdon Gilkey, *Shantung Compound: The Story of Men and Women under Pressure* (New York: HarperCollins, 1966), 35.

4. Ibid., 111.

5. Mary Taylor Previte, "A Song of Salvation at Weihsien Prison Camp," Weihsien Picture Gallery, August 25, 1985, http://www.weihsien-paintings.org/Mprevite/inquirer/MPrevite.htm.

6. David McCasland, *Eric Liddell: Pure Gold: A New Biography of the Olympic Champion Who Inspired Chariots of Fire* (Grand Rapids, MI: Discovery House, 2001), 285.

7. Florence Liddell to Eric Liddell, unpublished letter, August 23, 1943.

8. Ibid.

9. David McCasland, *Eric Liddell: Pure Gold: A New Biography of the Olympic Champion Who Inspired Chariots of Fire* (Grand Rapids, MI: Discovery House, 2001), 265.

CHAPTER 23: DISCIPLESHIP

1. D. P. Thomson, *Scotland's Greatest Athlete: The Eric Liddell Story* (Barnoak, Crieff, Perthshire, Scotland: Research Unit, 1970), 196.

2. Langdon Gilkey, *Shantung Compound: The Story of Men and Women under Pressure* (New York: HarperCollins, 1966), 35.

CHAPTER 24: ERIC IS IN

1. David McCasland, *Eric Liddell: Pure Gold: A New Biography of the Olympic Champion Who Inspired Chariots of Fire* (Grand Rapids, MI: Discovery House, 2001), 268.

2. "The Story of Eric Liddell: Olympic Champion—Man of Courage," *Day of Discovery*, season 32, episode 22, aired December 5, 1999 (Grand Rapids, MI: Day of Discovery, 2008), DVD.

3. Lisa Adams, "Scots Olympic Great Eric Liddell Helped Me Survive Concentration Camp Horror," *Daily Record*, July 1, 2012, http://www.dailyrecord.co.uk/news/real-life/scots-olympic-great-eric-liddell-989642.

4. Eric Liddell, *The Disciplines of the Christian Life* (New York: Ballantine Books, 1985), 114–15.
5. Ibid., 128.
6. D. P. Thomson, *Scotland's Greatest Athlete: The Eric Liddell Story* (Barnoak, Crieff, Perthshire, Scotland: Research Unit, 1970), 198.

CHAPTER 25: GOOD NIGHT, SWEET PRINCE
1. Norman Cliff, *Courtyard of the Happy Way* (Evesham Worsc., England: Arthur James Limited, 1977), chapter 11, as quoted in Weihsien Picture Gallery, accessed September 27, 2017, http://www.weihsien-paintings.org/NormanCliff/Books /Courtyard/txt_Chapter_11.htm.
2. Ibid.
3. Langdon Gilkey, *Shantung Compound: The Story of Men and Women under Pressure* (New York: HarperCollins, 1966), 113.
4. Ibid.
5. Russell W. Ramsey, *God's Joyful Runner* (South Plainfield, NJ: Bridge, 1987), 166.
6. "Stephen Metcalf Talks about Eric Liddell," People's Recollections, Eric Liddell Centre, accessed September 25, 2017, http://www.ericliddell.org/stephen-a-metcalf/.
7. *The Scotland Register*, June 20th, 2014.

CHAPTER 26: ERIC IS OUT
1. David Michell, *A Boy's War* (Singapore: Overseas Missionary Fellowship, 1988), http://www.weihsien-paintings.org/books/aBoysWar/ABoysWar(LaTotale)-pages.pdf
2. D. P. Thomson, *Scotland's Greatest Athlete: The Eric Liddell Story* (Barnoak, Crieff, Perthshire, Scotland: Research Unit, 1970), 208–17. These and the following words are a composite of the many praises lauded over Eric at his funeral.
3. Mary Taylor Previte, "A Song of Salvation at Weihsien Prison Camp," Weihsien Picture Gallery, August 25, 1985, http://www.weihsien-paintings.org/Mprevite /inquirer/MPrevite.htm.
4. David McCasland, *Eric Liddell: Pure Gold: A New Biography of the Olympic Champion Who Inspired Chariots of Fire* (Grand Rapids, MI: Discovery House, 2001), 286.
5. D. P. Thomson, *Eric H. Liddell: Athlete and Missionary* (Barnoak, Crieff, Perthshire, Scotland: Research Unit, 1971), 212.
6. Eric Liddell, *The Disciplines of the Christian Life* (New York: Ballantine Books, 1985), 120–21.

CHAPTER 27: A LIDDELL EPILOGUE
1. David McCasland, *Eric Liddell: Pure Gold: A New Biography of the Olympic Champion Who Inspired Chariots of Fire* (Grand Rapids, MI: Discovery House, 2001), 289–90.
2. M. E. Breckenridge to Florence Liddell, unpublished letter, October 16, 1945.
3. Eric Liddell to Florence Liddell, unpublished letter, August 24, 1944.
4. Eric Liddell to Florence Liddell, unpublished letter, August 27, 1944.
5. Eric Liddell to Florence Liddell, unpublished letter, February 21, 1945.

ABOUT THE AUTHORS

Eric Eichinger loves to share the "glory story" of Christ in creative ways. He earned a BA in theatre from Michigan State University, where he also ran varsity track and field. Upon graduation, he served two years as a youth worker in New York and two more years with LCMS World Mission in China, where he met his wife, Kara.

With a developed passion in missions, Eric earned a four-year Master's of Divinity degree at Concordia Seminary, Saint Louis, Missouri. In 2006 he was ordained into the Office of Holy Ministry in the Lutheran Church—Missouri Synod at his home congregation of Zion Lutheran in Kalamazoo, Michigan, by the Rev. Dr. Paul Maier.

During his eleven years in the ministry, he also served six years as a pastoral counselor for the Lutheran Women's Missionary League of the Florida/Georgia district. He is currently senior pastor at Bethel Lutheran Church in Clearwater, Florida, and also coaches track and field at First Lutheran School in Clearwater.

Eric and Kara enjoy their family life and occasionally see each other while raising their three children and breaking in their maverick dachshund, Doppelbock. Amid work and family, Eric also enjoys writing, film, deciphering U2 riffs on the guitar, running, cheering for any Detroit sports team, and dressing his children in Michigan

State green and white on college game-day Saturdays. Eric notes that most of these activities increase in enjoyment when good coffee is included.

Eva Marie Everson is an award-winning, bestselling author of over thirty fiction and nonfiction titles, including *Five Brides*, *The Road to Testament*, The Cedar Key series, The Potluck Club series (with Linda Evans Shepherd), *God Bless Us Every One*, *Reflections of God's Holy Land* (with Miriam Feinberg Vamosh), and others. She is the president of Word Weavers International, the director of Florida Christian Writers Conference, and a member of a number of writers' organizations. She and her husband make their home in Central Florida where they are owned by a small black doxie.

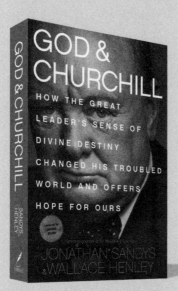 

Online Discussion *guide*

TAKE *your* TYNDALE READING
EXPERIENCE *to the* NEXT LEVEL

A FREE discussion guide for this book
is available at bookclubhub.net, perfect
for sparking conversations in your book
group or for digging deeper into the text
on your own.

www.bookclubhub.net

*You'll also find free discussion guides for
other Tyndale books, e-newsletters, e-mail
devotionals, virtual book tours, and more!*